QUEEN OF THE GOLDEN AGE

Queen of the Golden Age

THE FABULOUS STORY OF
GRACE WILSON VANDERBILT

by

CORNELIUS VANDERBILT, JR

GEORGE MANN *of* MAIDSTONE

QUEEN OF THE GOLDEN AGE
The Fabulous Story of Grace Wilson Vanderbilt

by Cornelius Vanderbilt, Jnr

First published in the United States of America 1956

This edition first published 1999

ISBN 0 7041 0276 5

Printed and bound in Great Britain by
J W Arrowsmith Ltd, Bristol
and published by
George Mann Books
PO Box 22, Maidstone
in the English County of Kent

DEDICATED

to

My Mother–Grace Graham Wilson Vanderbilt

a fabulous, exciting, gracious lady

ACKNOWLEDGEMENTS

Countless people all over have helped me piece this story together. To them I am greatly indebted. I have been actively working on it since 1950, and have used their information, old letters of and to my parents, faded newspaper clippings, and my own diaries and letters.

I am especially grateful to Betty Hannah Hoffman for her invaluable assistance in the composition of this book; and to Laura Lou Brookman, special projects editor of the *Ladies' Home Journal*; Nell Keyes Perry, assistant to the editor; Tina S. Fredericks, associate editor; and Marion Freeman of the same publication.

I am also grateful to Turner S. Catledge, managing editor of *The New York Times*, for the use of the reference library of that great organization; and to the executive directors of the New York Public Library and the Library of Congress in Washington, D.C., for the same.

I wish to thank Wayne Andrews, author of *The Vanderbilt Legend*, for historical information about the Vanderbilt family; Arthur Fowler of Loudon, Tennessee, for historical facts about the Wilson family; and Cleveland Amory, author of *The Last Resorts*, for several anecdotes about the social spas in their early days.

A large number of Mother's relatives and friends helped me immeasurably in the correlation of facts and dates. Especially, therefore, am I also indebted to Flew Johnston of Hartford, Connecticut; Syria Kalbfus of Newport, Rhode Island; Alice Roosevelt Longworth of Washington, D.C.; Henri de Bach of Paris; Nicholas Lelly of Athens; Roca de Torres of Madrid; and the late Lord Fermoy.

In addition, anecdotes and interesting bits of information were furnished by Winthrop W. Aldrich, Bernard M. Baruch, Alfred I. Barton, Lawrence S. Butler, Maria Goelet Bennett, Dr. Sam Brown (Father's personal physician for more than fifty years), Frederick W. Coudert, Weyland Echols, Katherine Mackey Hawkins, William Hoffman, Douglas and Ina Chandour, Lytle Hull, Harry Hooker, Mrs. Kelly-Evans, Ernesta Barlow, Marion Eppley, Peter Grimm, Frank Luther, James W. Gerard, Douglas Parmentier, Emily Post, Arvid Paulson, Henry May, Jesse Jones, Sen., Theodore Francis Greene,

Gen. John F. O'Ryan, Mrs. Walter Stokes, Gen. and Mrs. John Sherman, Gen. and Mrs. Anthony Drexel Biddle, Leicester Faust, Algara de Toreros, Robert R. Young, Mrs. Myron Taylor, Mrs. Charles Mitchell, Harry Woodring, Sheldon Whitehouse, Joe Werner, Ephrem Zimbalist, Bishop Ernest S. Stires, and Father Washington.

ILLUSTRATIONS

Chapter One

IF I close my eyes, I can see her now against the pale satin walls of her Fifth Avenue palace, a tall, slender, excitingly beautiful woman in a gold lamé gown by Worth.

Above Grace Vanderbilt's famous drawing-room were wardrobes filled with hundreds of other Worth and Pacquin creations, many of them so laden with jet and pearls and embroidery that they could not be hung up, but lay in clouds of blue tissue paper on twelve-foot shelves. There were closets just for hats, for parasols, for shoes—five hundred pairs of shoes, with as many handbags to match. Her jewels—including a rose the size of a peony, fashioned entirely of diamonds and platinum—were said to be worth more than a million. 'What do you have that's new and beautiful today?' she would ask the clerks at Tiffany's as they hurried up to her with deferential smiles.

Thirty-three servants, imported from ducal and princely households abroad, kept her mansions on Fifth Avenue in New York and on Bellevue Avenue in Newport running to perfection. She entertained every British monarch from Victoria to George VI, as well as King Albert of Belgium, the King and Queen of Spain, the crowned heads of Scandinavia and the Netherlands, and the King of Siam, to mention but a few of her royal friends. On her ocean-going yacht, the *North Star*, she wined and dined German princes and grand dukes, the Emperor Wilhelm of Germany, and the ill-fated Czar and Czarina of Russia.

Theodore Roosevelt, General Pershing, Mark Twain, Lord Rosebery, and Winston Churchill all added their lustre to the brilliance of her after-dinner *salons*. Rubinstein practised daily in her many-mirrored music-room, the finest in New York. Melba and Caruso and the de Reszkes came to sing for her.

When distinguished visitors from abroad arrived in New York, they paid their respects to Mrs. Vanderbilt before driving to City Hall. The number of her Fifth Avenue home, 640, was almost as well known on the Continent as 10 Downing Street is today.

To friends, she was known as the Queen or Her Grace. Spiteful tongues called her the Dowager Duchess or Kingfisher. There has never been a hostess like her. It is hard to believe there will ever be another. In a single year (and that was during the Depression) she entertained 37,000 guests. Her sway over society began in the gas-lit red velvet parlours of the turn of the century and—outlasting two major wars, the Crash, bathtub gin, flappers, and café society—survived for fifty dazzling years.

Throughout her lifetime, Mother never granted an interview.

She seldom, if ever, dined or lunched in public.

She never owned a mink coat, but had eleven white-fox neck-pieces.

Only once did she enter a night club.

She carried a fan to the opera, and was not often seen without her famous 'trademark', a bandeau about her forehead matching the fabric of her gown. Mother had hundreds of these, some jewelled, all made in Paris.

She believed that when entertaining royalty, one turned one's house over to them, and became royalty's guest.

She never gossiped, and declined to remain in a room where salacious tales were being spread.

'Grace Vanderbilt sees herself in a kind of perpetual fairy tale,' President Theodore Roosevelt used to say with admiration and affection. Perhaps it was this brightness and spirit about my mother, a refusal even to acknowledge the existence of tragedy, which endeared her to so many thousands—literally thousands—of people, great and small.

In many ways she resembled the late Queen Mary, her good and close friend. Like England's majestic sovereign, she wore for half a century a traditional costume by which she could be instantly recognized. She clung, with an unswerving passion, to a gracious and leisurely and elegant era long past. And lastly, like the Queen, she lived through some intensely unhappy family episodes.

When her son, King Edward VIII, abdicated the throne to marry an American divorcée, I saw the magnificent countenance of Queen Mary crumple into helpless and bitter tears as she stood on the balcony of Buckingham Palace. Mother went through equally soul-shattering experiences. But no one ever saw her cry.

'Your mother became, *against the heaviest odds*, the kind of person she most wanted to be,' a dear, close relative told me recently.

Mother's social influence became so powerful that friends would brave a full-scale hurricane to dine at her table, rather than incur the risk of being stricken—even temporarily—from her list.

Yet at the beginning of her battle for social supremacy, Mother herself was stricken from many lists. My Aunt Belle, Lady Michael Herbert, called the Vanderbilts' and their friends' treatment of Mother 'the greatest wickedness of the nineteenth century'.

Her candid comments about the strange feud I found among a treasure trove of family letters dating back to the 1880s. They reveal how Mother's family felt about the sensational quarrel she sparked, a quarrel which grew into a feud explosive enough to split the Four Hundred.

The Vanderbilt family fracas has a beginning which my Victorian mother never discussed with me. I am telling it now because I am filled with admiration for my intrepid mother, and because I feel that the pinnacle of social success she achieved is all the more remarkable in the light of what she had to overcome.

In the trunkloads of records she left behind, a vast memorabilia of her glamorous and fabulous life, I found an intriguing reflection of life among society's glittering circles both here and abroad. From these and many other sources, I have tried to assemble the pieces of the puzzle of Mother's truly extraordinary character.

The story starts before I was born, when my mother was a celebrated belle of Newport and New York. As I have reconstructed those Golden Era days of the late 1890s, this is when and where the Vanderbilt feud began:

One August evening in 1895 a parade of shiny carriages, driven by high-hatted coachmen in livery, carried a laughing crowd of young people in evening dress along Newport's splendid Narragansett Avenue. The coach lamps flickered over the women's round white shoulders, their huge dog collars of glistening pearls, their sparkling tiaras of diamonds. Bouquets of Jacqueminot roses and white jasmine and purple violets lay tumbled in each ruffled lap—gifts from swains who hoped to claim a waltz or two during the evening's *affaire de luxe*, young Gertrude Vanderbilt's coming-out party.

In the new *vis-à-vis* victorias the girls' escorts gazed at the ladies seated opposite them—intriguing visions of loveliness in chiffon and tulle. Past the girls' elaborate coiffures, they could see other great *calèches* following and hear the crack of the coachmen's whips, the whir of the rubber-tyred wheels, the rhythmic thud of the horses' hoofs on the gravel boulevard. At the end of the procession came a coach carrying the girls' personal maids.

A distinguished Parisian, visiting Newport that summer, had remarked that no watering-place abroad could compare with it in magnificence—not Deauville, nor Biarritz, nor even Cannes on the Riviera, splendid as some of its seaside villas were. As he hiked along the jagged Cliff Walk, which zigzagged for miles along the resort's easterly coast, with the dazzling blue Atlantic on one side and Newport's mammoth estates on the other, he marvelled at the unbridled lavishness of America's most social summer colony.

'On this tiny tip of an island, you will find more millionaires than in all London and Paris put together,' his friends had truly declared.

The *pièce de résistance* of his sight-seeing tour was a glimpse of the newly completed Breakers, a great square stone Italian *palazzo* five stories high, which occupied a small promontory jutting out to sea. For two years Newporters had watched the erection of the new summer home of Mr. and Mrs. Cornelius Vanderbilt. This was before the days of cement mixers, bulldozers, and mechanical cranes. Stone by stone, the seventy-room villa was built by an army of workmen wielding picks and shovels and driving horse-drawn scoops and carts. Tons of crated treasures from Italy and France arrived weekly and were dragged in great wagons to the Breakers' site. To build this great villa (which they intended to occupy only ten weeks of the year), my grandparents spent $5,000,000. But the Breakers could not be built for five times that amount today. In those days a dollar represented a day's wages for a labouring man.

Its top floors contained rooms for thirty-three servants. The great Vanderbilt stables, several blocks away on Coggeshall Avenue, contained twenty-six horses, the Vanderbilt coachman and his family, and thirteen grooms. Twelve gardeners were required to tend the greenhouses and the eleven acres of terraced lawns and gardens. And part of this staff would remain all winter, for the Breakers' art treasures must be preserved at a cost of some hundred and fifty tons of coal a season.

For weeks Newporters had discussed the interior of this fabulous new place. Gertrude's coming-out party was to be its housewarming. The bathrooms, it was said, all had French bidets and hot and cold water—in fact, rain water and even salt water, hot and cold, coming from their silver taps! The bathtubs were carved of solid marble and were so icy cold that young Reggie Vanderbilt reportedly refused his evening bath until his tub had been sufficiently warmed with hot water.

Downstairs, the kitchen was the size of a small house, with five immense wood-burning ranges, each with eight or ten burners. The butler's pantry was two decks high, and lined to the ceiling with fine glassware and china, all chosen from samples brought to Mrs. Vanderbilt's home, for it was said that she had never entered a shop. At the Breakers she could give a dinner party for two hundred, it was rumoured, without calling in extra help.

And each morning, Mrs. Vanderbilt, wearing immaculate white gloves, inspected her household, running a gloved finger over table tops and picture frames and stair railings. And when she was through, the gloves had better be white!

Some thirty young people had been invited to dine at the Breakers at eight o'clock the night of Gertrude's *début*; at midnight a second elaborate supper would be served to some three hundred guests who were to arrive for the ball. Most of these guests had dined earlier at various cottage parties, including one at Grace Wilson's on Narragansett Avenue.

And now, on the stroke of eleven, Grace Wilson's party in the parade of black victorias turned through the Breakers' thirty-foot black iron gates. The splendid Italian Renaissance-style villa was blazing with light, and by the glow of four immense outdoor bronze candelabras one could see white-wigged footmen assisting new arrivals from their carriages. A snatch of a waltz by Waldteufel floated out to the Wilson party as the girls, holding their bouquets with one arm, gracefully swept up their billowing trains to alight.

The girls' bustles swayed provocatively as they strolled under the towering *porte-cochère* towards the great oaken entrance doors. Inside, the floors were marble, scrubbed spotlessly clean. As the ladies moved across this great bare expanse, another set of doors, fashioned a heavy wrought iron, opened upon a second entrance hall, where a short flight of marble steps led to the galleried great hall.

Sixteen footmen awaited the guests in the maroon silk knee breeches of the House of Vanderbilt, standing at attention along a brilliant red velvet carpet, which seemed almost the size of a football field. Overhead, four immense crystal chandeliers, each large enough to hold several men, illuminated by hundreds of jets of flame, shone on the footmen's white wigs and gleaming silver buttons.

Past the blazing chandeliers a balcony could be seen, and higher still, great pillars of pink marble, soaring to what appeared to be a distant, cloud-filled blue sky some forty feet over the guests' heads.

The liveried footmen, bowing, directed the ladies to a great hanging marble staircase, leading to the balcony above, and the gentlemen to a staircase descending to dressing-rooms below. Like a shy covey of grey doves, the ladies' personal maids scurried after their mistresses up the red-carpeted stairs.

A few moments later Grace Wilson sat before a dressing-table mirror as her maid let down her honey-gold hair, and then, with a tortoise comb and bristle brush, expertly rearranged it. The gas-lit mirror reflected a young woman in her middle twenties with a face and figure of almost classic beauty. Her aristocratic features were chiselled and small, like her fine-boned body. Only her lips were, perhaps, a trifle too thin for the flawless perfection of a Diana.

Her eyes—green, or grey, or violet—dark-lashed, watched absently in the mirror her maid's deft fingers. How many times, in later years, I was struck by the radiant self-assurance of that calm, beautiful oval face gazing from the glass!

'Grace Wilson had so many points of gentility—her tiny, high-arched feet, her beautifully straight nose, her long tapering fingers—that I don't see how anyone could have possibly doubted her good blood,' a Southern relative of ours, Aunt Flew, used to say frequently.

About her throat that evening Grace Wilson wore a many-stranded pearl necklace. From her belt a chain of diamonds held a small ivory fan. Her white chiffon ball dress, deeply *décolleté* and intricately embroidered with pearls and appliquéd flowers of white satin, emphasized the elegance of her slim, high-bosomed, small-waisted figure.

This was Miss Wilson, the pet of international society, the particular favourite of the Prince of Wales, later to become King Edward VII. Accustomed to spending her summers abroad since her eleventh year, she was an accepted member of the most discriminating inner circles of London and Paris. Even in the exacting eyes of the *ancien régime* of France, she was considered a *jeune fille bien élevée*! Her French was flawless, her German good; she could distinguish at a glance a Turner or Millet or Manet, or place a piece of ancient Chinese porcelain. A devoted music lover, she knew by heart every aria from every great opera, having heard them countless times in the vast opera houses at Bayreuth and London and Rome. The great Polish tenor, Jean de Reszke—it was whispered—had given her both singing lessons and his slavish devotion.

Whether a foreign minister should follow or precede the Vice President of the United States in to dinner gave her not a moment's hesitation. She knew the proper temperatures, the right vintages, for a dozen kinds of wine, the correct measures to keep a sauce *béarnaise* from curdling (she had taken cooking lessons in Paris), the only way to board a yacht, how to curtsy without tumbling, and the precise intonation to use with everyone from a king to a chambermaid.

Now, as she rose from the dressing-table and moved towards the great gas-lit hall, her maid pressed into her hands her collection of swains' bouquets. I imagine they both smiled, knowing that the flowers would lie wilting all evening on some gilt chair—the object of envious stares from the small circle of girls who, partnerless and disconsolate, spent much of the evening on the side lines with the chaperones.

At the entrance to the grand *salon*, or music-room, the butler stood ready with a list in his hand to announce the guests. As Grace and her partner—tall, brown-haired Jack Astor—joined those waiting in line, waves of music greeted them from the two orchestras. Before them lay a scene of pure enchantment—young couples dipped and swooped about the great gold-and-white ballroom while, on the side lines, plumed and diamond-starred dowagers watched with hawk-eyed attention the flushed faces and heaving bosoms of the season's prettiest and richest *débutantes*.

In front of the white marble fireplace, with its high-backed gold throne chairs, Mrs. Vanderbilt and her daughter Gertrude were receiving.

Alice of the Breakers, as some Newporters called my grandmother, was at this time a *petite* woman in her forties, with plain features, tight lips, and piercingly cold grey eyes. She was wearing a red satin gown, her tightly whaleboned figure girdled with ropes of pearls and diamonds and her high pompadour adorned with ostrich plumes. Next to her stood a thin, serious-looking girl in white chiffon who was known to her friends as Gertie. This immensely rich heiress could not be called pretty, nor even very feminine, for she had inherited the strong, rugged features which made most of the Vanderbilt men so handsome. Known as a wholesome kind of girl, obedient, subdued, shy, who loved sports and the out-of-doors, Gertrude had already turned down several suitors for her hand, it was said, announcing that she would marry only for love.

It was no secret in Newport that Gertie was much taken with a former Yale classmate of her brother's, Harry Payne Whitney, whose prowess on the polo field (a sport he helped to introduce to America) had caused more than one feminine heart to flutter.

Young Harry, who would some day inherit a large slice of his family's Standard Oil fortune, seemed just the kind of clean-cut, sports-loving young chap who would make an ideal husband for Gertrude. But her mother, it was said, had greater ambitions for her eldest daughter.

There were some who insisted that Alice of the Breakers had no social ambitions, preferring her privacy and many philanthropies to the giddy social whirl. Others said that she was bitterly envious of the social success of her sister-in-law, Alva Vanderbilt, but that she herself lacked all facility and finesse as a hostess. She was not especially gay or amusing; her demeanour, at first glance glacial and forbidding, failed utterly to attract and to keep a following of attractive and attentive men, without which it was impossible to give a successful party, no matter how much money or energy was expended. In fact, it was a brave hostess indeed who attempted to give a ball in Newport during the nineties, so acute was the lack of dancing men.

My mother was always careful to silence potentially envious tongues with small acts of thoughtfulness and gentility. I can imagine that, as Mrs. Vanderbilt bowed stiffly and extended her hand, Grace Wilson floated towards her with a winning smile. I can almost hear her sweet and lilting voice saying: 'What a beautiful house! Everything is quite breath-taking! How wise you were not to use many flowers, Mrs. Vanderbilt—it all blends and balances so perfectly!'

Indeed, the four-foot vases of American Beauty roses were so dwarfed by the proportions of the ballroom that they might just as well not have been there at all.

Grace Wilson, still smiling her warm smile, revealing her quite perfect white teeth, now took Gertrude's hand, and by the gaiety of her remarks, effected a transformation in that stiff, reserved, and craggy face. Mrs. Vanderbilt, observing the two girls for a moment, the one so poised and beautiful, must have sighed as she turned her head away, searching among the dancers.

Neily Vanderbilt, her son, recently graduated from college, was dancing by. He was an extremely handsome boy, just under six feet tall, with the kind of square, clean-cut, manly good looks immortalized by Charles Dana Gibson. His thick brown curly hair sprang back from a well-shaped brow; his chin, accentuating a full and sensuous mouth, jutted out with the implacable determination becoming a future titan of finance.

Only his dark-blue eyes lacked the piercing fire of an Andrew Carnegie and revealed instead a shyness which was almost an incurable obsession. I can picture him blushing furiously as he caught sight of Miss Wilson and then, in his confusion, missing a step, his lean legs tangling with his partner's sweeping skirt. I can picture Grace Wilson, with her usual exquisite tact, observing nothing and sending him a gracious smile.

Neily was known to Newporters as a sweet and sentimental boy who composed love ballads and played the banjo. He was a good student, attended church regularly, and was generally conceded to be a most exemplary son. His health, however, was a subject of vexing concern to his parents, for he suffered greatly from recurring attacks of rheumatism.

I'm sure that the tender exchange of glances between Neily and Grace Wilson was not lost upon the host of the evening, Mr. Cornelius Vanderbilt, Senior, Neily's father. Just past fifty, the chairman of the board of the New York Central Railroad was a strikingly good-looking man with a powerful frame, a stubborn neck, and a square chin framed with black sideburns. Although his manner was generally mild and pleasant, a certain chilling look of command belied his quiet courtesy. One felt that here was a man who expected to be obeyed, and instantly.

No scandal had ever touched the hem of Grandfather Vanderbilt's sombre black garments; everywhere he was applauded as a model Christian gentleman, devoted to his church and family. It had been years—people said—since any flash of humour had illuminated the staid features of his devoted spouse, Alice, whom he had met while teaching Sunday School.

Although his father had possessed a personal fortune of $200,000,000, my grandfather's first job as a bank clerk paid him fifty dollars a month, and it was said that he then lived on this salary. For thirty years he had laboured twelve hours a day at his desk, engrossed in his ledgers. It was reported that when he assumed the chairmanship of the family's great railroad empire, no detail was too small or too trivial to escape him. Many times he had been pronounced the world's most expert accountant. Unlike his father, who used to say he did not know how many millions he had accumulated, Cornelius Vanderbilt II could produce a record of every dollar he had ever spent. On any day of the week he could estimate to the penny what he was worth, so people said.

Not that Grandfather was a miser—indeed, he was considered most charitable. Chauncey Depew said that for twenty years my grandfather had been giving away from one-fourth to one-half of his yearly income—anonymously, of course, as befitted his modest and publicity-shunning nature. His father and grandfather had left him a combined fortune of $72,500,000 and, as he had never owned any kind of yacht or racing stable and could not possibly be lured into any sentimental or bogus investments, Grandfather's yearly income could be estimated conservatively at $3,625,000 a year, tax free.

Intensely religious, this Episcopalian vestryman attended church every day and sometimes twice, if two services were held. His conscientiousness was a constant source of wonder to his business associates in those palmy days of the robber barons. 'Every matter which comes to him is first subjected to the crucible of its being right or wrong,' his closest confidant, Chauncey Depew, once said.

'Satisfied that the course he is to pursue is the right one, no difficulties, no dangers, no obstacles deter him.'

My cousin, Consuelo Balsan, his niece, has confessed to being
considerably intimidated by Cornelius Vanderbilt II, whom she
found always 'stern and serious'.

I never knew my grandfather, and so cannot judge his character,
but the stories I have heard about him reveal the deep puritanical
strain which I believe motivated most of his actions.

William Dodge tells, for example, of the first time he met
Cornelius Vanderbilt II. A mutual friend introduced them with
these extraordinary remarks: 'Mr. Dodge, I want you to know
my friend, Mr. Vanderbilt. He was my room-mate in college. I never
heard him say or do anything that he would not have done had his
mother been in the room at the time.'

My aunt, the Countess Szechenyi, explains her father's character
this way. 'He was a saint,' she says simply.

All his life, because of his position and immense wealth, Grandfather was surrounded by unctuous flatterers. People praised him
for his simplicity and lack of pretension—as if a simple, unpretentious soul would choose to live amid the terrible splendour of his
kingly dwelling places!

But perhaps this, too, was part of his intense conscientiousness,
a feeling that he had a kingly role to play. No one ever heard him
complain, unlike his brother Willie, the father of Consuelo, who, at
last, steeped in unfeigned ennui near the close of his sometimes
naughty career, remarked: 'My life was never destined to be quite
happy. It was laid out along lines which I could foresee almost from
earliest childhood. It has left me with nothing to hope for, with
nothing definite to seek or strive for. Inherited wealth is a real handicap to happiness. It is as certain death to ambition as cocaine is to
morality.

'If a man makes money, no matter how much, he finds a certain
happiness in its possession, for in the desire to increase his business,
he has a constant use for it. But the man who inherits it has none
of that. The first satisfaction, and the greatest, that of building the
foundation of a fortune, is denied him. He must labour, if he does
labour, simply to add to an over-sufficiency.'

In the light of events following young Gertrude's coming-out
party in 1895, I cannot help believing that, like his brother Willie,

my grandfather, Cornelius II, suffered from some deep-seated and ineradicable malaise of the soul which drove him to an unpredictable and tragic end.

It is part of the Vanderbilt legend, by now so overlaid with rumour, fiction, spite, and folklore that it is almost impossible to uncover the hues and shadings of the original picture, that every Vanderbilt heir has fought violently with his father. It was true in my case, and in my father's, and it runs clear back to the founders of the Vanderbilt fortune, the Commodore and his sons.

I would say, from my experience, that the Vanderbilt traits of stubbornness, pride, sense of duty, and explosive temper, coupled with a ready susceptibility towards the charms of the opposite sex, have accentuated the terrible rivalry between father and son.

'If brother Bill hadn't died in Yale, the whole history of the family would have been different,' my Aunt Gladys remarked sadly to me not long ago.

Bill Vanderbilt, Neily's brother, and the oldest of Alice and Cornelius' six children, had been trained since childhood to assume the position of head of the House of Vanderbilt. Never for an instant did my grandfather allow his oldest son to forget the lofty responsibilities inherent in that title, and, fortunately, Bill seemed perfectly endowed for it by nature. He was intelligent, aggressive, a born leader, and immensely popular with young and old. Like his father, he resembled in appearance a patrician of Rome; yet in manner he was easygoing, quiet, and democratic.

He and Neily were rooming together at Yale when suddenly Bill was taken with typhoid fever and died at the age of twenty. So stunned were his parents by this tragic turn of events that for several years Grandfather made no attempt to direct Neily's foot-steps towards the presidency of the family railroad, but allowed him to go along much as he had before, content to potter by the hour with his test tubes and boyish inventions and sailboats, all occupations which kept him supremely happy.

For Neily Vanderbilt's dream was to become a scientist. As a boy of sixteen he wrote to his parents from St. Paul's School at Concord, New Hampshire: 'Dear Papa, I am getting on pretty well with my sawmill, however I am at present considering what motive power to use. I have a great favour to ask you and that is if you will get me a bicyclette while you are in London. If you would get me this, I would sell my tricycle and buy a screw-cutting lathe for my workshop. It cost $70 which is the world.' He also complained, 'This cabling to you every week is killing me. $2 every time.'

When he entered Yale in 1891, Neily wrote that he had managed to spend the week-end in New York without taking any cuts in classes. 'New York seemed pretty empty,' he told his parents, 'that is on Fifth Avenue and in church. I thought the music in church was fine but perhaps that was because I hadn't heard any good church music for a long time.

'I am getting on here first rate and like it very much though I think I shall enjoy it more when I get more accustomed and know more of the fellows. Bill is perfectly well. . . . Now I must practise my banjo.'

After his brother's death, Neily's references to his rheumatism seemed to grow more frequent. 'I suppose you know I have had another attack of rheumatism from the cables I sent you, but I am recovering slowly and am still in bed. I am all right except my strength,' he wrote his travelling parents in 1893.

That summer his father packed him off on a world cruise in a chartered yacht, which was filled with fresh produce from the family farms in Rhode Island. This was to be the first step in the training of the future tycoon of finance, to pick up some knowledge of European art, manners, and language, and also to put some flesh on young Neily's skinny frame.

Neily came back tanned and fit and exhilarated (all his life he loved boats and was a marvellous sailor), but with little to show for his culture tour except a jaunting cart he had picked up in Ireland. Neily never had much use for 'culture' as such, for music, or art, or literature, or the artists who produced them. To him, everything had to be comprehended concretely, in terms of precise, scientifically measured reactions; the 'creative' mind, unless it created things one could see and hear and touch in a laboratory, had little point of contact with him.

This, then, was my father as he approached his twenty-second year. His school marks had indicated considerable engineering ability, and on the Yale campus he had acquired a kind of quiet popularity. He was proud to belong to the Scroll and Key, which in those days had only fifteen members, but on the whole Father dressed and lived very quietly and was in no sense of the word a social light. He was known to keep a careful budget and seemed utterly unaware of the worldwide prestige and influence enjoyed by his wealthy and powerful family.

Neily admired pretty girls and was naturally besieged with invitations to *débutante* parties. But he had never shown serious interest in any particular girl until the summer following his graduation from Yale. Then, into his life came a fascinating green-eyed beauty, a sophisticated woman of the world, named Grace Wilson. Neily straightway fell head over heels in love.

Newporters have for generations been marrying other New-porters, through, I suppose, that magic alchemy of hot young blood and hotter summer sun. Grace Wilson and Neily Vanderbilt had moved for years in the same tight, moneyed circles in New York, attended the same balls, the same dinner parties, the same *bals costumés* (fancy dress relieved to some extent the tedium of seeing the same people continually), but their romance began in Newport.

How fortunate were the suitors of those days! It was unthinkable that they should take a girl of gentle breeding to a public restaurant (without her mother, that is), and night clubs were unknown. Instead of spending one or two hundred dollars an evening in the company of a charming girl, an eligible male in the 1890s was besieged with invitations to sumptuous dinners and balls, replete with dry champagne and terrapin, his only expense being an occasional bouquet of flowers.

On the night of Gertrude's coming-out party, young Neily's obvious devotion to the cosmopolitan Miss Wilson aroused much curiosity and speculation. How old was she? She had been 'out', several ladies were sure, at least five or six seasons. However, since her engagement to Cecil Baring, son of Lord Revelstoke, had been broken, she had spent most of her time abroad. Some declared spitefully that it was because her fiancé had lost most of his fortune (which was in a private banking firm) in the crash of 1893; others said that Lord Revelstoke demanded such a high dowry that the intended bride's father, Richard T. Wilson, refused to accede to his outrageous proposition. There was no doubt, however, that Cecil Baring was still pitifully in love with the beauteous Grace, as were half a dozen other young men on both sides of the ocean.

Whispers about my fascinating mother carried back to servants' halls a half a century ago still linger there today. Did some significant scene take place the night of Gertrude's *début* between this gay and radiant belle and the stern and pious senior Vanderbilt?

All I know is that my grandfather Vanderbilt overnight developed a most inexplicable dislike for the charming Miss Wilson. Just as suddenly, Grandmother Vanderbilt began to display the same attitude.

At four o'clock in the morning the great Breakers' ball ended. Down the box-lined drive clattered pair after pair of superb glossy chestnuts guided by the yawning coachmen who had sat up all night gossiping about their employers at the nearby Vanderbilt stables. Within the great stone mansion, servants began wearily removing the vestiges of the party, for they knew that within a few hours Mrs. Vanderbilt would appear with her penetrating gaze and spotless white gloves.

I can see the shy and gangling Neily standing under the ornate stone *porte-cochère* watching the beautiful Grace depart, a brave and erect figure in her elegant ball-gown and jewels.

Then he turned and re-entered the splendid mansion which everyone supposed would some day be his, along with the major share of his father's seventy millions.

Chapter Two

THE following week, Grace Wilson's brother Dick gave a party at the Newport Golf Club. Sixty were invited for dinner, a hundred more for dancing. The *crème de la crème* of Newport society, as they liked to call themselves, were invited. From what I can learn, only a few sent regrets—among these Mr. and Mrs. Cornelius Vanderbilt, Sr., and their son Neily. He had accepted an earlier invitation for a cottage party at Mrs. Calvin Brice's.

The beautiful Miss Wilson stood beside her brother, her sister, and her parents in the receiving line in the richly decorated ballroom of the Newport Golf Club. 'Old-rose pink and maroon were the colours in the ballroom,' the *New York Times* reported in describing the Wilsons' 'interesting and brilliant affair'. Roses were used in great abundance on the face of the balcony mouldings and on the outlines of the arches. Above were bands of heavy green foliage, in which tiny electric lamps shone, and below, suspended from brackets, were heavy old Roman garlands with pendent wreaths of rose-pink flowers, caught up with red roses and broad sashes of apple-green satin ribbon.

Absurdly overdone as this sounds, it was chaste compared to the elaborate gingerbread effects popular in that day. Sometimes roses, lilies of the valley, pinks, and jasmine were fastened by the hundreds to chandeliers to waft down their heavy perfumes, and to drift down also, by twos and threes, into the dinner guests' hair and laps. A *débutante* on a whim, might wear one hundred dollars' worth of fresh violets pinned to the hem of her dress, to fade in an hour. Fifty dollars for a satin box filled with candy was a not uncommon luncheon favour, while a thousand dollars for luncheon for twenty-four, including flowers and favours, was by no means unusual.

The favours at the Wilson ball, distributed during the cotillion, were simple, in keeping with the theme of the party (many guests appeared in calico peasant costume), and consisted of canes, ribbon sashes, calico workbaskets, and lamp-shades. (At Gertrude Vanderbilt's *début*, gold cigarette-cases and fans, costing $10,000 in all, had been distributed.)

Who were these Wilsons who could attract with calico work-baskets and lamp-shades the most illustrious names in Newport to a *bal intime*? So difficult was it to crash Newport in the nineties that some families waited four summers to be invited to one of Mrs. Astor's parties. As Cleveland Amory has recalled in *The Last Resorts*, the late Mrs. Astor's major-domo, Ward McAllister, advised all social climbers with a daughter to launch to take her first to Bar Harbour. 'There,' he said, 'she can learn to flirt to her heart's content and vie with the other girls.' For her second summer, he suggested Newport—but only if she could have 'a pair of ponies, a pretty trap with a well-gotten-up groom, and Worth to dress her'. The safest technique, he advised, was to buy a yacht. Then, if snubbed by Newport, which was described as 'New York society's best dish, garnished with a little cold Boston celery and a fringe of Philadelphia and Baltimore parsley', one could always weigh anchor and slip off to the warmer shores of Southampton.

The Wilsons owned no yacht; they lived unpretentiously in a comfortable frame-house; and they didn't have as much money as some Newporters—no more than $15,000,000 at any rate. Moreover, before they came north from a tiny backwoods town in Tennessee, nobody had ever heard of them.

On the night of his son's ball, Richard T. Wilson, self-made banker and multimillionaire, might have been described as that tall, barrel-chested, slightly stooped gentleman in his sixties with the immaculate white waistcoat and closely cropped white whiskers. His manner was gentle, fastidious, smacking of old Southern chivalry; of Henry Frick, the Pittsburg steel baron, he once said that he should not be allowed in the same room with children.

Unlike many of his Wall Street associates, Richard T. Wilson put in an appearance at all the exclusive Patriarch balls in New York and at Mrs. Astor's dinner-table; he even dined with Mrs. Ogden Mills, a matron so selective that she had reduced society, in her own mind, to a mere twenty families. He was a friendly soul who enjoyed his morning gossip at Newport's ultra-social Casino, and his small black schipperke, Romeo, was said to be the only dog allowed to enter the sacrosanct male portals of New York's Union Club. Yet an air of mystery hung over Richard T. Wilson. His name was never in the newspapers; he seldom spoke of the past. His closest friend was another self-made financial giant, Andrew Carnegie.

His son Dick was a slight, dark young man in his twenties, with the look of a dandy. As the host of the party, he stood beside his mother welcoming the guests. A small white-haired woman with an aristocratic profile and an air of great sweetness and distinction, Mrs. Wilson would greet new arrivals in her soft, slurred Southern accent, then introduce them to her daughter Belle, a strikingly attractive woman with honey-blonde colouring, who was visiting Newport with her husband, the Honourable Michael Herbert, presently stationed in Constantinople as secretary at the British Embassy.

Richard T. Wilson's married son, Orme, stood at the far end of the room with his plain-looking wife, Carrie Astor. One of the four daughters of *the* Mrs. Astor, she had inherited none of her mother's social aplomb.

May, the oldest Wilson daughter, was a plump woman in her late thirties. In the costume of a milkmaid, she stood under a Roman wreath of roses, laughing at some witticism of her slight, frail husband, who suffered from chronic asthma. Some eighteen years ago she had married the scion of the fabulously rich Goelet clan. May, with less social charm than her sisters, was nevertheless so full of life, so generous with her hospitality in her palatial yachts and villas, that she and her husband, Ogden, became leaders of Continental society.

It was May who really launched the Wilsons socially in New York, although her mother's beauty and grace of manner had already won them an honoured place in London society.

The Wilson odyssey began with my maternal grandfather, Richard T. Wilson, a husky, clever, and capable boy born in Gainesville, Georgia, in 1829, the son of a Scottish tanner.

As a travelling salesman, young Richard bought supplies of small articles in Atlanta to sell upcountry in exchange for cotton. While travelling between Knoxville and Chattanooga, he stopped at a handsomely cultivated 712-acre farm with a manor house and slave quarters, owned by one Ebenezar Johnston. Mr. Johnston had a cultivated Virginia-born wife and, more important, a beautiful daughter named Melissa, the eldest of ten children.

People in Loudon, Tennessee, near the Johnston plantation, say that Richard T. Wilson was the 'poor-but-honest' type, a man of large appetites, ambition, and charm. The rumour persists that Margaret Mitchell based the character of Rhett Butler on the legend of Richard T. Wilson's swashbuckling charm and good looks.

There can be no doubt that he was a sensational salesman, for not only did he talk Ebenezar Johnston into financing him in business, but he talked him out of his eldest daughter as well. With the Johnston money behind him, Grandfather Wilson opened a small general store in Loudon and, over its counter, sold clover seed and bacon, tobacco, window-sash, bellows, and just about everything else he had previously lugged about in suitcases. And within the year he made Melissa his bride.

My Aunt Flew who, like Richard T. Wilson, married into the Johnston family, recalls that he was a handsome man with 'a delicious sense of humour'. One night when she was visiting the Wilsons in New York, she found that she had left her handbag in the living-room and slipped downstairs to get it. 'There stood Richard, with a candle in each hand, gazing at a big oil portrait of himself on the wall. I crept up behind him and suddenly remarked, '*Damn* good-looking fellow!'

'Yes,' he agreed calmly, 'isn't he?'

There's an old saying that it takes two generations to make a gentleman in America, since the first one seldom arrives married to a lady. But my grandmother, Melissa Johnston, was undoubtedly one. Although she had never been more than a few miles from Loudon before her marriage, she lived to be named by the Reverend de Lyon Nichols, in his snobbish book *The Ultra-Smart Peerage*, as one of the three most fashionable dowagers in America, a group that included Mrs. Astor. A woman of sensitivity and feeling, of great moral rectitude as well as physical grace, Grandmother Wilson succeeded in smoothing over a great many rough corners in her husband's character. Still, she was never domineering or obvious, but remained to the end of her days, when I was privileged to know her, a sweet gentlewoman, still with her soft and clinging Southern ways.

Grandmother Wilson's first three children lie buried by three small white tombstones in the Loudon, Tennessee, cemetery.

Perhaps this was the reason she returned to Loudon so seldom in later years, and never after her Virginian mother died.

When the War between the States began, Grandfather Wilson, who was then in his early thirties, joined the commissary department of the Confederate army with the rank of major. Along with his wife and two small children, May and Orme, he moved to Atlanta. It was fortunate that he was able to remove his family from Loudon, Tennessee, for that little town, being on the direct highway and rail route between Knoxville and Chattanooga, suffered greatly from marauding troops during the war. Melissa's sister Mary, who had been left on the family plantation with her elderly, ailing parents, wrote that the cotton fields were 'a sea of tents' and that 'the military have commandeered our bake-ovens' and 'we are living on fish and a mess of Mustard'.

In January, 1864, Mary reported to her husband on the Wilsons in Atlanta: 'Melissa writes that they are all well and getting along as well as they can under the circumstances. They are keeping house in the Marshall Ormes' house in Atlanta. Mr. Wilson bought things to make her room comfortable . . . got a nice Brussels carpet, a bedstead, bureau, washstand, sofa and other things . . . Sister says she has formed the acquaintance of several nice ladies.'

Several weeks later Mary wrote again: 'We had two letters from Mr. Wilson, the last one dated the 28th of January. Sister had given birth that day to a fine little daughter. He said she and the babe are both doing very well, says they are living very well and comfortable in Mr. Orme's house in Atlanta, have two rooms comfortably furnished and enough provisions to last six to eight months . . . This is the business part of Mr. Wilson's letter. He says: "*Have sent father's bonds to Richmond, have not heard from them yet. Have purchased for father a bond on E.T. and V.R.R. for $1000 . . . I have reliable information of the sale in Europe of the bonds of the $100,000,000 loan at 30¢ on the dollar. I think you had better try them. If sent by mail I will take the risk of their loss on the way. The matter is well worth the experiment, and if they bring the price we can try again. You can purchase them in E. Tenn. without difficulty.*" ' (Italics mine.)

Apparently, Grandfather's speculations on the foreign market were successful, for soon the Johnston daughter wrote again to her absent husband: 'I hear that Mr. Wilson has bought a plantation on the Alabama River near Selma worth $150,000 and a house in Atlanta worth $25,000.'

In June, 1864, there was a final letter from Mary Johnston to her husband: 'Mr. Wilson has gone to Europe, the family remaining in Atlanta, and if the Federals take it they will be looked after. We all feel very uneasy about them.'

At this stage in the war, Grandfather Wilson had been selected to go to England to represent the Southern cotton growers, who were desperate for a market for their crops. With all the Northern markets closed to them, foreign outlets remained their only source of revenue. My Wilson grandparents with their three young children ran the blockade of Union warships patrolling the harbour of Wilmington, North Carolina. My Uncle Orme Wilson often mentioned his excitement in peering out the portholes to look for enemy ships.

They all reached England safely and remained abroad until the war ended.

Apparently, English society was charmed by the Southern Wilsons. And Richard T. Wilson must have sold a great deal of his own cotton abroad, for he returned to this country, some said, with $500,000 to invest. Others maliciously called him a war profiteer, and I am afraid that this was the impression he left upon the South; for at the time of his death, fifty years after the War between the States, when he had become known as one of the financial wizards of Wall Street, the newspapers of Atlanta, Georgia, afforded him no more than one obituary paragraph. The New York newspapers gave him columns.

I can't believe that Grandfather, with all his Victorian propriety and gentleness of character, came by his fortune dishonestly. At any rate, he did not act like a robber baron. The first home he bought in New York, immediately following the War between the States, was a plain brownstone up at 812 Fifth Avenue. At this time much of the land north of 59th Street was rugged, hilly, rocky terrain, dotted with frame farmhouses and squatter settlements, and it did not become a desirable sector until the advent of the steam shovel made it commercially profitable to level the ground.

It was here, in the house at 812 Fifth Avenue, that my mother was born in 1870. Perhaps that is why she always loved simple, quiet, country pastimes, and always turned to them when wearied by her glittering days. Mother frequently said that when she was a small girl in pinafores, her older sister was having babies of her own, and this was true, for Aunt May Goelet was sixteen years older than Grace. Aunt May's children were almost contemporaries of my mother. Coming late in her parents' life as she did, when they were just beginning to be able to afford luxuries, young Grace was greatly pampered and spoiled, so I'm told. She was called nothing but Baby for three years, until she herself decided upon the name Grace Graham (after her great-grandmother, Margaret Graham, who had emigrated from Ireland to Virginia).

Every summer until she was seven, Grace returned with her mother to Loudon, Tennessee, to visit her Southern relatives. There she helped dam up the creek and went swimming in it, picked blackberries, and climbed about the old peg-constructed barn.

'After her mother died, Mrs. Wilson never returned to Loudon, Tennessee,' a relative there told me. 'And we never saw Grace again, but we were clothed in things they sent from New York. We were just little country tykes, wearing calico and percale. The clothes the Wilsons sent were practically new—some of them had probably only been worn once. They were lovely silks and brocades and laces. I can still remember playing in the red clay gullies in Grace Wilson's blue satin slippers.'

Once settled in New York, Grandfather Wilson began to help reorganize and rebuild Southern railways, which had been wrecked during the War between the States. First he reorganized the East Tennessee, Virginia and Georgia Railway, of which he became president in 1870. Later he rebuilt the Macon and Brunswick, as well as other railways in Georgia.

He was one of Andrew Carnegie's first customers for the new steel rails in the 1880s, when he built the Yazoo and Mississippi Valley Railroad, known as the 'millionaire's railway', which is now part of the Illinois Central. Eventually he owned lines in Iowa and the Midwest, and had large financial interests in street railways in Detroit, Cleveland, Brooklyn, and Yonkers. Grandfather invested his money shrewdly but always improved, never exploited, the properties he acquired.

He also had many manufacturing interests, and helped form the Mathieson Alkali Works in Saltville, Virginia, makers of caustic soda and bleaching powders, which has since become the Olin Mathieson Company.

It can be seen that Grandfather was, in his way, gifted with the same kind of vision, ability, and business acumen as the old Commodore Vanderbilt, founder of our family, who expanded a loan of $100 from his mother into a fortune of $105,000,000.

But the Wilsons never made the social columns in New York until their oldest daughter, May, married, in 1877, young Ogden Goelet.

By this time, twelve years after the War between the States, Richard T. Wilson was a millionaire and the head of his own banking firm, which was located at 33 Wall Street. He was well able to afford a rather elaborate summer cottage at New London, Connecticut, with a large parlour where his eldest daughter, May, could entertain her various beaux. One of her swains was Ogden Goelet, a short, sensible young man who rather shunned society and who was considered no great matrimonial catch.

In no time at all, however, he captured May's susceptible young heart. In an old family trunk I found a letter she penned to him, in her large, generous hand, back in the 1870s: 'I never liked you so well, or wished more to be with you, than last night and yet you left me—heedless of my entreaties, left me with a man too prone to say sweet nothings, which some think mean so much, or so little.

'I am convinced you have no jealousy—I shall *really* be awfully disappointed if I do not see you tomorrow, and prefer of course seeing you in the evening. Forget the other girl and I will do the same with the other man.

'It was very sweet of you to come to the ball, I know it must have been a great bore to you, I appreciate your martyrdom. I am reading Denzil Place and think it very naughty. Yours truly and sincerely, May Wilson.'

Before long, Richard T. Wilson was writing to young Goelet: 'As the day of your marriage with my daughter May arrives tomorrow, I feel it proper to state to you that I have given her a total of $75,000 in bonds. I will hold these bonds in trust for my daughter, and shall be pleased to have your counsel and advice in the management of this trust. I beg to offer you a most hearty welcome on behalf of Mrs. Wilson, the children and myself into the new relations which your marriage will create and we do most sincerely ask God's blessing upon the union which is to unite you and our daughter in the sacred and we pray happy relations of husband and wife.'

Although Ogden and May began wedded bliss on a modest scale, it was not long before his uncle, Peter Goelet, died, leaving to Ogden and his brother a fortune in Manhattan real estate roughly estimated at $25,000,000. As the Goelets made a policy of never selling their holdings, charging land rents instead, it was a fortune which soon soared in value as New York City grew.

So while Grace Wilson was still in pinafores, her sister May moved into a grand red brick mansion at 49th Street and Fifth Avenue, which was then considered 'way uptown'. 'I have never seen such a stream of carriages passing this corner,' May wrote to her husband while he was away on a yachting cruise in the spring of 1885. 'By moving up here I thought we would be out of all that for at least another generation. Mrs. Mills has asked me to lunch with her on Sunday . . . Write me all about everything, about your dearest self and believe that I love you fondly and miss you more every hour until your safe return. Kisses from my soul and from the babies to you, Sweetheart, and a big hug from Your Ever Loving Wife.'

A lot of people made fun of Aunt May, whom they called a 'pusher'. Although as a young girl she barely tipped the scales at 102, she grew to be very fat. This, plus the fact that she dashed back and forth across the Atlantic so often during the year, earned her the nickname of Steamboat Mary. After a few cocktails, she loved to reminisce about her gay life on the Continent for, like the Marchioness of Ripon, that pale, swanlike beauty of London society, Aunt May could boast that she had passed her life between princes and tenors.

I can remember her sitting on the broad terrace at Ochre Court, her French chateau at Newport, sipping a *crème de menthe* after luncheon. My mother was drinking plain Poland water, as she never touched a drop of alcohol. I can recall how shocked she was when Aunt May dipped one plump jewelled finger into her glass and let me taste the peppermint liqueur with the tip of my tongue. I could not have been more than seven or eight at the time. Father had offered me $1,000 if I abstained from drinking until my twenty-first birthday; I not only won the bet but never tasted a cocktail until I was thirty-three.

When the Goelets came into their money they chartered a luxurious yacht named *White Ladye*—from Mrs. Lily Langtry, I believe—and on this they sailed along the Riviera and attended the boating races at Cowes and Kiel. In those days there was a great rivalry between the Prince of Wales (later Edward VII) and Emperor Wilhelm of Germany, each trying to stage the most spectacular races, with the world's fastest and sleekest sailing yachts. Any American yachtsman with enough manners and money to be acceptable to court circles found himself welcomed with open arms. And the *bon vivant* Prince of Wales, it was said, was enchanted with American women, their wit and charm and their blooming-rose beauty; it was he, more than anyone else in the eighties and nineties, who let down the bars of London society to young American ladies.

Yet, oddly enough, it was Belle Wilson, a ravishing honey-blonde several years younger than her sister May, who was first granted an audience with the awesome Queen Victoria.

'Your letter with account of your audience with the Queen was most interesting and, after the children and I had thoroughly enjoyed it, we posted it to Mamma last evening,' May wrote to Belle from her mansion at 608 Fifth Avenue. 'The titles which always attend such ceremonials must have given you a few moments of discomfort. I mean your description of the interview is quite what I imagined such a function to be—a great fluttering about the heart and an unnatural voice as though one's very life depended upon the effect of the visit—a feeling of intense relief when it is over. I think you are enjoying yourself more than at Newport!'

The beauteous seventeen-year-old Belle Wilson, travelling abroad with her father, was indeed having a wonderful time.

Mother always used to say that the strength of the Wilsons lay in the fact that they always stuck together. Unlike many wealthy families, who lived side by side as total strangers in the same house, the Wilsons displayed a passionate affection for and interest in each other, even when separated by thousands of miles of ocean, as they frequently were. Uncle Ogden suffered so acutely from his asthma that he and my Aunt May found it best to remain most of the year in Beaulieu, between Cannes and Monte Carlo, going to

35

London only for the season, and occasionally coming to Ochre Court in Newport for a month or two.

In the summer of 1884, when my mother was fourteen, Grandmother Wilson wrote to May from Newport: 'I am writing this letter under difficulties as Grace is studying her French grammar lesson. She takes two lessons a week with Madame du Caylee and two music lessons with Professor Wilson, and also has one lesson in English an hour each day with Mrs. T. Cushing's governess, who we think is excellent. She really has more lessons and more to do than she had in the winter. She has also joined a dancing class that Mrs. Cushing and Mrs. Wetmore have made for girls between 14 and 16 years. I do not think she will be able to go every day as she has most of her lessons in the afternoon.'

My mother never attended a regular school but had, instead, private tutors, winter and summer, whether home or abroad. Perhaps because her governesses were mostly well-born foreign ladies with no knowledge of American slang, Mother always spoke the English language with scrupulous perfection. She never slipped into such sloppy habits as saying 'phoned' for 'telephoned'; she always 'motored', never 'drove'. 'Children' were never, never 'kids'.

When Ward McAllister organized the Patriarch balls in the early 1880s he resolved to make them the most exclusive, best-run balls ever given in New York, and to a large extent he succeeded. He and Mrs. Astor chose twenty-five so-called 'patriarchs' of New York society, who were allowed to invite to each ball four ladies and five men. Each Patriarch was held personally responsible for the social acceptability of his guests. There were no Vanderbilts and no Wilsons among the Patriarchs. But after their famous fancy-dress ball in 1883, Alva and Willie K. Vanderbilt were regularly invited to the Patriarch balls and, gradually, so were the other Vanderbilts.

The Wilsons won the same recognition with a lot less effort. Orme Wilson, the oldest son, simply married one of Mrs. Astor's daughters.

At first, it was said, Mrs. Astor vigorously opposed the match. Then, one day, while leaving church, she saw her daughter Carrie coming out of the holy portals, hand in hand with the young Columbia College graduate. There was something so touching about the scene, friends say, that Mrs. Astor capitulated. By this time, Richard T. Wilson could afford to give the young couple $500,000 as a wedding gift; the Astors did the same and added a house, so that on their wedding-day Carrie and Orme Wilson began a domestic career with a Fifth Avenue mansion, a houseful of servants, and a tidy million in the bank.

It wasn't long before my mother, then in her teens, became a special protégée of Carrie's mother, Mrs. Astor, the so-called 'Queen of the Four Hundred'.

'My dear Grace,' Mrs. Astor wrote her, 'I am giving a dance on the 11th of January and I write to ask you if you will lead the German for me with Mr. Dyer. It will give me so much pleasure if you will do so and please look your prettiest. Affectionately yours, Caroline Astor.'

As this invitation was to Mrs. Astor's annual ball, conceded to be the most dazzling event of the New York winter season, a request to lead the cotillion was a very special honour indeed.

None of Mrs. Astor's four daughters could compare in grace or beauty or social flair with my mother (although they all made very wealthy marriages). Perhaps this explains why my mother and her sister-in-law, Carrie Astor, although friendly, were never really very close. I was told once by one of the Astors that Carrie's brother, John Jacob, who eventually inherited about $60,000,000, was very keen on marrying my mother at one time but that his sister, Carrie, talked him out of it. On the other hand, my mother told *me* that she never considered marrying Jack Astor, whom she found 'gross and vulgar'. (He married twice before losing his life tragically in the sinking of the *Titanic*.)

'Darling daughter Belle,' wrote Mrs. Wilson to her travelling daughter in the winter of 1887. 'My longings for a few words with you overcome me and I am seated for a few moments with you before dinner . . . Carrie and Orme dined here last evening for the first time since the birth of the baby. She looks better than I have ever seen her and is as homelike and friendly as anyone could be. She inquires after you once in a great while but, strange as it may seem, never speaks of May or her children. I have avoided saying anything in my letters to you purposely as it is not worth thinking about when you are away from here; it will keep up toward May when she comes back, but I hope she will be more decent toward you. I really do not think she has much to do with her sisters when her mother is not here . . .

'The opera season is drawing to a close. It has been very successful. There have been crowded houses every night but it seems it will never be able to pay. I fear the people will soon get tired of the great expense of owning boxes and having to be assessed so heavily [the Wilsons owned Metropolitan Box number 3].'

Grandmother Wilson then went on to recount all the recent New York gossip, discreetly referring to the ladies and gentlemen involved by their initials, and ending with 'You must *burn* this letter and by no means allow anyone to see what I have written.'

'I have such treats in reading your letters . . .' she continued. 'I think you will be among the best people there and not among the fast ones. You must tire of the numerous Americans there but it must be something new for you to see so many new people and very interesting to meet distinguished foreigners. Is it not very monotonous not having any young men where there are so many beautiful young women? I don't think it would be at all interesting.'

My grandmother's concern over her daughters' associaton with the fast set may refer to the Prince of Wales' circle, to which the Ogden Goelets belonged. The Prince was always grateful for the intimate dinner parties Aunt May arranged for him aboard the *White Ladye*, parties to which he knew the Honourable Mrs. George Keppel would be invited. His wife, the statuesque Princess Alexandra, naturally received an invitation as well, but it was tacitly understood that she would graciously decline. So understanding was the Princess on the subject of Mrs. Keppel that when her husband, then King Edward VII of England, lay on his deathbed, it was she who summoned his Scottish friend to his side.

Such situations, which Aunt May learned to accept with tolerant amusement, turned my Presbyterian Grandmother Wilson 'pale with horror', as Belle used to say.

The summer that Grace turned eighteen, the Wilson family was again travelling abroad. In Paris both Dick and his father came down with measles, each suffering from a sore throat, headache, and fever. Their eyes were 'bright coals of fire', so Belle reported. Then Grace became desperately ill with typhoid fever.

Just before Grace took sick, Belle wrote to May describing their social doings in London and Paris: 'London looked empty,' she reported in a letter of April, 1888, 'so many people being still away on Easter parties. I sent a note to the Prince so late that I hardly thought that he would answer it before I left, but he is punctuality itself. He thanked me for letting him know that I was passing through London but regretted that I was leaving the next day as he loses out therefore from the pleasure of seeing me—to thank my sister and brother-in-law (the Goelets) for their kind messages and to send you his best regards.

'It amuses me how the outrageous scandals are going on in the same way as when I left.'

The next day Belle wrote again: 'I must send you another line before I leave Paris to thank you for the present you put into the envelope for Grace and me. I cannot tell you how much it means. Too dear and thoughtful of you and I expect to turn it into something very pretty if I don't lose it all at Monte Carlo! The gambling fever is growing on me—it seems such an easy way to enlarge one's possessions, but I am afraid my dear parent [Richard T. Wilson] will restrain my wicked impulses.

'Grace went with Amy Bend under the care of Mr. Winthrop to the E's yesterday. Mr. Winthrop says Bennett is being very attentive to that big handsome Miss Mary this winter at Nice and that *en plus* he had not only one but two ladies there besides! This page had better be expurgated before passed on to the male members of the family. It's too naughty. Good-bye dearest sister and thank you again and again for that dear remembrance.'

In November of 1888 Belle married the Honourable Michael Herbert, who was then *chargé d'affaires* of the British Embassy in Washington, D.C., at a very fashionable wedding at St. Bartholomew's on Madison Avenue. Grace Wilson was her sister's only bridesmaid, wearing a trained gown of yellow satin and a large hat of dark-brown velvet with plumes to match. Her only jewellery was a gift from the bridegroom, a necklace of pearls with a diamond and pearl pendant.

With this marriage the Wilsons became related to one of England's oldest and most distinguished families. For four hundred years the Herberts have occupied Wilton House, a celebrated castle originally designed for them by Holbein. 'Wilton is the Paradise of England,' wrote the English poet, Sir Wilfred Blunt, 'with three rivers eternally beautiful and unchanged when its owners change or perish. One passes by and finds Herberts there as one finds swallows in the village . . .'

How well I can remember the portraits of long-dead Herberts, lords and ladies, painted by Van Dyck, gazing down at me from the walls of the great gilded drawing-room where every afternoon we had tea. Better still, I can remember the velvety grass tennis courts stretching in front of the ivy-covered stone castle where I took my first lessons in this sport. On the other side of Wilton House one strolled through acres of beautifully cared-for formal Italian gardens. The Prince of Wales, his lovely wife, Alexandra, and his brothers were frequent week-end guests at Wilton. They were all on affectionate terms with Belle's husband, whom they called Mungo.

So once again society buzzed with the Wilsons' astonishing luck in contracting advantageous marriages. A joke current at the time went:

'Question: Why did the Diamond Match Company fail?'

'Answer: Because Mrs. Richard T. Wilson beat them at making matches.'

Chapter Three

IN the comic and cruel struggle for social supremacy among America's brash new moneyed aristocracy, nothing seemed to elevate a family quicker than a series of advantageous marriages. After her sister's marriage into English society, Grace Wilson's social horizon widened immeasurably. Her life began to assume the pattern it followed for many years afterwards. During the early part of the winter, she remained in New York for the opera season and the Patriarch and Assembly balls. Then, early in April, she sailed for Paris to have a summer wardrobe fitted, then on to visit the Goelets on the Riviera, perhaps to take a short cruise with them, ending with a 'cure' at Bad Nauheim that lasted for several weeks. By the first of June she was always in London for the season. After that, off to Scotland for grouse hunting, or a Scandinavian cruise, or perhaps a visit with le Duc et la Duchesse de la Rochefoucauld in their lovely chateau, or a stay at Deauville.

Then a rapid rush through the enchanting shops of the great couturiers on the Rue de la Paix, a flurry of orders and fittings, and off to the United States and a six-week 'cure' at the Homestead at Hot Springs to prepare her for the strenuous New York winter season.

As Aunt Flew recalls it, Grace would cable from Paris: 'Father, what shall I do? I'm supposed to sail on the Teutonic, and Worth doesn't have my dresses ready.' So Richard T. Wilson would say to Aunt Flew's husband (who was employed in the Wilson bank), 'What are we going to do about Grace?' And my uncle would say: 'Well, Major, I guess I better go bail her out again. When do you want me to leave?'

R. T. would say, 'This afternoon at three.' So my uncle would go over to Paris and take the hide off Worth's and get Grace's dresses and they'd sail as scheduled. There was never any blame for Grace. Mr. Wilson just thought it was outrageous that those people should keep his daughter waiting.

'Grace has never looked so well,' Grandmother Wilson wrote

to Ogden Goelet following a trip of Grace's to visit her sister Belle and her husband in Constantinople. 'She and Dick seldom dine at home and Grace goes from morning until midnight. They say they have never had so many invitations . . . Tonight Grace is dining at Cornelius Vanderbilt's. . . I suppose the Herald announced to you the arrival of Lord Ava in New York. He was met when the boat arrived by the terrible reporters to know if he was coming to marry Miss Wilson [Grace]. He was so frightened by them that he only came to see her once. He told her that he was so sorry for her and wondered what her father would think of all this talk. He only stayed three days and went on to Canada and, after reaching there, wrote her a nice letter saying he hoped that it would make no difference in their friendship but I am sure it will . . . It was hard for Grace but there was no way to stop people's mouths . . .'

In 1894, a year before Grace's romance with young Neily Vanderbilt, she wrote her 'darling parents' from aboard the Goelet yacht, *White Ladye*, anchored off Kingston, Ireland. At this time she was twenty-four and still unmarried, but obviously not lacking for beaux.

'We have been in Ireland since Friday morning and I am greatly enjoying myself. May and I got over here most comfortably, the Irish channel being very smooth.

'On Saturday Arthur Paget took us all to his races at Leopardstown, where we lunched and spent the day in the Lord Lieutenant's stand. He, Lord Houghton, is a very good-looking, charming young widower of about thirty-five. Rich, clever, and everything! He was so nice to us and immediately asked us to come up to Dublin and stay in the Vice Regal Lodge with him.

'On Sunday we drove about—the country is too, too lovely. Then on Monday we drove out to the races again and lunched and spent the day with the Lord Lieutenant [Lord Houghton]. Prince Francis of Teck is here and seems *such* a nice young man. I have seen him quite often. The young Duke and Duchess de Luynes are staying with Lord Houghton and came to the races yesterday. Tomorrow the great Dublin Horse Show begins and we are going with Lord Houghton and then we shall return with him and all of his suite and outriders to the Castle where there will be a large dinner, followed by a ball, and we shall stay there for a night or so. The Italian Princes, the Duke d'Aosta and Count Turin will also be staying there. What fun it all is!

'You really don't want me at home, do you, Mama, just yet? I should like to stay over here all winter if only you and Papa could come over!'

The following week she wrote from London: 'Since I arrived here last Saturday morning I have been having a very pleasant week of town life at this season, which means doing the plays, etc.

'Monday Belle and Mungo were in town so we were together most of the day. In the evening May and I, Arthur and Seymour Fortescue dined at the Savoy and came home about 10 and when we got here we found Hedworth [Sir Hedworth Lambton] had come to pay an evening call! It sounds so old-fashioned but at this season of the year they call in the evening.

'Wed. Ogden arrived looking very fat and well, but Sister says it is *puff* not fat. That afternoon he had quite a number of visitors and in the evening we went with Hedworth to see Constantinople, which I was curious to see on account of Belle and Mungo!!!

'Thursday was a quiet day, and Sister, Ogden, and I shopped.

'A most wonderful fortune teller is quite the rage here at present and has told most strange things to several people we know which have come true. She gave me a splendid future and told me the name of the man I am to marry and wrote it down for me and it is someone I know and like but I won't say who!!! I was so startled when she spelled it out of my hand. She also told me that years ago I was engaged to a fair young man with blue eyes and she told me other things that were true and of course she had no idea who we were. So it was very wonderful.

'Sister and I go to Paris on Monday.

'Hedworth has just come also so must close. Devotedly, Grace.'

Was the fair young man with the blue eyes to whom Grace admitted she was once engaged Bill Vanderbilt? All the sons of Alice and Cornelius of the Breakers had blue eyes, but Miss Wilson must have had dozens of suitors on both sides of the Atlantic who would fit that description. All I know is that what is left of old-guard Newport society today still insists that there was a romance between Grace Wilson and the oldest Vanderbilt boy, who was about her own age. After Bill Vanderbilt died at twenty of typhoid, Grace became engaged to Lord Revelstoke's son. When this engagement was broken, she returned to America and soon began focusing her charms upon young Neily, fresh out of Yale, and the presumed future head of the family.

Her actions were interpreted by Neily's parents as part of a calculated campaign to marry a Vanderbilt *en tout cas*, and for this, so say the gossips, Grace Wilson incurred the senior Vanderbilts' wholehearted disapproval.

I never heard my mother mention a romance with Bill Vanderbilt, and I have found no record anywhere of such an engagement.

It is clear from the letters my mother wrote her family from abroad about her various beaux that a dozen distinguished foreign titles could have been hers, titles carrying far more social cachet than the name of Vanderbilt.

If ambition alone had led Grace Wilson to encourage young Neily's infatuation, she never would have chosen to marry into a family which had only 'arrived' on the New York social scene simultaneously with her own backwoods Tennessee people.

It was Father's Aunt Alva, Mrs. William K. Vanderbilt, who first got the Vanderbilts into society, something which two generations before her had failed to accomplish. Almost as soon as Alva, a bouncy, pushy belle from Mobile, became Mrs. Willie K. Vanderbilt, things started to hum.

'Until Mrs. William K.'s advent,' commented the New York *World*, 'the Vanderbilt family was unheard of in New York society, except occasionally when it was abused for watering railroad stock or damning the public. Mrs. W. K. thought that better things could be done with their opportunities. She took Willie K. by the hand and led the way for all the Vanderbilts into the gay world of society, Fifth Avenue, terrapin, Newport, dry champagne, servants in livery, men who don't work, women with no serious thoughts, and all the other charms of fashionable existence.'

My great Aunt Alva boasted afterwards: 'I always do everything first. I blaze the trail for the rest to walk in. I was the first girl of my set to marry a Vanderbilt.'

Aunt Alva did not attempt to crash society until she was thirty-one. Then, in 1883, she threw a *bal costumé* so dazzling in conception, so lavish in its details, that it is still remembered as *the* Vanderbilt fancy-dress ball.

The affair was held in Aunt Alva's and Uncle Willie's newly

completed $3,000,000 French chateau of limestone and Caen stone on the north-west corner of Fifth Avenue and 52nd Street. (Alva, according to her contemporaries, was always 'knee deep in mortar'.) Twelve hundred invitations were issued. Up until this time, Aunt Alva had never been invited to one of Mrs. Astor's balls, nor had that famous arbiter of society ever deigned to call upon the young Mrs. Vanderbilt. Alva was careful to see that no invitation was extended to the Astors.

Unsuspecting, the lofty Mrs. Astor (who had long ago dropped the 'William' from her calling cards and begun using the sublime inscription 'Mrs. Astor') in the meantime had fallen into Alva's clever trap. She encouraged her daughter, Carrie, to form a quadrille of her young friends to perform at the ball. Alva waited until they had drilled to perfection, then quietly let it be known that, since Mrs. Astor had never dropped her pasteboard at 660 Fifth Avenue, it would be quite impossible to invite either her or her daughter to the ball.

Mrs. Astor smouldered in quiet rage for several days, but finally the entreaties of her daughter won out. She summoned her coachman, so the story goes, and a footman in the blue livery of the House of Astor, and delivered her card to the maroon-liveried footman at the portals of the House of Vanderbilt. Immediately afterwards, the Astors received an invitation to the ball.

For Alva's first big social splash, the florist Klunder was given *carte blanche*. Throughout her chateau he distributed thousands of Gloire de Paris and Baronne de Rothschild long-stemmed roses at the fantastic cost of two dollars apiece; he transformed the second-floor supper-room into a tropical forest with palm trees festooned with orchids. For his efforts, he rendered a bill of $11,000.

On the evening of Alva's fancy-dress ball, my grandfather, Cornelius Vanderbilt II, left his offices at the Grand Central Depot and returned home, where a costumer and hairdresser awaited. On the stroke of eleven, curious mobs standing along the avenue, kept toughly in check by squads of horse-mounted policemen, were rewarded by the sight of King Louis XVI emerging from my grandfather's house. He was wearing breeches of fawn-coloured brocade and point d'Espagne and a coat of reseda trimmed with real silver lace. A diamond-hilted sword hung by his side. His wife, hanging on his arm, appeared rather incongruously as 'The Electric

Light'. Her white satin dress and headdress produced a 'blaze of diamonds', according to the onlookers.

Mr. and Mrs. W. K. Vanderbilt received, with Lady Mandeville, in the dining-hall of their palace. Uncle Willie K., a rather short but dashing-looking fellow, appeared as the Duc de Guise in a pale-yellow silk doublet with a black velvet cloak embroidered with gold. Alva, the hostess, was a Venetian princess, dressed in shades of deepest orange to canary and wearing a superb jewelled peacock in her hair.

All in all, the *World's* reporters estimated, the costumes for this ball, to be worn once and then discarded, cost in the neighbourhood of $156,000. Just the other day I met a dear old lady, born in 1860, who had actually been one of the guests. 'It was magnificent,' she said, 'but you know, I can't recall having much *fun*. People are always so self-conscious in fancy dress.'

Nevertheless, the ball accomplished Alva's purpose. Shortly afterwards, her husband was admitted to the ultra-exclusive Coaching Club, and then to the Metropolitan, the Knickerbocker, Union, Racquet and Tennis, Turf and Field, and the New York Yacht Club. The following January they attended Mrs. Astor's annual ball, to which only four hundred were invited, since the Astor ballroom could accommodate only that number. Alva was 'in', and after her trooped all the rest of the Vanderbilts.

But she never managed to crash the sacred circle of box-holders at the old Academy of Music, where the Bayards and Beekmans, the Schuylers and the Livingstons held their opera evenings. So the Vanderbilt clan, along with the other new millionaires, formed a corporation to build their own opera house. They chose a site at 39th Street and Broadway and called it the Metropolitan Opera House.

By 1892, when the Diamond Horseshoe was added, its thirty-five boxes selling for $60,000 apiece, the new opera house had become so fashionable that *Town Topics* remarked, 'Millionaires would willingly crawl on hands and knees up the red velvet stair to the Diamond Horseshoe and feel that the dust accumulated on their knees in the painful odyssey was a hallmark of social progress.'

For the next fifty years, only twenty families occupied the thirty-five boxes of the Diamond Horseshoe. By 1926, Frazier Jelke was happy to pay my cousin Harold Vanderbilt $200,000 for his box. Nor was this the final cost, for the yearly assessment on the boxes amounted to $4,500.

Irving Kolodin, commenting on what was wrong with the Metropolitan as an opera house—poor lighting, no place to store scenery, no stables or shelter for coachmen and horses, who were forced to wait outdoors through the bitterest winter weather—remarked that it 'served only one purpose perfectly; display of those who occupied the boxes, for which it was built'.

And what a display they made! Grace Wilson's parents owned a box, as did her sister and brother-in-law, Mr. and Mrs. Ogden Goelet; the various branches of the Vanderbilt family owned five. 'Let royal coffers be what they may,' a fashionable clergyman commented in appraising the jewels of the Metropolitan box-holders, 'the collective contents of the jewel caskets of the ultra-fashionable set in New York society approximate closely one hundred and seventy millions of dollars. White ropes or Oriental pearls of almost priceless purity enchain the necks and shoulders of the smartest set; the coronets of diamonds worn at the Opera cost, on the average, not more than twenty thousand dollars. Of a few of the more imposing tiaras, however, each of the pearl-shaped brilliants capping the apex could easily command five thousand dollars. If a woman aspires to regal effects in evening dress, beside her diamond tiara, a corsage piece of diamonds valued at, say, seventy-five thousand dollars is requisite.'

Both my Grandmother Alice Vanderbilt and her sister-in-law, Alva, owned jewels valued at a million dollars. In appearance these two were somewhat alike—although Alva was credited with considerable sex appeal. In the early part of 1895, Alva scandalized society by divorcing Neily's uncle, Willie K. Vanderbilt, who found his money such a handicap to happiness. Moreover, she had the audacity to divorce him in New York State, where, as everybody knew, there was only one ground for divorce. This behaviour should have put Alva beyond the bounds of polite society, in a day when ladies rose and left the room when divorce was mentioned and 'adultery' was an embarrassing word in the Ten Commandments. But Alva continued to maintain her position as one of the great triumvirate of Newport, the others being the *grande dame*, Mrs. Astor, and the *enfant terrible*, Mrs. Stuyvesant Fish.

The moment her divorce went through, of course, my Great-aunt Alva was cut dead by the rest of the Vanderbilt clan. A particularly bitter feud had existed for years between her and her sister-in-law, Alice of the Breakers, my grandmother. It was no coincidence that in 1895 both were building villas which were the most elaborate ever seen in Newport. Alva's marble house, with its outside Corinthian columns larger than those of the Temple of the Sun at Bazlbek, cost only $2,000,000 to construct, but she made up for this by spending an additional $9,000,000 on the furnishings. As it happened, both Marble House and the Breakers, housing the two feuding ex-sisters-in-law, were completed just in time for the *débuts* of their two marriageable daughters, Consuelo and Gertrude Vanderbilt.

'A marble palace is the right place for a woman with a marble heart,' was a phrase that went the rounds at Newport that summer of 1895. It referred to Alva's obvious attempts to break up Consuelo's well-known romance with a thirty-year-old New York bachelor, Winthrop Rutherfurd.

Not that anything was amiss with the young Winthrop's pedigree. The Rutherfurds moved in the most impeccable circles of Newport and New York society and—unlike some members of the old-guard Dutch families who lived well, dressed expensively, and did little else—Lewis Rutherfurd, the father of Winthrop, was a distinguished astronomer who had taken some truly extraordinary photographs of the moon. But, above and beyond their considerable talents and wealth and family tree, the Rutherfurds were celebrated for really breathtaking good looks.

'My mother tore me from the influence of my sweetheart,' Consuelo testified years later to the Catholic Court. 'She made me leave the country. She intercepted all the letters my sweetheart wrote and all of mine to him. She caused continual scenes. She said I must obey. She said I knew very well that I had no right to choose a husband, that I must take the man she had chosen, that my refusal was ruining her health, and that I might be the cause of her death. There was a terrible scene in which she told me that if I succeeded in escaping, she would shoot my sweetheart, and she would, therefore, be imprisoned, and hanged, and I would be responsible.'

Consuelo's aunt testified: 'Consuelo broke down and wept when first told she must marry the Duke. . . . She had nobody to whom she could turn, not even her father, because her mother and father were separated by divorce. . . . That Consuelo was coerced is further shown by the fact that her mother, fearing that she might, at the last moment, change her mind and retract her consent to marry Marlborough, placed a guard at the door of her room on the day of the wedding so that nobody could speak to her or even approach her.'

'I forced my daughter to marry the Duke,' Aunt Alva admitted to the Rota. 'I have always had absolute power over my children. . . . When I issued an order, nobody discussed it. I therefore did not beg, but ordered her to marry the Duke.'

Consuelo's engagement to the Duke of Marlborough was the sensation of Newport in the late summer of 1895. It was even remarked, rather spitefully, that the Duke had proposed first to young Gertrude Vanderbilt, whose fortune was larger than Consuelo's, and that she had straightway turned him down, so that finally, on his last day's visit with Aunt Alva, he had turned to Consuelo.

And so that Newport summer of 1895 sped by in a whirl of *fêtes champêtres*, coaching parties, polo matches, tennis matches, brilliant balls and dinners, and what Grandfather Wilson referred to as 'the usual hurrah' of those fabulous diamond-studded days.

Early in September, young Neily Vanderbilt, who had been Grace Wilson's most constant squire all summer, succumbed to a severe attack of rheumatism. So concerned was his father (he had lost one son two years previously) that he is said to have had a bed moved into his son's room and remained by his side nightly until the attack subsided. Then he sent Neily to Hot Springs, Virginia, for a long rest.

'I have been getting on here very well indeed,' Neily wrote his father on October 6. 'The baths I now take bring out the rheumatism more and more . . . I have written Orme Wilson, as Frank Polk [Neily's room-mate at Yale] could not come, and am very much hoping that he will be able to get away. Neither Regi, nor Alfred, nor Gertrude [his brothers and sister] have written, so I haven't heard any news at all.'

The 'news', such as it was, was that Neily's mother had paid a social call on Mrs. Richard T. Wilson and, between cups of tea, had casually inquired whether young Grace was going abroad that winter. She learned that no such trip was being planned.

A few weeks later Neily departed for a grand tour of Europe and the Near East, supposedly to build up his health.

With the young lovers separated, temporarily at least, attorney Chauncey Depew, known as the Vanderbilt prime minister, since he handled so many of their affairs, both public and private, sent a note to Richard T. Wilson requesting an interview on the subject of his daughter.

My chivalrous grandfather, who doted upon his lovely youngest child, refused indignantly, saying that he would discuss the matter with Mr. Vanderbilt, Sr., and no one else.

Subsequently he received a second note from Depew saying that a meeting had been arranged between the two parents to take place on November 26, 1895, at the Depew house.

Aunt May then wrote to Grandfather Wilson in evident distress: 'Ogden is so *positive* you ought not to accept an interview at Mr. Depew's house for your own dignity's sake that I have to send you this—

'The point is that Mr. Vanderbilt is making a request of you and he should come to you and not you to him—especially as you should not have it at the house of the man *you have declined* to accept as an intermediary. You have declined to have an interview on the subject of your daughter with anyone but Mr. V.

'Ogden doesn't think you could tell Mr. Depew verbally to get out of his own house. If you could come and see Ogden for a moment before answering his letter—Ogden thinks you can't go to Depew's.'

Where the meeting took place, I do not know, but the result was an open declaration of war. For Grace Wilson sailed abroad with the Ogden Goelets and before long a small item appeared in Paris newspapers to the effect that Cornelius Vanderbilt, Jr., was stopping at the Hotel Continental, while Madame Goelet, her family, and Miss Wilson were at the Hotel Bristol.

Soon Neily and Grace were observed holding hands in a carriage, driving down the Champs Élysées.

Just before Christmas the Honourable Michael Herbert, Belle's husband, who was then secretary at the British Embassy in Turkey, wrote to Mr. Wilson from Constantinople: 'This is to wish you and my dear mother a very Happy New Year in spite of Mr. Cleveland and the McKinley Washington politicians. I am afraid you must be lonely with so many of the family away and Grace's worries must also disturb you a good deal. I cannot sufficiently express my indignation at the way in which I hear the young man's precious parents treated you and Mrs. Wilson. Confound their cheek and their audacity. I should like to give them a piece of my mind. Who the deuce do they think they are to talk so? One Wilson is worth dozens of them any day in my opinion. We hope Grace will come out here as things are settling down. . . .

'I was very glad to have Belle back after our long separation and could not let her stay away any longer, although I expect Grace was disappointed at not meeting her in Paris. I am keeping pretty well and my weight does not fall off, which is satisfactory. Write me the news when you have time and let me have your opinion on Venezuela and also that of the business community and the sensible people among whom I am unable to claim the politicians of Washington. Love to Orme and Dick, yours affectionately, Mungo.

'P.S. Will you send us another letter of credit for £2,000 made out to Hon. Michael Herbert and Mrs. L. B. Herbert.'

It was not Grace but Neily Vanderbilt who hastened to see the Herberts in Constantinople. In January, 1896, Michael Herbert wrote to Grace: 'I am sure you will be dying to hear our impressions in regard to a recent visitor here and will reproach us all for being so silent, but we have thought it preferable to delay writing until further acquaintance with him enabled us to form a more definite opinion as to his character and his intentions.

'He arrived here a fortnight ago and two days after his arrival I received a telegram from his father asking "Is my son in Constantinople?" I replied, "Yes, Pera Palace Hotel." Since then he has received several letters from his family and one from Chauncey Depew, the first few appealing to his affection for his family and the later ones, I regret to say, adopting the lowest and most despicable means of pressure, i.e. calumny.

'His Uncle George has written him a most monstrous letter which he showed to Belle and containing sentences of this kind: "I hear a rumour that a certain young lady is paying you the most pressing attentions." "I wish I could see you as I could tell you certain interesting facts about her which I cannot write." "All I can say is do not commit yourself," and so on and so on. No name was mentioned by the wily scoundrel in this abominable letter which was worded like an anonymous one. His mother has also written to the poor boy in the same strain, or perhaps saying worse things, as he told us he had burned her letter at once, it was so horrible. It makes one's blood boil, but as he showed me the letter from his uncle privately, I do not suppose we have the right to take any notice of it. But I should like to write to the father and frighten him and tell him at the same time that if ever his precious brother dares to——' (Rest of letter missing.)

A little later Aunt May wrote to her husband at Monte Carlo: 'Neily left this evening. He could remain no longer without Grace. His father sent him a most horrid and disagreeable cable yesterday to the effect that unless he separated himself from G., his remittances would cease beyond honouring his letter of credit which he was obliged to do. I want to talk all this over with you and ask what you think is best to be done. Poor fellow, he is terribly cut up and depressed. He took the train which is most uncomfortable and full of changes, because it was cheaper. I enclose his wire. More loving wishes for the New Year from Your Wife. M.'

Despite the threats and imprecations from his father, Neily later that winter joined Grace at Cannes, chaperoned by her two married sisters, Belle and May. Together with Ogden Goelet, they spent weeks lazily cruising on the *White Ladye*.

Meanwhile, the Wilsons in New York were sending frantic inquiries abroad. A fragment of a letter from Belle to them begins: 'Papa and Mamma, do not let it disturb you one way or the other. And try *not* to exaggerate the consequence of the *animosity* of that family. Of course *nothing* could exceed their vulgarity and the dreadfulness of their conduct, but I for one should not be knocked down by anything they can do.

'Grace still intends and feels it is certainly for her ultimate happiness to carry the thing out. She is really very fond of the boy and one can understand that what he proposes doing for her and all the sacrifice it involves appeals to her very much.

'He *wants* her to go home. He *wishes* to give them one more chance. He intends doing this. To tell them that he still proposes to marry her and will give them one more chance to reconsider their threats. This he wishes to do soon, and Grace is crazy to get home so that he can *follow*, not precede, her. We (Mungo and I) think he hasn't in the least changed in his affection for her, but we cannot tell if he will still be strong enough to stand face to face with his family and receive their vituperation and abuse. Ogden is going to have a serious talk with the boy and point out to him that he has a serious trust put into his hands, and that altho he must, he believes, give in to the separation question if he still desires it, he must see that Gracie's family can no longer allow her to be talked about with him without some definite promise. He himself is getting nervous about this equivocal situation and says something must be done, but does not seem to know how to do it.

'Is it *absolutely* impossible for Dick to take three weeks' leave and come over and get Grace? I think it is *so* necessary that she should go home with one of the family, as they might say all sorts of things about her if she crosses the ocean alone. Do think about this. Three weeks would do it. Of course it would be awfully hard on Dick, but if I hadn't my children and husband to think of I would do it. Can't Brother take his place for that short time? People here are all asking a great many questions and talking a great deal about it. It's almost impossible to know what to say. Everyone answers when I say she is a little older, "Oh, but what difference does that make—it would be *better* to have it the other way, but if they care for each other what does it matter?" And Grace is so tremendously admired by foreigners that they can't make it out.

'The Prince of Wales is here and has already tried to pump me on the subject. We are all to dine this evening, we three sisters, at Lord Brougham's to meet the Prince and she has asked Neily to come in afterwards, so he will have the honour of meeting H.R.H. There is, of course, the usual excitement that the Prince's presence brings to Cannes. We dined in company with him at the Hoffmans' on Wednesday. He went out on "White Ladye" yesterday and we have several dinners and fêtes ahead where we are asked to meet him. People are awfully kind to us. I never realize that my attractions justify so much consideration and I am always *surprised* that we are asked out so much wherever we go. The Prince has been so nice and pleasant to us. Has asked a great deal about all the American difficulties and has had some interesting conversations with Mungo. He thinks Mungo looking very thin and seems anxious about the climate of Constantinople for him. I hope "Britannia" has won today or else he will be in a dreadful humour at dinner. He has got the pleasant Fortescue in attendance which makes his presence all the more desirable!

'Now, darling parents, don't get so depressed that you cannot fight the enemy! I hope it will all turn out well in the end. And darlingest of mothers, please let us know how you are and I *pray* that you may be kept well. Your loving daughter, Belle.'

Neily returned to New York and a job in the engineering department of his father's railroad in the spring of 1896; Grace returned a few weeks later. She arrived in New York the end of May, and soon found this letter from Belle: 'Darling Child: All of my thoughts are with you this morning for you ought almost now to be disembarking unless you have had the luck to reach home last night. What a thrilling moment for you! I think I must telegraph in a day or two to know the result of your triumphal entry! What an awful ordeal for you, but only the knowledge that so much earnest and true love is waiting for you must give you strength and help him and you through it. I can fancy Mamma and Papa's happiness at having you back and you will be able to give the very last news of us all.

'I got your ship letter yesterday. You may imagine how greedy I was for it, and how I at once devoured it, having had no news of you since I left. This time, of course, I understood. I was so glad you wrote as you did—and I shall count on you to *act* also. That is the line and the feeling to have—you will find how happy you can be living more in someone else's life, whose life is also yours, and whose life is consecrated to you. And evidently *he* knows and realizes this solemn part of the contract so well that it cannot help touching you and making you see the great and good side of marriage, so much more than the ordinary person. Give him my love—for I admire him very much. He has got such an enormous depth of character and so much to know and study!

'Long before this reaches you, you will have been through scenes, tumults, battles, struggles, threats, insults—perhaps blows!! I shall look for telegraphic news in my N. Y. Herald. If I were in your place I should have one preliminary canter over the course, and then I should coolly go in to win—with or without their consent. And with no fuss and feathers. Wait a week or two to see if there is any attempt to retract their bitterly insulting conduct, and then you and Neily must realize that you have got your own lives to lead and that you have perfectly proven the fact that you are all in all to each other, and the outside world must be dismissed from your minds for some years to come. I even advise you to dismiss *us*. Live for yourselves.

'I do *pray* for your mutual happiness, though I am tied at this distance from offering anything except my prayers.

'I sent Darling Mother a cable yesterday for her birthday. It is not nice to be always separated like this. I hope next year we may be nearer home, so that to jump on a steamer occasionally will be possible. I couldn't keep this wandering life up for ever.

'People have asked a great deal about you and if you were coming back this summer—*not* a word about your engagement, so they either think it is a delicate subject or that it is off.

'How dear and nice Bee [Lady Herbert] was to you. Isn't she a dependable, dear creature?

'The children are well and happy. We had a tea party in honour of the 3rd birthday of Prince Bo-Bo, and the Queen was at the same time taken notice of. Candles and flags and books. Toys from all the secretaries. Very grand.

'Write everything possible. Kisses to the darling parents, B.'

For several weeks after Grace's return she was not seen in public. Nor was Neily's phaeton observed near her door. There was talk that Neily's father had threatened to disinherit him and that the romance was finished. Then, one bright June afternoon, New Yorkers peering through two layers of white lace curtains from their Fifth Avenue brownstones saw the happy lovers ride by in a maroon-coloured Vanderbilt victoria. With them, beautifully gowned, sat one of the most charming and respected pillars of society, Mrs. Richard T. Wilson.

On June 10, 1896, the New York *World* published the announcement of an important coming marriage. Large pen-and-ink sketches of Grace Wilson and Neily dominated the front page—Mother in a high-collared lace dress and enormous white tulle hat, Father in a high stiff collar and four-in-hand tie with a determined expression on his face.

The announcement stated that Cornelius Vanderbilt, Jr., eldest living son of Mr. and Mrs. Cornelius Vanderbilt, would be one of the richest men in the world. 'It is said,' the *World* continued, 'that one of his wedding presents will be one of the biggest yachts afloat.'

The front-page article then went on to describe the blond-haired beauty of Miss Wilson and reiterated the chain of wonderful marriages made by the children of Mr. and Mrs. Richard T. Wilson. 'Miss Wilson's trousseau was all made during the spring in Paris and is said to exceed in magnificence any yet brought over. The bridal gown is quite marvellously lovely.

'Mr. and Mrs. Cornelius Vanderbilt, Sr., gave up their usual European trip this summer because of the coming wedding.'

The next day the story read quite differently. For Grandfather Vanderbilt overnight gave his approval to the long-discussed marriage of his nineteen-year-old daughter, Gertrude, to Harry Payne Whitney and at the same time expressed in no uncertain terms his disapproval of his son's intentions. Both engagement announcements hit the front pages of the New York morning newspapers on June 11.

The *Times* indicated that the Wilson-Vanderbilt nuptials would be a hurry-up affair, 'probably in two or three weeks' time.' I can imagine the effect of this announcement on society circles in New York, where a proper engagement lasted at least five or six months.

Richard T. Wilson was quoted as saying, 'Though the time has not been fixed yet, my daughter's wedding will not be deferred long and will doubtless take place in the present month.

'Cornelius Vanderbilt, Sr., is opposed to the marriage—on what grounds I do not wish to discuss.' Then he added: 'It is untrue that my daughter is eight years older than Mr. Vanderbilt. She is twenty-five years old, and he is twenty-three.'

From the Vanderbilts came the cold and stuffy statement, 'The engagement of Cornelius Vanderbilt, Jr., to Miss Wilson is against his father's expressed wish.' Nor would the famous capitalist add anything to that statement.

The *World* pointed out that young Vanderbilt had 'not a dollar in the world' aside from the salary he earned. Actually, this was not strictly true, as in his twenty-first year my father inherited a trust fund which gave him a yearly income of about $6,000. This, however, represented his entire personal fortune.

'Just how far Mr. Vanderbilt is likely to go if his son insists in opposing his wishes in marrying Miss Wilson it is difficult to say, but those in a position to know assert that he is likely to go to extremes,' commented another newspaper.

Since no Vanderbilt, not my father or grandfather, or any of their friends, would ever condescend to discuss such a matter with reporters in those days, there is little doubt that 'those in a position to know' were household servants bribed to talk.

Wherever the *World* reporter got his information, the next statement has a ring of truth to me. 'Mr. Vanderbilt's objection to his son's marriage is that he has not seen enough of the world. He is much younger than Miss Wilson. His father wants him to travel, to mix in society here and abroad, and to widen his ideas of life before he selects a wife.

'Miss Wilson is the only young lady he has ever manifested any affection for and Mr. Vanderbilt is reported as thinking that lads should not commit themselves to their first love until they have had time to learn something about the ways of women—or try to.'

What a nine-day wonder the scandal was, what rumour, what talk! Grandmother Vanderbilt and Gertrude were at Newport, at the Breakers, busy with preparations for Gertrude's marriage to young Whitney, oldest son of William C. Whitney, former Secretary of the Navy, and a childhood sweetheart of Gertrude's. Grandfather Vanderbilt and Neily were both staying in the great brick mansion at 57th Street. During the week, each rode separately to his New York Central office, where they did not meet or speak. Neily was then employed in the engineering department of his family's railroad.

It is not hard for me to imagine my father's reaction to his family's stubborn opposition to Grace. The most evasive person in the world if he did not choose to face an issue, Father could, once forced into a corner, explode with all the violence of a volcano.

And Grace Wilson? This proud, independent, pampered daughter of a multimillionaire, the darling of the courts of Europe? She publicly disregarded the entire fracas, then and for evermore.

On the day on which she sent out the wedding invitations she gave a luncheon for a few close woman friends. Thus society learned that the engagement so suddenly begun would end as abruptly, for the pair planned to marry within a week. Grace Wilson calmly proceeded through the day, driving in the afternoon with her fiancé in Central Park in a fashionable little runabout. A reporter said they attracted much attention coming down Fifth Avenue.

From the Metropolitan Club, Neily sent a note to Mrs. Goelet at Beaulieu, near Nice: 'At last everything is arranged and by the time you receive this we shall be married.

'I wish I could tell you how very happy we are over it and how pleased all our friends seem to be.

'Grace and I will feel quite lonely with no trouble to mope over, and I hope we will become more natural as we get back to our normal selves again.

'I am sure you are quite as pleased as we are, happy that all is settled and arranged, for all our difficulties are forgotten now and the prophecy that you told us you had heard in Paris, that a wedding was to take place in six months, is coming true.'

That evening Neily remained to dine with the Wilsons.

The gossip of the Four Hundred, languid since the preceding winter when Consuelo became a Marlborough and Alva became a Belmont, now stirred with new zest about the Vanderbilts.

Richard T. Wilson, pressed for his reactions to what the young couple would do if Neily was disinherited by his father, remarked testily: 'It makes no difference what Mr. Vanderbilt does. I am not concerning myself about his intentions. Whether he cuts his son off without a cent or not, the wedding will take place at the time and place arranged.'

The wedding would presumably be performed by Dr. Wesley Brown, rector of fashionable St. Thomas' Episcopal Church, at the Wilsons' Fifth Avenue home, where a wedding breakfast for a hundred and fifty would be served. The guest list was kept small, it was said, because so many fashionable New Yorkers had already departed for watering places for the summer.

On Saturday, the week-end before the wedding (scheduled for Thursday, June 18), the Wilsons departed for the country. May Goelet was reported rushing across the Atlantic to attend the wedding.

Reporters besieging the big old-fashioned Wilson house at 511 Fifth, former home of Boss Tweed in his days of glory, found all in confusion. Servants informed them that there would be no bridesmaids; that even the best man had not been chosen. The floral decorations would be 'white' but nobody knew what kind. The minister had not yet said whether he would perform the ceremony.

Richard T. Wilson, deserted by the rest of the family, when asked about his marriage settlement on his daughter, smiled pleasantly and said he didn't care to talk about it. He knew nothing about the details of the wedding, he said. If a European honeymoon trip was being discussed, he had not heard about it.

'To tell the truth,' remarked someone identified only as a 'society person', 'it's a good deal of a hurry-up affair. The young couple got tired of trying to win over Cornelius' father and decided that they might as well get married at once. While everyone was looking forward to the marriage, I do not think that the persons most concerned thought that it would take place so soon.'

By the following Tuesday, the *New York Times*, which had managed to stay aloof from the debate, published a small announcement that the wedding would take place on Thursday. The newspaper added that one of the ushers, Frank Burton Harrison, a classmate of Neily's at Yale, had quite suddenly decided to sail for Europe Thursday morning and regretted not being able to attend the ceremony.

The matter of a clergyman was discussed. The Vanderbilts belonged to St. Bartholomew's Episcopal Church—in fact, Grandfather Vanderbilt had given so much money to it that it was known informally as 'the Vanderbilt church'. Fortunately for the rector, the Reverend Greer, a European sojourn removed him from the scene and the possibility of having to wed a Vanderbilt against his father's wishes.

Even the rector of the next-most-fashionable church, St. Thomas', was playing coy. 'The Reverend Dr. John Wesley Brown of St. Thomas' Church was asked if he was to officiate at the wedding. His only answer was, 'If I were, I would not tell you.'

Still more humiliations were to be endured by the Wilson family. Of the hundred and fifty invitations sent out to 'the usual list'—meaning the cream of New York society (excluding all Vanderbilts)—only about a third accepted. Many announced hurried departures east, west, south, and abroad, anxious to escape the risk of being permanently cut off the Vanderbilt list, and possibly snubbed by all the Vanderbilts' influential friends as well.

The newspapers printed every scrap of information they could find or invent. Young Neily's college record was recalled. At Yale, it was said, 'he was always regarded as unambitious for a man of his opportunities. One of his friends said yesterday that he was pleased at having escaped from the business career his father had planned for him, as he believed himself unsuited for the responsibility of managing the great Vanderbilt estate and the various business properties to which he would have become heir in the natural course of events.'

While these speculations were filling columns of newspaper space, the wedding day finally arrived—but no wedding. Instead there was a typed statement sent to the newspapers, signed by two doctors:

'Mr. Cornelius Vanderbilt, Jr., has an attack of acute rheumatism and is confined to his bed and cannot safely leave his room, Thursday, the 18th inst. Dr. William H. Draper and Dr. E. G. Janeway.'

To understand the sequence of events it is necessary to backtrack to the preceding week-end, when Grandfather Vanderbilt left for Newport, apparently convinced that he was unable to break his son's resolve to marry Miss Wilson. The Wilsons returned to New York from the country Sunday evening, and Neily went to their house to dine.

Afterwards, he walked home through a summer rain to the great, empty, echoing Vanderbilt house with its vestibule 'slightly larger than the Supreme Court of the United States'. This is just the kind of thing Father would do. He loved to walk, rain or shine, and always conspired to leave the house without the umbrella and rubbers which his valet would anxiously proffer him.

The next day, Monday, Father ordered his bride's wedding bouquet from the florists, which was to be 'hundreds' of sprays of lilies of the valley (a favourite flower of Grace's) and white orchids and orange blossoms.

That night (it was reported from Newport) the owner of the Breakers received an urgent telephone call from New York, and shortly afterwards departed on the Fall River overnight boat. Grandmother Vanderbilt followed soon afterwards.

On Tuesday, the prospective bridegroom was seen at the New York Yacht Club in his 'usual health and spirits'. Yet later that same day, after the arrival of his mother from Newport, it was announced that the wedding had been indefinitely postponed because of the illness of young Vanderbilt.

The story, as I heard it, was that my other grandfather, Richard T. Wilson, at once sent his family physician, Dr. Draper, over to examine the bridgroom.

Wednesday, the day before the wedding was scheduled to take place, reporters received conflicting information from the Wilson and Vanderbilt households. At the Wilsons'—where it was said Miss Grace Wilson was receiving no callers—Mr. Wilson said that young Vanderbilt's condition was 'very serious'.

At the Vanderbilts', however, the attendant at the door said he had been instructed to say that young Mr. Vanderbilt had a 'slight attack of rheumatism induced by walking home in the rain from the Wilsons' Sunday night', and that his condition was 'not serious'. The same story was repeated by another Vanderbilt footman later in the evening.

That same evening, Grandfather and Grandmother Vanderbilt 'went out' together for the first time since their son's engagement had been announced. Shortly after eight o'clock they were observed walking past the great iron gates of their Fifth Avenue house and strolling up the avenue to 60th Street. Mrs. Vanderbilt wore a black gown with a sage-green silk bodice and drapery on the front. Neither appeared to be the least bit anxious over the health of their son.

They dined in the ladies' annex of the Metropolitan Club, where they chatted briefly and pleasantly with their many friends, returning home at nine-thirty.

What a contrast to their behaviour the preceding September when young Neily—who, as everyone knew, had never been strong—suffered a similar attack of rheumatism in Newport!

On the day before his daughter was to become a Vanderbilt, Richard T. Wilson cancelled all orders for the wedding. The floral decorations, consisting of 10,000 lilies of the valley, 10,000 white, pink, and red roses, and many boxes of orchids, were directed by his order to city hospitals. The caterer was dismissed, the orchestra's engagement cancelled.

Apparently abandoned, the bride-to-be was left with mounds of wedding presents—silver candelabra, a massive gold-lined compote, silver tea-sets, cut-glass decanters. Young Neily was also incommunicado.

The Wilsons, it was reported, would leave at once for their summer place at Newport.

It looked as though the Vanderbilt Seniors had won.

But the battle was not yet over. And for my beautiful and brave and cruelly reviled Mother, there was far worse calumny to come.

Chapter Four

ALTHOUGH Grace Wilson's mother, the shy and family-loving Mrs. Richard T. Wilson, did not publicize her feelings in the titanic battle over her daughter's engagement to a Vanderbilt, Grace's two older married sisters, Belle Herbert and May Goelet, responded with reams of sisterly advice and sympathy.

'What *is* there left for you to go through with?' Belle wrote to her younger sister when she heard that the wedding had been cancelled. 'One can't believe it all possible. It is what is called an *interesting* life!

'As for Neily, I "adore" him! He is splendid. But it is incredible that such bad luck should have come to people who have already been through so much. I suppose you must have grown *callous* to all the talk and gossip . . .

'Of course I can't (put my mind to it as I will) begin to realize the terrible agony you have been through until all these newspaper accounts and your letters come. How loathsome of Fred V. [Father's uncle who lived at Hyde Park] to write like that, too, the Brute! And the house prepared and all that. Dear me, it is just like a "bad dream". But then there *must* come the happy awakening, and Darling how I long for it to come to you.

'I am having a rest in bed today and of course my mind turns topsy-turvy trying to see what is now going on. We are dining on board our yacht Imogene this evening—the silly but nice little Commander Morgan is giving me a dinner in honour of the 4th of July. I shall sit on the American flag and I should not wonder if he didn't expect me to come dressed in one! Just now I am not feeling any increased patriotism and this rubbing it in rather bores me.'

A week later Belle again wrote from the British Embassy in Constantinople to Grace: 'I am still waiting, every nerve on edge, for further developments. . . . I feel, with your love for Neily and his undoubted and much-tried affection for you, things *must* some day be right. But the misery you have been through!

'Lady Herbert [Belle's mother-in-law] is so nice and interested about you and so unhappy that the Vanderbilt family she had always thought so nice should have disappointed her as they have done! She *can't* understand it and you know when she can't understand a thing there is no use trying to make her. She arrived here last Wednesday by sea from Rome undaunted by distance or age. She is really a wonder. Her energy and interest in life are very encouraging. I like being with her when I am quiet and have time to devote to her.

'We are so deliciously comfortable. Do you remember the hall of the Embassy—the round part with the pillars? I have got it furnished as a room and we sit here most of the time. It opens out into the garden and is so bright with flowers and plants. I only wish I had a sister to go with it. When one has been three sisters, one always wants *one* at least about, and I am lonely, darling, without you. . . .'

With this letter, Belle addressed a separate note to Neily: 'I got your nice happy little letter a few days after you should have been married. I felt so broken down in spirit for your sakes that anything I could have put on paper would be but a wail of distress. For this reason I have refrained from writing. I am sitting mentally bound, waiting for Fate to have done with you two young people, for you seem *fated* to experiences of every kind. You are certainly brave and splendid—and that you should have added to your many troubles this physical suffering is too terrible. I am *so* sorry for you, dear Neily. My telegrams say that you are better now and I am so thankful! I have been thinking of you through each step, and wondering what your position would be and what line was being taken by your people during your great illness—and how poor Grace would be *able* to stand being separated from you by the barriers of cruel opposition when she felt you were in such dreadful pain and distress. It must have all been too dreadful for words. Grace has written me wonderful letters. So strong and beautiful there in the midst of her great misery. I admire her more than ever, but it makes my heart ache that I shouldn't have been at home to share some of the trials that must have been going on.

'I still hope that the very near future holds better things for you both. This is a purifying fire of affliction but certainly it is all over now and you will both be happy and quiet in your minds before this reaches you.

'Loulie Baylies has written me such splendid letters on the subject. I think you both ought to feel some consolation in the admirable way your friends have come to the front and rallied round you.

'I have my Mother-in-law stopping here now. It is a great pleasure to me as she is such a dear old lady. She is so interested in you both, but it never ceases to puzzle her why there should have been any trouble about your marriage! Every day when the N. Y. Herald arrives she rushes to see if you are married yet! I try in vain to make her realize that perhaps you will be so kind as to send me a cable. She is very anxious to know what you both want for a wedding present. She has just come along and begs me to say she is 'so longing to hear of your happiness'. I wish you were both here with us—except for your rheumatism—for it is really lovely and we have all sorts of grandness in the way of yachts, etc., at our disposal. My dear Neily, I *hope* you are better. I can't write any more till I get more news.'

Commented *Munsey's* magazine after the wedding had been called off: 'Not only society but readers of newspapers all over the country have looked with interest upon the love story of the young prince of millions and his sweetheart. Cornelius Vanderbilt, Jr., the prospective heir of a fortune of something like a hundred million dollars, has expressed the prerogative of all young men, rich and poor, and fallen in love with a young society woman whose face has charmed many . . . For some reason, Cornelius Vanderbilt, Sr., objected to his son's early marriage and has done everything in his power to prevent it. All the world loves a lover and it is doubtful if the father gets much sympathy in his objections. We cannot help settling him down with the "cruel parents" of literary tradition.'

Commented the *Times*: 'With the wedding of Mr. Vanderbilt and Miss Wilson off for a time, at least, New York Society has turned with renewed interest to the engagement of Mr. Harry Payne Whitney and Miss Gertrude Vanderbilt, which appears to be one of those rare engagements which meet with universal approval and with the general dictum that it is eminently suitable and charming. Mr. Whitney and Miss Vanderbilt are congenial in temperament and tastes, and Mr. Whitney's own fortune and prospective inheritance relieves him entirely of any suspicion that his courtship of Miss Vanderbilt, one of the three richest heiresses in the world, was prompted by other than sincere liking and affection.

'The many friends of Mr. and Mrs. Cornelius Vanderbilt are

pleased with their pleasure in their daughter's engagement which to some extent mitigated their somewhat different feelings regarding their son's engagement to Miss Wilson. No definite date has been set for Miss Vanderbilt's wedding, but it is generally thought it will be celebrated in this city next November.'

In other words, a most proper engagement of six months' duration.

Friends who knew the degree of iron in Cornelius Vanderbilt, Sr.'s resolve were placing bets that no wedding would ever take place between his son and Grace Wilson. Neily would be shipped off on a world cruise as soon as possible, probably with his family to prevent any clandestine meetings aboard the Goelet yacht, and that would be the end of it. In time, he would fall in love with another pretty face. They did not reckon with the stubborn, implacable Vanderbilt streak in my quiet and reserved father.

I have heard some faint echoes of the violent scenes which took place between father and son after the wedding was cancelled. I have heard that young Neily, shouting his defiance, actually struck Grandfather, causing him to suffer a paralytic stroke.

Knowing how my father reacted when pressed and nagged and pushed into a corner, I cannot say that this was impossible. It may have occurred. To the world, my father was the epitome of gentleness, sweetness, and courtesy. This was his real nature, but, like his uncle, Willie K., who found money such a handicap to happiness, Father's life was so moulded and shaped by pressures beyond his control, that I can imagine him as a young hot-blooded man, deeply in love for the first time in his life, striking out against the harsh authoritarian who was his father.

I do know that one month after the wedding was postponed Grandfather Vanderbilt suffered a near-fatal stroke, and also that in this month Father left his family and moved into a small New York apartment. How family patterns repeat themselves! Years later, I, too, as a rebellious young man, fought violently with the ultra-conservative, tradition-bound male (or so I thought my father at the time) who was attempting to run my life. I, too, walked through the massive front doors of a Fifth Avenue palace, thinking never to return.

The *New York Times*' society editor called the whole affair a 'nine-day wonder' and remarked: 'It is not to be believed that Mr.

and Mrs. Vanderbilt have any decided personal objections to Miss Wilson, who is a very charming and attractive girl, but it is said that they do not approve of what they have considered too evident a disposition on her part to receive the attentions of their son, knowing that his parents were opposed to these attentions. The entire matter is, however, too delicate a one to be publicly discussed.'

This was a love story which caught the imagination and sympathies of millions. All over the country, newspaper readers followed the romance with intense and passionate interest, applauding the young lovers and urging them on in letters by the barrelful. It was as though everyone who had ever suffered from the harsh hand of parental control wished the rebellious young millionaire the right to claim the girl of his choice.

And everyone I have ever talked with who knew young Neily and Grace says that this was a love match beyond all possible doubt and that the devotion of the young couple, one to the other, was a heart-stopping thing to see.

And so, in spite of everything, they were married. It occurred very quietly one August morning in New York, about two months after the engagement had first been announced. Reporters who had been camping on the Wilson doorstep awaiting developments, wrote fulsome accounts, one of which (New York *Journal*) is reproduced here. My cousin, Orme Wilson, as a boy of ten, was present at the wedding, and from what he has told me, this account is substantially correct:

VANDERBILT AND MISS WILSON ARE MARRIED

Ceremony Performed at Noon at the Home of Her Parents

No Member of the Bridegroom's Family Attends the Nuptials

Made Man and Wife by the Rev. Mr. Pott in a Room Bare of Floral Decorations

Courtship So Bitterly Opposed by the Young Man's Father Thus Ends with His Loyalty and Scorn of Disinheritance

CORNELIUS VANDERBILT, JR., AND MISS GRACE WILSON ARE MARRIED
The ceremony took place at noon yesterday in the Wilson parlours. There was no representative of the Vanderbilt family present, nor any

one outside of the bride's family except one or two college friends of the groom. Even Chauncey Depew, who was half expected to give unofficial sanction by his presence, failed to appear.

The Wilson mansion is a brownstone of the regular Fifth Avenue type. There were no preparations visible from the outside; no canopy, no carpet to keep the wedding-guests' dainty footgear from the pavement when they stepped from their carriages; no long line of coupés.

The policeman on the beat was mildly interested and the windows of neighbouring houses were crowded with heads anxious to see the bridegroom go in and the bridal couple come out.

The first sign of what was to come was manifest at 9 o'clock, when a young man left the house.

ONLY A FEW FLOWERS

'That's R. T. Wilson, Jr.,' whispered a lady in a window two or three doors below to several girls on the stoop.

Somehow it became known that young Mr. Wilson had gone to order the flowers. These came later.

Eight boutonnières of lilies of the valley were ordered, and some cut flowers, principally lilies of the valley. With these were gladioli, hydrangeas and American Beauty roses. One man brought them all in three medium-sized boxes and one parcel.

At 10.30 the butler rushed down the stoop, gave the address of a well-known photographer to a hansom-cab driver, who then drove down Fifth Avenue, with instructions to bring the photographer and his camera to the house at once and take the bridal party's pictures. When the photographer arrived he was told he had come too late.

Meanwhile Mr. and Mrs. M. Orme Wilson, with their two little sons and maid, drove up at 11.05 o'clock in an omnibus, which backed up to the sidewalk to let them alight. Mrs. Wilson was dressed in tobacco-brown cloth, with spinach-green ribbon at the throat. She wore a small black bonnet. The little Wilsons were in white duck sailor suits, trimmed with navy-blue braid.

A cab drove up from the Hotel Savoy at 11.15. It was a critical moment for the persons in the windows and the interested policeman, for the cab contained young Mr. Cornelius Vanderbilt and his best man, Mr. Frank Polk. The watchers saw two well-groomed young men in black frock coats, light trousers, patent leathers and high hats. They differed principally in that one wore a white waistcoat while the other's was black. The white vest marked the bridegroom.

By and by another young man came, he came afoot. His air and band collar told why he was there. He was the Rev. Mr. Pott, of St. Thomas's

Episcopal Church. He carried an ample travelling bag, and the policeman, by virtue of his connection with the detective department, announced to a friend that it was to be a 'full-blown' wedding, as the clergyman evidently had his vestments in his bag.

Then there was a long wait with nothing to interest the policeman or the persons in the windows but their surmises. A butcher's car and a grocery wagon stopped and the drivers inquired the reason for the attention that was being bent on No. 511 Fifth Avenue. They were told, and then they contentedly waited.

At 12.30 the suspense was practically over. The Wilson brougham, driven by the family coachman, drew up at the door. Within ten minutes the front door opened and the splendid Negro butler, who had come all the way from Newport for the occasion, stood forth. A moment later Mr. and Mrs. Cornelius Vanderbilt, Jr., both smiling, both apparently very happy, ran down the long flight of brownstone steps.

The bride's blue travelling dress of light Summer silk with ruffles of lace set off her figure prettily. The watchers on the other side noted with interest that young Mr. Vanderbilt had changed his raiment for a light grey suit with cutaway coat and double-breasted waistcoat, and a straw sailor hat with band of black. The bride carried her bridal bunch of sweet peas with her.

The groom opened the door of the brougham, the two little Orme Wilsons threw a few grains of rice, young Cornelius helped his bride into the brougham and stepped in himself, and as they drove off, the presumably disinherited young millionaire leaned out and waved an adieu to the Wilson family, which crowded the parlour windows. Then they drove away and the outsiders resumed their usual avocations.

THE WEDDING CEREMONY

What happened inside the Wilson mansion, and which window-gazers would have given anything to see, was this:

The bride came down the broad stairs with her father, and passed into the rear drawing-room, where the Wilson family, Mr. Vanderbilt and his best man awaited her.

The rustle of silken skirts was all the music that announced her arrival, for orchestra and the usual etceteras that go to make up a swell wedding were entirely wanting at this one, which was, strictly speaking, a family affair.

The bride wore the gown made for the first announced wedding, which had to be postponed at the eleventh hour because of Mr. Vanderbilt's illness. It was of the heaviest and richest of white satin of shade of whipped cream, and was made with a long train. Ruffles of the most exquisite point d'Alencon lace trimmed the skirt in front, and a quaint cape of this fell over her shoulders. Her veil was a very old piece of point lace, and fell from a wreath of diamonds, in which sprays of orange blossoms were tucked away as 'porte bonheurs'.

At her throat was a heart brooch—the bridegroom's gift. It contained thirty large diamonds surrounding an immense sapphire.

The usual bridal bouquet was dispensed with, and its place taken by a small ivory prayer book and a bunch of lilies of the valley, which Mr. Vanderbilt had ordered at Thorley's.

There was no floral chapel, no altar rail, not even a prie-dieu for the bride and bridegroom to kneel upon.

Dr. Pott stood under a large oil painting of Miss Wilson, at the east end of the room, where he performed the marriage ceremony.

KISSES FOR THE BRIDE

Five minutes and this was over. Mr. Vanderbilt kissed his bride. Her father kissed her, and her mother kissed her, and her brother and sister-in-law, Mr. and Mrs. Orme Wilson, kissed her. Their two little sons followed suit, and the bride's brother, 'Dickie' Wilson, and her nephew, Robert Goelet, second, did the same.

There was a perfect love feast for a few moments. Young Vanderbilt looked defiant, though happy, and his bride looked so fascinating.

Her mother wore canary silk, with black lace frills on the bodice. Mrs. Orme Wilson, who is not over demonstrative, showed that she heartily approved of the wedding. In fact, the whole company seemed to be perfectly in tune, and not a jarring note marred the harmony of the entire affair.

After the kissing and congratulations were over, the bride and bridegroom disappeared to prepare for their wedding tour. His clothes had been sent to the Wilson residence early in the morning by a messenger, and one of the rooms on the second floor was placed at his disposal; likewise a valet.

When they had completed their travelling toilets Mr. and Mrs. Vanderbilt returned to the drawing-room, where the family party was resumed until 12.35 o'clock, when the Wilson carriage drew up and took them off to the depot. The bride's parents followed her to the front door.

There is nothing tell-tale about their appearance and the brougham might have been destined for a shopping expedition, so far as any stranger meeting it would have known. The horses had no flowers or white ribbons, the coachman and carriage groom no bouquets. Mrs. Vanderbilt wore a simple little garden dress, just the sort of thing she would go morning driving in at Newport.

But it was Frenchy, of turquoise blue batiste, sprinkled all over with a tiny design in black. The skirt flared very little and the sleeves showed a decided tendency towards tight-fitting. The bodice was made in full blouse effect in front, the fullness being laid in gathers under a black velvet belt fastened with a velvet bow on the left side. These rows of heavy white lace appliqué were gathered in with the material, but in such a deft way that the pattern appeared to excellent advantage. The sleeves were puckered all the way from the wrist to the elbow. They wrinkled like mousquetaire gloves until they changed into short unpretentious puffs.

Over these puffs, little epaulets fell. These were cut like long tabs, pointed where they hung over the sleeves, and coming from under the collar. Were entirely tucked and edged all around with ecru lace. The collar was of white taffeta silk. In the back a fine narrow pleating of this stood up, stretching from ear to ear.

The bride's hat was one of those rough straw, sailor affairs, so popular just now. It was deep straw colour and had a band of gladioli and pink taffeta ribbon.

Some plaited tails of ecru lace flapped up and down on the brim whenever the breeze caught them, and tucked between the hat and her hair were a lot of crushed pink roses, which were almost hidden under a black dotted veil, drawn tightly across her face.

Mrs. Vanderbilt wore no jewels on the train, but she had on a lot of gold trinkets, several gold bangles on her left arm, with enamel medallions dangling from them, and a gold coin purse, which hung from a slender gold chain around her neck.

Her gloves were pearl-coloured glacé kid, and she carried a bunch of lilies of the valley. In her belt were some gardenias, about half a dozen.

Nods Goodbye to Servants

As the bride left her father's house she caught sight of a group of servants in one of the basement windows. She nodded them a goodbye and kissed her hand to them as the carriage drove down Fifth Avenue. It went as far as Thirty-eighth Street, then through to Park Avenue, to Thirty-fourth Street to Lexington Avenue, and up to the Grand Central Depot.

They left the carriage at the waiting room of the New York Central & Hudson River Railroad and seemed in no special hurry to join the crowd inside. Mrs. Vanderbilt looked amused when she discovered the flutter of excitement her presence created and the way the railroad porters nudged each other to look at her. Even the other travellers in the station caught the infection and stared at her, knowing she was some one of unusual importance without knowing just who.

The photographer who followed at her heels amused the young bride more than anybody. She was so happy herself she could afford to consider other people, so she faced him several times and stood still in some characteristic poses and let him take a few snapshots of her.

Mr. Vanderbilt was less at ease. He seemed nervous and fidgety. He fumbled in his pockets for the tickets, and when he had fished them out, said something to his wife. They walked towards the ticket office, then turned towards the ticket taker's door, and afterward went out to the carriage, where Mrs. Vanderbilt gave some orders to the coachman. Later she gave some instructions to the groom, who by that time had reappeared from the baggage room, and then she and Mr. Vanderbilt took their train.

After they reached their section she discovered the photographer was still after her.

'Oh, the horrid fellow!' she exclaimed. Then recollecting she was too happy to be vexed, she raised her head and smiled.

Then the train puffed out of the depot.

Mrs. Wilson's Matchmaking

The bride's mother, Mrs. R. T. Wilson, is called the greatest matchmaker in America. The first great marriage into a family of wealth which she arranged was that of her oldest daughter, May, to Ogden Goelet, who is reputed to be worth all of $50,000,000. The Goelets are, next to the Astors, the greatest owners of real estate in New York. Then Marshall Orme Wilson, her oldest son, married the late William Astor's daughter Caroline, whose fortune is quoted at $15,000,000. Miss Belle Wilson, the second daughter, became Mrs. Michael Henry Herbert, marrying the son of Lord Herbert, of Lea, and brother of the Earl of Pembroke. Now Grace, the youngest daughter, is wedded to the principal heir (maybe) to a fortune of $110,000,000.

When the bridal carriage returned, R. T. Wilson, Jr., gave out this statement for publication:

'Miss Wilson and Mr. Vanderbilt were married today at 12 o'clock by the Rev. William H. Pott, assistant to the Rev. Dr. Brown, of St. Thomas's Church. There was no one asked to the ceremony except Miss Wilson's immediate family and Mr. Frank Polk of Boston, who was Mr. Vanderbilt's best man.'

Cablegrams were received, young Mr. Wilson said, from the Prince of Wales, the Earl and Countess of Pembroke, who are relatives of the Hon. Michael Herbert, whose wife is Belle Wilson Herbert, a sister of the bride, and from the Duke and Duchess of Marlborough.

And now society is wondering what the head of the house of Vanderbilt will do. Maybe the withholding of his presence from the ceremony will be considered punishment enough, and young Cornelius may not be kept out of the ancestral millions after all.

Saratoga, N. Y., Aug. 3. Cornelius Vanderbilt, Jr., and his bride, arrived here at 6 o'clock this evening. They are at the United States Hotel, where they have engaged 'a cottage', as it is called. The cottage, which is what would be called a flat in New York, consists of five rooms, and is so separated from the rest of the hotel that its occupants can be as exclusive and as much to themselves as they please.

The cottage to which young Cornelius took his bride today is the same one that his grandfather used to occupy while sojourning here. The young couple will stay here for a week, and possibly longer.

When the train reached Albany at 4 o'clock Mr. Vanderbilt and his bride, followed by a man servant and maid servant, walked out of the New York Central Depot and around the block to the Delaware & Hudson Depot, where they were to take the 4.40 train for Saratoga.

On the way the bridal party was halted by its leader. A news-stand was the cause. A copy of every afternoon paper in sight was purchased. Mrs. Vanderbilt unfolded one of them and was reading with great interest when her husband caught her by the arm and hurried her along to the depot. Nothing was seen of the young couple about the hotel during the evening. Supper was served for them in their private dining room. During the concert in the court, they appeared on the balcony in front of their rooms for a few minutes.

Newport, R. I., Aug. 3. It was impossible to see Cornelius Vanderbilt, Sr., this evening, or to get any word to or from him concerning his son's marriage. The attending physician, Dr. McLane, allows no one outside of the immediate family to see him. Mr. Vanderbilt is in no condition to be informed of his son's marriage. No one at the Breakers would say anything upon the subject of young Mr. Vanderbilt's marriage.

'Thank God you have at last succeeded in entering upon the Holy Estate of Matrimony,' Belle wrote her at-long-last-wedded sister. 'We were made so happy by receiving your telegram. During my toilette, chiefly in my tub, I was concocting another cable stronger than the last (!) to enquire what in the world was *now* happening, when in burst Mungo with such a radiant face and excitedly waving the first telegram from Mrs. Vanderbilt. We are so full of joy! It has made the sunshine brighter and my whole outlook bright—so what must it have done for you!

'Oh, I am so glad, dearest Neily and Grace, and I do hope and pray you will have a little quiet and peace now. Forgive my last letter with all the numerous instructions. It's another example of what a useless waste of time giving advice from this distance is. Every situation is changed so long before the letter reaches you.

'You certainly have had more trials and sorrows than any other two people (out of a book) I have ever heard of. I hope the present chapter is ending with "and they lived happily ever after". Darling little people, don't ever lose sight for a minute of how far better being really *in love* with each other is than anything else in the world. Having experienced it, I can advise. All life goes so much smoother, and each little simple day seems to have held so much and things no longer "bore one" like they do when one is alone or unloving. I have said all the rest once before but I am still bubbling over with admiration and affection for my new brother-in-law—so full of strength and sincerity and things I also, as well as you, Grace, admire most in men. I can't help telling him how I love him and how I willingly confide to his tender care and devotion the person who is *nearly* the dearest to me on earth. God bless you both.'

The immediate effect of Neily's marriage upon his family was the sudden announcement that his sister Gertrude's wedding, scheduled for November, would take place within three weeks, in August. Plans for an elaborate wedding at St. Bartholomew's in New York were cancelled, and the wedding, it was said, would take place quietly at the Breakers in the presence of only sixty guests.

From a hotel cottage at Saratoga the new Mrs. Vanderbilt wrote to her father at Newport: 'Darling Father, Neily and I are thinking of staying on here another week or so, as he has been feeling much better the last few days. Hardly any rheumatism and his heart not bothering him either. We should prefer to be at a place which would be more in the country. The drives here are simply beautiful but there are very few nice country walks.

'All the hotel people treat us royally and the people in the hotel run to peer at us when we pass in and out. You have never seen such behaviour. They follow us in the streets!! The number of letters we get is dismaying, most of them are from people we don't know congratulating us, etc.

'Neily telegraphs to his brother Alfred every few days asking about his father and he, Alfred, answers as to Mr. V.'s condition, but that is all the communication we have had with them.

'I want you to tell people that Neily is very much improved. I shall send this to Newport so it must be an answer to dearest Mother's letter, too.

'Neily seems much against our going to Newport in August—he says we might go for a few days in Sept. before sailing. I suppose you will send my ponies to Newport. Do write, dear Papa and Mama, for I, too, naturally miss you very, very much in spite of my being perfectly happy and content. He is the most darling creature that ever lived! I want you to know and realize this and be happy that I am married to him.

'My maid seems an excellent woman and so nice. I have no time for more, so with kisses and love from your fond daughter. Grace.

'I am sending you this old letter of credit thinking you may wish to do something with it. By the way, have I a bank account and, if so, may I have the cheque-book? Send letters here for another ten days.'

On the following day she wrote her bachelor brother Dick: 'I advise you to go and get married at once! I've not written because, as you correctly surmised, I am too happy to write. Was glad to get your dear letter and also the charming contents. Really you have been too generous but I shall keep it all the same and get something very beautiful which, being your gift, will be the one I shall ever treasure, dear Dick.

'You arranged a very nice, comfy honeymoon for us when you sent us here and Neily is so much improved that we think we shall remain on another ten days.

'August 16th. Have not sent this yet! I wish you could see the way people watch us and follow us about. Read today's World and you will get quite a fair idea of it all.

'How are you feeling, dear Dick, and are you going to Newport? Neily is strongly of the opinion that we should not go there, and any way now we can't go as he had a letter from Dr. McLane day before yesterday saying that his father was still too ill to be told [of Neily's marriage]. I enclose the letter. Let me know what you think about it and show to Papa and then return to me. Today he got a letter from one of the confidential business advisers of Mr. V.'s saying he had seen Mr. V. this week and had been asked by him to write to Neily and request him to come to Gertrude's wedding. They have sent Neily an invitation. Neily answered Dr. McLane saying we were not going to Newport as we were going abroad but that he did not wish to leave the country until his father was better.

'I hope you will see Belle's letter about my getting married— exactly your and my views. Do write and tell me how you are getting along without me to bother you. Neily and I are delighted with Marriage, etc., and he is even dearer as a husband than he was as a fiancé!!'

Since Grace had not been invited, the newlyweds did not attend Gertrude's wedding in Newport. *Town Topics* reported that on that day Cornelius Vanderbilt, Sr., still critically ill, was confined to his rooms.

'There was no return of the prodigal son, no scene of weeping reconciliation, no welcoming of a new daughter-in-law, who had married the eldest son in defiance of his parents' wishes, and when she knew that one of these parents had received an almost fatal shock from this defiance,' remarked that notorious tattle sheet. 'Finally, no announcement of disinheritance for this rebellious son.'

From their honeymoon spit, 130 miles away at Saratoga, the bridegroom wrote to his father-in-law: 'Dear Mr. Wilson: Grace got your letter last night and we shall arrange to sail Wednesday on "Majestic".

'I think it is really much better that we should be away from this country for a while. We think it necessary to go to town Saturday instead of Monday, as I have several things to do in town.

'I have had no other word from my family and do not expect any.

'Grace and I will be very glad to get away to some place where we will not be so conspicuous, though the climate here agrees quite well with me. I am rapidly gaining my health, but am still rheumatic and get tired very easily.

'I am quite a different person from when I came up here. Grace sends her love. Believe me, ever yours, Cornelius.'

At the end of August, the honeymooners left on the *Majestic* for Liverpool, to remain abroad for the next five months. 'They went to the pier in a public hansom,' one paper reports. 'None of the Vander-bilt family appeared to see them depart. They were not recognized by the crowds on the pier and made their way unnoticed to their staterooms. Subsequently they promenaded on the deck, arm in arm.'

'Such a delightfully smooth trip,' Grace wrote her parents a few days later. 'Thus far I have not felt the sea once.

'I am so glad we came as it's a far greater change and rest than anything else would have been. The reporters flocked to the steamer and tried to photograph the staterooms we had taken. I expect there were any number of articles in the papers after we left. By the way, Neily has subscribed for some newspaper cuttings and we want them forwarded. I expect we shall only be a week in London, so send everything to Munroe and Co., 7 Rue Scribe, Paris.

'I felt awfully, awfully sorry to go away and leave you and Papa to face all those people alone but feel sure it would have broken us both down to stay and hear every day new tales. Mr. Depew told Neily that morning not to get too depressed as he was sure there were better times in store!!!

'Of course I will write often, dearest Mother. I pray you will keep well. I am perfectly strong and well and am encouraged about Neily. We sit at the Captain's table, I on his right and Neily next to me. He seems a nice agreeable man and the other people are not bad. We are happier than ever. Each day seems to bring us greater happiness than the past ones. Neily is *goodness* itself. He never leaves me for a second. I will close this but add another line before posting it at Queenstown tomorrow. Love from both of us. Grace.'

Then, from Piccadilly in London, Grace reported their arrival: 'Darling Mother: I must send a line by this steamer. I am in bed today, having a rest. We felt awfully tired upon our arrival here last Wednesday afternoon but the journey from Liverpool was made most comfortable for us owing to Mr. Ismay's [chairman of the board of the White Star line] kindness. He got on board "Majestic" at Queenstown and, hearing we were passengers, came to our cabin and introduced himself to Neily and me and begged that he might do all in his power to make us comfortable. So he had the one large Saloon carriage reserved for us and sent us someone who got us through the luggage place and into our train without a moment's delay. So it was delightful for us. When we got here we drove to this hotel, and, finding it a very nice, comfortable place, we engaged a charming little suite of rooms on Piccadilly and from the sitting-room I can see all the way down St. James St. and almost to the park. It is the brightest, nicest spot I have found in London.

'Neily seemed very tired on Thursday, went to see the great rheumatism specialist's assistant as he, M., is out of town. The assistant said Neily's heart was going every which way and that he must go home and lie down, so he spent Thursday lying down. Friday the Dr. came and examined him and said his heart was better and that there was nothing dangerous about the condition of Neily's heart but that it was serious and that he must take great care and never overtire or tax it. He said he had heard about our marriage, etc., and that he was sure, from a medical standpoint, Neily should have got married as it would be much better for him to have the suspense over with and that he thought he had done the wisest thing, but he says now that Neily needs a good long rest and *no* worries. He does not recommend any cure just at present, and does not think Aix the place for Neily, but he said he will think more about it and let us know in a few days. He does not advise our going yachting but rather that we shall keep by ourselves and be quiet. I think we shall remain here till end of next week and then go to Paris. May and Ogden are cruising for a month around Scotland, Loulie Baylies arrives here today. I shall see Bessie Belmont in Paris. Lady Herbert and Gladys are out of town.

'I am tired so must stop. Much love from Grace.'

'I have almost lapsed into my old habit of not writing, have I not?' Grace wrote her mother next from the Hotel Campbell, Paris. 'We came back to Paris from London a week ago, after a pleasant little glimpse of Belle, Mungo, May, Baby May—all of whom were in good health and spirits and it was great fun all being together again. All three of us married and only Baby May to look after now.

'We came to this hotel on our return and are delighted with it. We are way up by the Arc de Triomphe on the next parallel street to the Champs Elysées and I assure you the difference in the atmosphere is very great from the old Bristol. Also the difference in the price!!

'We both took cold in England but are all right again. Since getting back we have been to a few plays and were to have dined with Mrs. Moore tonight, and gone to the opera, and last night we should have dined with Susie B. and her charming husband but now we have been obliged to give up everything on account of the sudden death of Neily's grandmother. Mr. Depew cabled Neily immediately and Neily sent a cable to his father and got a cable from his father (we don't know whether it was sent in answer to Neily's or before). It said, "Your grandmother died Friday after an hour's illness. Funeral Tuesday. Father." This is the first message of any kind Neily has had from his father and he was *so so happy* to get even this. Of course Neily will wear mourning for a while and we think (at least Mrs. Moore came to see me and said she thought it would be better taste for me to wear black, *not* mourning) I had better wear black for a while, as my husband is in mourning. But about this I shall not decide till I hear from May and Belle.

'I had a long letter from Loulie Bayliss which I will forward when Belle returns it. Neily rather thinks he would like to try returning home in Dec. or Jan. to see if his father would let him see him, but this is only an idea. Please be careful of all my letters. Why don't you get one of those tin boxes from Lewis and Conger and lock them all up? I beg of you to do this.

'I send a delightful letter from Belle. Was so thankful to get your line in pencil and Papa's dear letter by last ship. Did I tell you about Mrs. Martin's wonderful present to us? It is a *huge* silver gilt bowl— at least 18 inches high and 20 inches across the top. A magnificent present. Please be *very* nice to her this winter.

'So McKinley was elected. I do hope it will give Papa and Dick easier times now. I will get your dress as soon as possible and don't you think you could afford a new evening dress? I think you *must* have one. Do write soon and often and beg Dick to do so. Tell him we are looking for his pearl studs.

'I pray that you are not too lonely. Neily keeps on improving— is looking very well and has not nearly so much pain around his heart or rheumatism. I am very well and in my normal state of happiness.'

Neily's grandmother who died so suddenly was Mrs. William H. Vanderbilt, born a Kissam, daughter of a Brooklyn clergyman, and a sweet, lovely, and gracious lady. Neily had always been a special favourite of hers. From abroad, he sent flowers to her funeral, for in an old trunk I found a small envelope, with a mourning band around it marked '1896—Lilies of the valley, from C. V.,

Jr.' Although many persons expected that Neily might share in his grandmother's fortune, in her will she overlooked the Vanderbilt family entirely, leaving all her wealth to various needy Kissams.

Father often told me that when he was first married, his income was $6,000 a year. Richard T. Wilson gave my mother a trust fund of half a million dollars, which yielded a yearly income of about $25,000. Mother was accustomed to spending that much money on her wardrobe alone! Severe economies were in order, and Mother must have set about them matter-of-factly, with head high, with the somewhat tactless assistance of her two older and immensely wealthy sisters.

'I saw a *little* footman for you yesterday but he wouldn't do at all,' Belle wrote from London to the new Mrs. Vanderbilt in Paris. 'Too small. I think you had better see people yourself when you come over. But I don't much approve of your taking one home as the duties are so different. You see footmen do not valet as a rule. Do you mean you will not keep a butler? Or do you want a man in livery who does everything? You were not very explicit. It is horribly cold here today, bright and a light wind and it gives me dreadful neuralgia.

'You haven't answered any of my letters or questions so I don't know how to prepare for you. I will come to London on Thursday morning, Dec. 10th, to be with you, as Mungo says he knows you will not care to spend your last few days in the country.'

The question of what kind of jewellery to give their younger sister for a wedding present appeared to vex both Belle and May greatly. 'Dearest Grace,' May wrote from London. 'We have all been trying to help you about your presents and both Boucheron and Hamelin's jewels are lovely. It is most difficult to say which would be best.

'I don't think you would like the Fontana necklace unless you have seen one made up in that style and it pleased you. Even when a design is set up in wax it is difficult to know if the same would be becoming on. (Heavens what a pen this is!) Belle liked Boucheron's diamond chain and emerald drops very much and I did too—she also thought that a great pin with sapphire and two diamonds would be nice for her present. I think on the whole she preferred

Boucheron's things altogether. That stomacher of Hamelin's would make such a nice set of pins, all of which you could wear in the daytime, but when divided it does not make very important ornaments.

'I haven't seen Morel's designs but I know he does make up most wonderfully effective pieces and I should think *you would* need a necklace to go with your tiara.

'We all think Boucheron's necklace with the emerald lovely and chic as well. That would be part of Belle's present but I think she will probably write you herself tonight.

'May [her daughter] and I are coming over to Paris on Wednesday so you might delay your decision. I do think you had better get a necklace of some sort. It is despairing work to decide and I quite sympathize and pity you. You see that large piece of Boucheron's is only one set thing and I think you want your jewellery just at present to make more useful things—those little pearl pins would always be so pretty. I like that piece—but it, like everything else, seems dear. It has been bright and fine here today but it is getting so cold for hotel living and travelling. I am beginning to wonder how we shall ever exist all winter without a house or home. Your loving Sister May.'

'Darling Grace, Please order me *at once* either at Pacquin or Doucet (as you think best) a tea gown,' Belle instructed from Herbert House on Belgrave Square, London, to Grace in Paris: 'Mungo thinks pink or pale yellow and I think some imitation turquoise trimming would be pretty. Soft with lace but *confined* at the waist. I don't like them sacque and they don't wear them so here. It *must* be here for next Friday. Do get something ravishing. I want to wear it at Lord Elcho's party where there will be most delightful people! Use discretion about where to order it and have it made fully *two* inches *shorter* than your clothes. Also one very *pretty plain* blouse, not too smart to wear with blue tweed dress. I wonder if you can do this for me.

'How is the maid getting on and why don't you write? I am not enjoying myself as I have spent this entire week answering advertisements and looking for nurses and I haven't found one, and I am awfully cross and disgusted, for life isn't worth living. Now answer my questions *at once*. Will you come to Wilton on Monday week Dec. 7th if Bee [Lady Herbert] asks you? Do you think it would hurt Neily to be here for a week before you sail? If you do, you must *not* come. In great haste and love always, Belle.'

On the same day she wrote again: 'Darling Grace, I wrote you this morning respecting my own wants and must now send you a line in regard to the jewels. I have seen both Boucheron and Hamelin. Boucheron I am rather inclined to think the best of; this is what Mungo and I liked—a dear little chain necklace with emerald drops—lovely if you decide to stick to emeralds and then sister *ought* to give you a lovely thing for the front of your dress with an emerald centre and two emerald (pear shape) drops price about 35,000 pounds [$175,000]. But I see no disposition in her to invest more than 25,000 pounds [$125,000]! Now the little emerald necklace might be made more important as it does not come up to our limit. Besides this at Boucheron's for us to give you is a *stunning* sapphire with two diamonds on each side—splendid and very rich looking and you could wear it in the daytime on grand occasions. It is Mungo's choice and I think it magnificent! I really think if I were buying for myself it is what I should choose. You have got three large stones for future use and I think it beautiful.

'From Hamelin I like the pear-shape diamond necklace very much indeed but could not very well tell the effect without seeing them set. Of course it would be an advantage to have diamonds alone, as you could wear them so much oftener, and either of those necklaces is very chic and the sort of jewel we ought to wear. There was the huge pendant of the ruby necklace that could be set on a chain for about our price. They call it 18,000 but with the discount it would come down to almost 15,000. Think seriously of the sapphire.

'The stomacher from Hamelin, Sister seems to admire very much. It is lovely, no doubt. I have had it in the front of my dress and it is light and beautiful, but I don't believe I like it *quite* so well as the Boucheron pieces. I think sister *ought* to give you rather more than that! I can't make out why she doesn't when they buy such lots of things for themselves! This is very naughty of me—but it would come out!

'Either of those three things from us satisfy us as I think they are *lovely*. It depends whether you really *need* a necklace or not. I rather wish you would get my necklace that Sister gave me copied here exactly. It had such a success at Eton.

'Answer about Wilton. Will go there Wednesday. Yours, B.'

In the meantime, the Wilsons in New York were keeping the newlyweds posted on events there. In early December, 1896, May wrote to Grace: 'This is really a nice short letter from Father and I must say I can't help agreeing with his ideas and views. It makes one revengeful for they openly give out to the world that they will have nothing to do with you two and yet rather expect you to exile yourselves *on their account*. This is most unreasonable and unjust. If it were not for Neily's health I should most certainly go home— but we will talk this over tomorrow. Scandal evidently is subsiding.'

Soon Neily wrote from the Hotel Campbell in Paris to Dick Wilson: 'Dear Dick, We have decided to go home and are sailing on Dec. 16 on the "Teutonic". If I can't stand the climate, Grace has made me promise to come away again.

'I am so very anxious to see my Father that I feel I must make the attempt, as he has been and still is so very ill.

'We think we shall want rooms at the Buckingham (in N.Y.C.) on our arrival on the 23. Then decide after we have looked about where we shall stay and what sort of an apartment we like. Could you engage us rooms there? A sitting-room, a double bedroom and dressing-room, I think, will do, and not on a lower floor but pretty well up, as I think they are so expensive.

'There are a good many advantages about going home for the winter and I hope we shall be able to stay.

'The Martins cross in the same ship. Grace is looking very well and we have enjoyed Paris, though not going anywhere on account of my grandmother's death.

'Do come and meet us and see if you can't get us through the Custom House as Grace has some silver, etc. Must stop to catch this post. Yours ever, Neily.'

But Grace and Neily never sailed on the *Teutonic*. Instead, a succession of shocking pieces of news reached them as they made ready to end their voluntary exile from New York.

'I am sure our cable of yesterday must have been a great, great sorrow and disappointment to you,' Grace wrote her 'dearest Papa and Mama' on December 4 from Paris. 'And no one could be more upset than I am at present. You know that after Neily got that letter from Dr. McLane he was really quite alarmed about his father's condition, as until that letter came he had thought his father was recovering in a most satisfactory way. So after Dr. McLane's letter reached Neily about four weeks ago, he decided that he must and would go home to try to see his father as he felt so unhappy and miserable at the thought of his father's condition of health and he felt that if his father should suddenly get worse and anything happen to him, he, Neily, would never forgive himself for not having seen him again or at any rate not having tried to see him.

'So he wrote to his father (just after hearing the news of his grandmother's death) telling him how sorry he was to hear of her sudden death, etc. Then a few days after that (and after receiving a cable from his father announcing the news of his grandmother's death, which came after Neily had sent off the other letter) he wrote again to tell his father that he so much wished he would see him and that we were going to sail December 16th and he hoped his father would not refuse to see him.

'Of course he could not tell his father his reason for begging him to see him (namely the alarming letter from Dr. McLane). He also wrote to Dr. McLane by the next steamer saying he had written to his father and that we were going home for the purpose of Neily's trying to see him, but that we did not know if we could stay long as the climate might not agree with Neily. He is perfectly well, but it might be too cold for him at home.

'Now the reason for our putting off sailing (as we cabled you yesterday) is that Neily got yesterday morning (Thursday, December 3rd) a cable from Dr. McLane which was as follows: "Your Father has read your letter he is doing well and making slow but steady progress he does not wish to see you at present and as his physician I must insist upon exemption from worry do not return an interview impossible. Have written you— McLane. December 2nd New York."

'After receiving this there is nothing more we can do. Neily and I are both sorry, but it can't be helped. May and Baby May arrived here day before yesterday. We of course have not yet thought of plans for passing the winter over here. Must close as we are going skating with Baby May. Of course in a rink. Please try not to be too disappointed. Will write again soon. Your devoted daughter, Grace.'

Soon after my parents received the peremptory order 'do not

return' from the senior Vanderbilts, the senior Wilsons cabled in great agitation about a vile rumour circulating about the newlyweds in New York. Grandfather Wilson explained by post.

'To begin with the slanderous reports, referred to in our cable of the 12th,' he wrote, 'it came on us so suddenly that we were amazed, so to speak. On Thursday night December 10th about 11 o'clock a reporter from the Journal called and showed me a letter signed by someone who did not exist, addressed to the Editor of the Journal. This letter said that, according to club gossip all over town, there had been an addition to the Vanderbilt family, that you had given birth to a child at some place in Switzerland. The infernal reporter said that he would hunt up the man or rather go to see if such a person existed as purported to have signed this letter and that he would not publish it and so far as we could see from a careful examination, he did not publish it; but on Saturday there appeared in the Journal over the Cholly Knickerbocker column the enclosed piece which is not seemingly intended to be bad.

'Fearing that the wretch would publish the letter, I went to confer with Mr. Choate [Joseph Choate, Grandfather Wilson's lawyer] to see if anything could be done with them if they did publish it. He could not see his way to advise legal proceedings, as he said we could not afford to mix up with such a low and slanderous lot. I then cabled you that it was necessary for you to come home in order to protect your name from scandalous reports, thinking that, if you came, people could and would at once see that the whole thing was a lie and that none of the papers would publish anything.

'I found last Monday (yesterday) that this story had been talked all round—in fact when I went last night to see Choate, he told me that one of his own clerks in his office had told him last evening that he had heard in a club that you had a child. He was to get me the particulars today but I haven't had time to see him, nor do I think it worth while to see any further about it as I am certain it has been talked all round.

'I showed Mr. Choate your letter, containing a copy of the cable from McLane, for the purpose of enabling me to get his counsel as to whether or not I should cable you to come home. After carefully thinking over the matter, he decided that if he were in my place he would not cable but would wait and write you.

'From Choate's, and after consulting him as to the advisability of my doing so, I went to see Dr. McLane. It was nearly 7 o'clock and he said he was dressed to go to a dinner at 7 o'clock. He only talked for about two minutes. I told him of the infamous report about you and that I thought it was necessary for you to come home and that I did not see what damage could be done to Neily's Father if you returned and no interview was sought, and that I wanted him to cable Neily to this effect.

'He said he had not given the advice to Neily hurriedly but after mature reflection and that he thought the whole thing of your return would be in the newspapers and might do Mr. Vanderbilt serious injury. He said he had heard the report also. I asked him how he accounted for it; and he replied that it was probably started by the same party who started the report last summer; to the effect that your then condition made it absolutely necessary for you to get married.

'I then asked him who he thought started these reports. He replied "I do not know" and after pausing a moment he said it was certainly not any of his [Neily's] people. I replied, "Do you think it is not?"—and he replied, "It *could* not be any of them, for they did not know about them, that is these reports."

'McLane said that he never permitted any such rubbish to worry him, that everybody would know that there was not one word of truth in any of them and that he would not pay one particle of attention to them, etc.

'Here my interview with him ended but I asked him what time he would be in today and he replied about six p.m. So I went in again and had quite a talk, again appealing to him to know if it could not be arranged so as to have Neily come back without doing his Father an injury. He adhered to what he had said yesterday and added a good deal about the great importance of Neily's stopping for the winter in a warm, dry climate and that he understood from Neily's letters that Neily's doctors had impressed upon Neily this course.

'In respect to Neily's desire for an interview with his Father, he said his Father would not grant the interview and that, as his physician, he could not permit it, even if Mr. V. were willing, as he feared the effect might be very injurious; that he thought from every standpoint it was better for Neily to remain abroad until next spring. I asked Dr. McLane if he could name a time when he would not object to Neily's return. He replied that he hoped in a few months Mr. V. would be so far recovered as that the excitement incident to Neily's return would not injure him.

'I then returned to the subject of his reasons for thinking it was so much better for Neily to remain away, and he expressed the belief that time might and probably would make it easier for Mr. V. to forget his disagreement with Neily, not that he had any particular reason upon which to found such a belief except his confidence in the efficacy of time to soothe wounds etc.

'In the interview today I asked him when he first heard the report that it was necessary for you to get married and he replied that it was some time last summer. I asked him how he heard it; if it was from an anonymous letter. He said, "No, I don't recall; I think I just heard it." This closes my report of what occurred with Dr. McLane.

'I must now tell you what Mr. Edmund Baylies, who came into our box at the opera last night, told Dick and myself in the back box as he was going out. I asked, or rather told him I wanted to ask him if he had heard anything about you recently. He said he had heard that some five or six days ago the Journal had had a piece saying that you had to get married when you did, but that he had not seen it, nor could he tell the date of the paper. He did not seem to have heard the other story. He said they were infamous, and that anyone ought to be shot who would start such things.

'We then went into the advisability of your returning. He said that, while under ordinary circumstances he would say come home, yet in view of the fact that Dr. McLane had advised against it on account of the possible bad effect on Mr. V.'s health, he thought this should be a controlling reason against it.

'I have not given you the whole scandal stories, horrible as they are. Both McLane, Baylies and also Choate said no one would believe them but, whether they do or not, I don't now know that you can do anything to help the matter. If you had only returned here one month ago, or possibly if you had come on the 16th, it might have been in time to put a stop to the whole thing. It is a great pity that Neily ever wrote to Dr. McLane. If he had not done so, but had come home with Mrs. Martin, the chances are twenty to one no damage would have been done to Mr. V. or anyone else except these wretched scandalmongers—and it would have been such a good opportunity to have taken your place at home in society.

But, inasmuch as he did write to Dr. McLane, it gave him an opportunity to shut you out again and, while it may have been best for the reasons McLane gives, I greatly doubt it. You all will have to decide—in case we want you to come home we will cable. I think however that I may leave it entirely to you.

'Of course we are greatly worried and upset by these outrageous reports and at not getting you back with us but we shall have to bear it as best we can.

'With love to all and wishing you a merry Christmas, Father.'

The 'enclosed piece' Grandfather Wilson referred to in this letter was the following newspaper clipping:

A MOMENT WITH THE CHAPPIES

Somebody in the Knickerbocker Club has so far forgotten his manhood as to write me an anonymous letter in a disguised hand.

If it were not that the envelope containing the communication had been fastened with wax and stamped with the Knickerbocker Club seal, I would have concluded that the fellow had stolen the club's stationery, for anybody who would be guilty of writing an anonymous letter would not hesitate to steal the paper on which to write it.

Of course the purpose of the writer was to stab somebody in the back under cover of anonymity.

He first takes me to task for having said something pleasant about some very well-known New Yorkers the other day and asks how much I was paid for saying it.

This was the fitting prelude to his own proposition that I should publish in this column a scandalous story about a recently married young couple who are now abroad.

He concludes with this cowardly injunction: 'You had better publish the truth about this matter. You need not mention names. Everyone will understand.'

I am fully aware that the story to which he alludes has been common gossip in club and church circles, at fashionable teas, in public restaurants, and even in newspaper offices for the last fortnight, but I do not believe there is a word of truth in it.

In the first place, the character of the woman assailed has always been above suspicion.

In the second place I have absolutely trustworthy advices from Paris that the whole thing is a lie.

Now let the scandalmongers, both those who whisper in the vestibules of the church and those who write anonymously from the Knickerbocker Club, look elsewhere for sweet morsels to roll beneath their libellous tongues.

The Lord knows there is enough of evil within the sacred circle of our holy Four Hundred without charging wrong-doing to those who are innocent.

Ogden Goelet, the first to marry one of the famous Wilson sisters, wrote to his wife: 'What you write me about Grace and Neily I can hardly realize. I never in my life heard of such a dastardly attack. It is enough to drive her mad and they have my heartfelt sympathy. But *surely* this lie can be traced to some one and for him no punishment can be too great. Your father sometimes gets too excited over things, but something must be done. It will never do to let this pass. I do wish your father had some sensible man of the world to advise him rightly. It is no place for lawyers and to them he always seems to go when in trouble. It is awful. I do hope Dick will act like a man and not rest until he gets at the bottom of this plot. It makes my blood boil. And I feel it deeply for all of you and myself as well, and I do wish I could be of some use.'

Aunt May sent this letter to her youngest sister, Grace, and added: 'This is what I forgot to enclose. What will he think when he receives Father's letter and knows just how far it has gone and how dreadful it is?'

The 'stories' about my mother which both May and Richard T. Wilson found 'too dreadful to reveal' were by this time common backstairs gossip and—incredibly enough—are alive even today. They assailed Grace Vanderbilt's character in a manner both unbelievably vicious and absurd. I have never known a more proper person than my mother.

Grace Vanderbilt was gay and beautiful and charming, and she loved the company of men—accordingly, throughout her lifetime, she was able to attract and keep a devoted following of males. This was the essential key to the success of her always-well-attended parties. Yet because as a young girl she was an accepted part of certain Continental circles whispered to be racy, envious tongues branded her as 'fast'. They even insinuated that the gloomy and upright Cornelius Vanderbilt, Sr., almost died of a stroke over his son's marriage because he himself was madly infatuated with the beautiful Miss Wilson!

Thus the public wildly and melodramatically surmised why the senior Vanderbilts were so bitterly opposed to my gracious and lovely mother.

I see the feud beginning as a kind of rivalry between the Wilson and Vanderbilt families. No one is more snobbish about other hopefuls than the parvenu to society. The Wilsons' brilliant succession of marriages—none of them calculated, to my mind, but a result of good luck and the Wilsons' great personal charm—must have aroused considerable envy in the Vanderbilts.

Then, too, I believe Grandfather Vanderbilt realized that Neily was a serious-minded scientist, loving hard work and solitude, with no hankering after fashionable society. Grandfather felt, I'm sure, that such an earnest young man could not be happy for long with a woman so beautiful, so brilliantly gay, and so superbly gifted to play the social role for which she had been trained since birth by her two older sisters.

Chapter Five

ALL her life, even when she was being maligned, Mother adored the limelight. Father, on the other hand, deplored the slightest publicity. I am sure that he regarded the furore in the press surrounding his marriage as one of the most harrowing experiences of his life. He did not enjoy being pictured (as he was in some papers) as a rebellious, disobedient, and selfish son. His father's near-fatal stroke, following Neily's refusal to give up his fiancée, must have caused this heretofore dutiful and devoted son deep pangs of guilt. After his repeated requests to see his father had been refused and he had sailed abroad with his bride, he undoubtedly felt extreme distress when he heard in Paris for the first time what people were whispering about Grace in New York (scandal which was sure to reach his straitlaced parents).

'This has been a dreadful week for us,' wrote Grace to her father from Paris on December 18, 1896. 'Your first cable telling us there was a scandalous rumour about me came just a week ago and it upset us both. We felt at first we must start off immediately and sail the 16th. Then when your other cable came saying "It had been sent paper but not published", we all thought it was probably only scandalous gossip and May, Belle, and Mungo, to whom we wrote everything, sent us word not to act too hastily. We got everything ready, however, and were going to leave here Sunday but Saturday night we dined and went to a play.

'After the second act was nearly finished Neily left the box suddenly and *fainted*. It was terrible. When he got a little better we all left the theatre and he and I came home in a cab. He was rather done up all the next day, Sunday, and Dr. Robin said that the attack must have come from some worry or anxiety he had had. So we kept him in bed and on Monday he was better and is now all right again only he has had since this worry began a great deal of pain round his heart.

'We are now awaiting your letter telling us what all this scandal and nonsense is about. I can imagine what they are saying owing to the postponement of our wedding and the long time I stayed at Bay Shore and in town without Mamma, but then how any story about my being ill here in Paris now could have the slightest weight is more than we can understand or see. If we were in some out of the way place it *might* be believed but, you see, people see us here, walking about etc. every day, and people who are on their way home see us and they must tell people at home—we now feel that if this wicked rumour is believed by people in general or if it has become public we can perfectly well sail the end of this month or some time in Jan. as it *must* be disproved or else it might hang to me always and I have been in a frightful state about it all.

'Your letter came last night saying you had just received our cable explaining our reasons for changing our plans about sailing and also telling us the V's are giving it out openly that they will never have anything to do with us. What if they do say this? It does not in the least affect us, or matter. What else could they say after the way they have acted all along? You see, after Neily got that letter from the Dr. we all thought—Belle, Mungo, May and all—Neily *must* make some sort of offer to go home to be near his father in case he died. Otherwise, had he paid no attention to the Dr.'s warning about his father, they could forever after have called Neily a brute.

'Please understand that it was no mere offer made hastily etc. It was all carefully thought out. Now that his father has repulsed him etc., he must never again have anything to do with them—and he does not intend to, I assure you. However, if we should have to sail soon, he will have to give some reason to the Dr. for coming—I hope Dick will also understand this and not just think we have been trying the "making up" business.

'I really am awfully afraid of the climate at home for Neily. Dr. Robin wants us to leave here at once, and he advises returning to America or doing anything to keep Neily from worrying but we shall wait until your letter comes. Love to all and, as Christmas will be past when you get this, we both wish you, dear Father and Mother, and Dick a happy New Year and a *quieter* one I pray than this last has been for you.

'With a heart very full of love from your devoted child, Grace.'

In the midst of all this furore, Uncle Mungo, the calm and sage diplomat, wrote to Grandfather Wilson from his family's ancestral castle near Salisbury, England: 'My dear Mr. Wilson: Just a line to wish you and my dear Mother a very happy New Year and a cessation of all the worries which have beset you this year. Grace will give you all our news as she spent Christmas here. I should not let her fuss too much or pay exaggerated heed to all these frightful lies. I think we can all be above paying any attention to them, and her presence in New York will be sufficient to refute them. What scoundrels some people are. We go back to Constantinople next week. It is a wrench but if I want to stick to the career I must make the best of it. Will you kindly pay the enclosed dues to the Racquet Club and also to the Metropolitan from Belle's acct.? Love to all the family, yours affectionately, Mungo.'

And, finally, when Grace and Neily at long last were about to sail for home in January, after an absence of five months, Belle wrote her from Wilton House: 'I sent the letter back in another envelope. It is exactly what I expected, but you must not pay any attention to it as far as your personal feelings go. You must only go back to face it, and to hunt out the starter of it, if possible. I think *all* evenly balanced and strong minds would scorn the idea of letting it in any way take hold. Dr. McLane's advice was correct in that way and Mr. Choate's. I am glad papa went to them, as it is good to have some support from the beginning.

'I know how *terrible* it will be for you but I am *sure* you will find a lot of friends. I should like you to keep me informed about that part of it. I don't think it will be safe to write anything particular to the steamer so do not look for letters there. They often do not catch the ship and are then opened and read.

'Now my darling, take courage. Of course I want to hear everything—by the time you reach home you had better write direct to Constantinople. Give heartsfull of love to all the very dear ones and a good account of us. God Bless you. Belle.'

When the newlyweds reached home, they moved into Grandfather Wilson's house at 511 Fifth Avenue. Within a week of their return, they were welcomed into their old circle of friends, with a few exceptions who sided with the senior Vanderbilts.

At Mrs. Henry Sloane's ball in January they were, according to a society reporter, 'the centre of attention all evening'. He went on to write: 'Mrs. Vanderbilt, Jr., is looking remarkably well and bears no traces of her recent rough trip home across the Atlantic. Her graceful figure is even slighter than when she sailed away as a bride, and she danced with an animation and zest which disproved any stories of her having been ill abroad.'

Thus even the Press backed up my popular parents.

Aunt May apparently still thought that the Vanderbilts would not be able to hold out indefinitely against public opinion, which was strongly in favour of Grace and Neily. For this reason, May thought that her sister and brother-in-law had made a mistake in moving under the Wilson roof.

'I am grieved that things go no better with you both,' Aunt May wrote Grace from Geneva in April of 1897. "It is something I suppose we shall never be able to fathom, the mystery of those attacks, or the reason N's parents should ever have taken the line they have—I think it would be better for all concerned to let the whole thing die a natural death——

'It seems almost a pity that you should have taken N to 511, as even if any of his people had wished to be civil to you, your being there quite put it out of the question as their hatred and animosity is centred and directed more against *your* people than *you personally*. And it must have been a dreadful aggravation having Neily under a roof so hated. I am glad you have had some steadfast friends. I feared they might drop off, but people on the whole seem to have been nice.

'We saw a great deal of the Prince, always the same kind friend to us, and Beatrix Herbert here with May made all the difference in the world to May's pleasure. Beatrix was mad keen about everything and they had great fun together. I can't say I enjoy chaperoning girls of 18 and Beatrix is a host in herself— She has grown very handsome, I think. Beautiful eyes and will have a future if I know anything about girls. We banqueted nearly every night with H.R.H. and some of our parties were very interesting and nice— more so than those stupid entertainments at Cannes.

'I wrote Robert about our great excitement and presentation to the Queen [Victoria] the day Her Majesty visited Greenock. The Prince had been on "White Ladye" to wish us Goodbye and we were all admiring the preparations made to receive the Queen. A great platform was built and covered over with canvas so that H.M. stepped from her carriage into her chair which was rolled on board by her Indian servant.

'We were all peeping as best we could when suddenly Seymour appeared and said we were all to come at once and be presented. It was altogether a hurry-scurry, no time for being frightened. We walked on board and the Prince presented us. The Queen *shaking hands* with us all. A few pleasant words and a beautiful smile and we were dismissed. It was interesting and certainly a very great honour for us.

'Well, time is going on and next week we go to Paris. How I dread and hate that—and so on home, sailing some time in June. Not in Mayflower [the Goelets' new yacht] although Ogden will, of course. I don't look forward with pleasure to returning, although I shall be so happy to see all the beloved ones again. It does seem ages since Robert left us and so long since I have seen dear Mother and Father. If you and Mamma want me to do any shopping for you *please* send me your commission at once.

'Yesterday May and I went out racing in Ailsa with Arthur in command (owner not here). I almost died of fright as we were struck by a squall and pinned over in a manner I never dreamed possible—I thought we were done for. I am too old for such business and hate the sea beside— Now I must stop and send this off. I wonder where it will reach you. I hope Neily is much better and that you both are happier. Let all the old trouble go. It is time enough to forget the past and live in the present. Love to you both from your loving Sister May.'

Belle was the romanticist in the Wilson family, like her highly emotional Father. May was always bedrock practicality, and my mother—perhaps because she leaned upon both of her sisters so much—was by turns both romantic and realistic.

That spring she and Neily went down to the Homestead at Hot Springs, Virginia, for the 'cure'. Father had taken the hot mineral baths there upon several different occasions, and Mother, who had been there with her parents, was considered by the aristocratic guests at the Homestead to be one of its most ravishing belles.

Southern belledom was still in flower in 1897. 'The South,' said Percival Reniers, 'in its contemplation and adoration of its belles got as much satisfaction as the North got from counting the cost of Cornelius Vanderbilt's horses or Jay Gould's yacht.'

At the Homestead, these lovely, fragile creatures spent their days strolling under parasols along Lovers' Walk, taking tallyho rides, or playing euchre on honeysuckle-laden porches with a bevy of beaux. In the evenings, there were dances called Germans and cotillions in the vast ballroom, illuminated with candlelit paper Japanese lanterns and decorated with boughs of spruce and laurel. When darkness fell, it was generally supposed that a raging beast awoke in every gallant's breast, and a belle could lose her honour by five minutes spent alone in a man's company.

'The last oil lamp on the porch was by the water cooler,' Mrs. Lavalette Keiley, greatest of the old Sweet Springs belles, told Cleveland Amory. 'You could walk with your beau that far but no further. It was considered breathlessly fast even to go a few steps beyond. It was almost like going away for the week-end, although of course we hadn't heard of *that*.'

The immense sprawling wooden Homestead, colonial in appearance and painted a gleaming white, was but one of the resort hotels on the grand tour of natural mineral springs followed by the aristocrats of the South since the time of Thomas Jefferson. The total tour covered some 170 miles, most of it tortuous carriage trails winding circuitously from valley to valley through the Allegheny Mountain country. At Warm Springs, the hotel landlord, Colonel John Fry, used to speed departing guests with 'Go get well-charged at the White, well-salted at the Salt, well-sweetened at the Sweet, well-boiled at the Hot, and then return to me and I will Fry you.'

For a hundred years, accommodations at these various mountain springs were so primitive that Northerners flocked instead to the luxurious establishments abroad at Bad Nauheim, Carlsbad, and Aix-les-Bains. Then, in the early nineties, a syndicate of New York financiers, including my Grandfather Vanderbilt and J. P. Morgan, acquired Hot Springs and turned it into a resort spa so fabulous that even staid Bostonians were induced to desert their beloved Cape Cod in favour of the uncertain novelty of travel below the Mason-Dixon line.

Mr. Amory in *The Last Resorts* also quotes Col. McKee Dunn, whose farm covers a whole mountain: 'In the old days we had everybody. We had the Vanderbilts and Whitneys and we had Mrs. Stuyvesant Fish and Governor Livingston Beekman from Newport and we even had a Miss Postlethwaite from Boston—oodles of people like that. Now we don't have anybody. Everything has gone to hell in the past twenty years. Roosevelt and Truman and all those people have given everyone the idea that they're just as good as everybody else.'

Only a few mad radicals held such rash ideas back at the turn of the century when, to get a reservation at the Homestead, it was practically necessary to produce the family genealogy.

In the spring of 1897, when my mother and father arrived at the Homestead, there were, I imagine, seven private railway cars belonging to as many railway presidents sidetracked at the depot close to the hotel. Drawn up close beside them, patiently waiting, was a coloured coachman in livery seated on an immensely high shining black Brewster victoria.

'Good morning, Henry!' Mother greeted him delightedly. This was her usual coachman and carriage provided by the Homestead stables for her exclusive use during her stay. Henry would not be needed until three in the afternoon, but he knew that my mother liked to see him the moment she stepped off the train, so although it was only seven o'clock in the morning, he had risen at five to get himself and the horses and carriage ready for her inspection.

As my parents started up the steep path towards the small white cottage which they had engaged, followed by their maid and valet and porters pushing ten large trunks, Henry turned his team back towards the stables. At the same time, the Homestead manager, Mr. Sterry, and the hotel housekeeper, were waiting to greet the Vanderbilts in their cottage, along with the waiter, housemaid, and bellhop who had been selected to devote their entire daily efforts to keeping my parents comfortable.

When the housekeeper observed the Vanderbilt procession coming, she touched a match to the fire set in the cottage fireplace and dispatched the special waiter to the kitchens for the Vanderbilt breakfasts. In a few moments he came racing back, balancing on his head a tray covered with dazzling white napery, and containing such delicacies as Southern hot breads, ruby-red mountain strawberries, cinnamon rolls running with hot butter and brown sugar and crisp pecans, country eggs, and slices of peach-fed Virginia ham cooked in champagne.

After they had breakfasted (Mother eating, as usual, nothing but tea and toast), and the servants were busy exchanging the hotel linen on the beds for the Vanderbilt linen sheets and blankets and silk bedspreads, Mother and Father liked to sit on their little porch near the tennis courts. Together they gazed out over the sloping velvety turf, clipped yew, and magnificent copper beeches towards the Pleasure Pool, where vapours from the hot springs rose mistily into the spring air. Beyond stood the gentle Alleghenies in April's freshest green, necklaced with white dogwood and the flaming-red flowering Judas.

Whenever Mother reached the Homestead—and she went there continuously for some sixty years—a kind of subtle change seemed to come over her. She was no longer the vivacious, cosmopolitan Grace Graham Vanderbilt, pet of princes and kings, but the little girl in heelless prunella slippers who gathered blackberries on the rugged hillsides of 64th Street, and raced along the red clay gullies of Tennessee. For hours she sat in her rocking chair, a soft pink French blanket pulled over her knees, her small brown rae pinscher in her lap, watching the restless surge of beautifully gowned women cross and recross the shade-dappled lawns. Each morning at ten, she strolled over to the four-storey bathhouse where—in a private cubicle—she sat in a tub of piping hot mineral water which flowed constantly over the sides of the tub to the floor, while an attendant wrapped her steaming face and head in icy cloths. Then, wrapped like a mummy in heated rubber sheets and woollen blankets, she would lie gently steaming on a cot, a relaxed smile on her lips. This was followed by a cold shower and an hour's body massage; precisely the routine she had followed for years at Bad Nauheim.

She and Father lunched alone in their cottage, and often in the afternoon took a leisurely victoria ride to Warm Springs, some five miles away. The carriage followed the lovely old Valley Road with its tiny weather-beaten farmhouses and stony fields, its flowering peach and apple orchards, and ancient worm fences which snaked up and down the green mountain slopes. The road, little more than two ruts, occasionally turned off through forests fragrant with laurel, heavy with the scent of hemlock and moss which mingled with the sharp smell of hot leather upholstery and sweating, foam-flecked horses. On such carriage rides, Mother customarily said little, but sat beautifully erect, holding her lace parasol, gazing about her with delight. Father often appeared to fall asleep, and the silence was broken only by the creaking and straining of harness and carriage and the snorting and blowing of the chestnut team. Near the end of the valley, my parents alighted and separated to bathe in the round wooden bath-houses built at the time of Thomas Jefferson.

After donning a shapeless Mother Hubbard coverall, Mother slipped into the five-foot-deep pool; the water was warm and as clear and bubbling as champagne. Over in the men's establishment, Father was bathing in the nude, while a respectful black attendant awaited the command to float out to him a tall frosted mint julep balanced on a cork tray.

At dusk Mother and Father, back in their cottage, with the fire lit and the curtains drawn, would dine in full evening dress with a few intimate friends. Often for two full hours they lingered over their eight-course dinners, superb examples of Southern cooking at its finest—perhaps roast turkey with oyster sauce, broiled mountain trout, corn fritters light as fluffs of cloud, soft-shelled Maryland crab with mayonnaise of celery—topped by a Madeira which had rounded the Cape.

The guests often left early, and then, rousing herself from the settee where she had been sitting with Father gazing into the flickering fire, Mother would change into one of those French dressing-gowns which a native of that country once described as 'revealing while concealing all that fires a gentleman's imagination'.

In spite of his great hard-won happiness, Neily (still only a youth of twenty-four, still with his boyish and tender and sentimental heart) could not seem to find peace of mind. The attitude of his family astounded him. It suggested that his crime against them had been a terrible one—but he could not figure out what it was. Could his rebelliousness alone have caused his father's illness? He still loved his parents dearly, and he was tortured by the image of his handsome and vigorous father reduced overnight to a feeble, half-paralysed old man vainly seeking his lost vitality in the great spas of Europe. All interest in work seemed to have deserted the elder Vanderbilt, who now appeared but rarely at the desk where once he slaved twelve hours a day, and the management of the great railway empire, which once he guarded so zealously, was now in the hands of his gay and cosmopolitan brother, Willie K.

But what must have puzzled Neily most was the attitude of his mother, who had always been such a kind and loving and devoted parent. Surely she would not cast her son from her heart for ever for a single act of disobedience? And *why* did she seem to hate Grace so much? How could she have written such things about her, in a letter to him in Constantinople so horrible that he had immediately burned it in a wave of revulsion and shame?

If she had ever had any question in her mind concerning Grace, why had she invited her, time and again, to her balls and dinners in New York when Grace was a leading *débutante* and the Vanderbilts had three unmarried sons? And why had his sister Gertrude aligned herself so uncompromisingly on the side of her parents? Could her jealousy of Grace's great beauty and charm lie behind the family's opposition?

Finally—if for some unknown and incomprehensible reason they found Grace unacceptable as a daughter-in-law—why must they close their hearts to him as well?

Apparently Father seemed to feel that the anonymous letter circulated at the time of his wedding had much to do with his parents' attitude, for he knew that their family pride was such that they could not bear to have the slightest scandal touch the Vanderbilt name. If only he could run down the author and expose the culprit! Perhaps then his mother and father would condescend to welcome him and his bride into their various kingly dwelling places.

'Am very sorry that you have no news,' he wrote to Dick Wilson, his brother-in-law, from the Homestead on the subject of the anonymous letters. 'Did you show the experts the specimens of ink from the Clubs, to find if the letters were written in the buildings or outside and then returned and sealed? The sealing-wax would also tell.'

With this letter, Neily enclosed a copy of a note he had written to his mother just before leaving New York: 'My dear Mother, I received yr. note a few days ago. I feel terribly that you refuse to see me. What there has been in my actions during the past eighteen months to make you refuse to see me I do not know.

'I considered the question of my own happiness lay with me, and I persisted in my choice. This is all I have done during that time and you *know* I have done nothing but what was perfectly open and just.

'And yet I am treated as if I were a scoundrel by my own family when there is nothing I have done that I am ashamed of, or regret, or that I would not wish to have the whole world know. My dear Mother, will you not allow me to see my sick Father? He is ill, and though you do not seem to *believe* it, I am very wretched at not seeing him.

'I ask this of you, and pray you will not refuse it. As ever, Yr. Aff son C.'

But Grandmother Vanderbilt turned a deaf ear to her penitent son's request.

Later that summer Neily wrote to his wife at Newport from the Metropolitan Club, which was just three scant blocks away from his parents' great Fifth Avenue chateau in New York: 'Dearest Grace: This is, I think, the first letter I have written to you since our marriage. I arrived here about an hour ago and have had dinner, in anticipation of the arrival of my bag, which has not turned up yet.

'The journey down was uneventful. The train was not so hot as I had expected and, with a very interesting magazine on Marine Engineering, I managed to get through it.

'I am thinking of you continually, you may be sure, and find our separation far from pleasant. But let us hope it is the only one we will ever have. I think of stopping in New Haven tomorrow if I can make connections so will probably arrive in Newport at 7.

'How many recollections this great building brings up to me. For I came here so often during the time we were engaged and that immediately preceding it. I could feel as I did, sitting at my dinner the day before I was taken ill—and then my last bachelor meal was eaten in the same place. But tonight all is so changed and different. Changed for the better.

'I hope you found "mommer" better and are not too lonely. Anyway it is better for you to sleep at your home than to be kept awake by all the noise of the carriages. I must stop now and send this for I want it to catch the night train. I am arriving very soon so don't worry, Darling Wife. Your affectionate Husband, Neily.'

Meanwhile, reports were coming from abroad that young May Goelet, or Baby May as the family usually called her, was engaged to the Duke of Manchester. This inspired the usual headshaking in New York over the Wilson family—'the most successful matrimonial schemers in the world outside of the royal House of Denmark.'

As I always heard the story, the Duke was an unprepossessing little fellow and Cousin May a person of considerable vivacity and charm, if not exactly a great beauty. At any rate, Uncle Ogden was reported furious over the reports and even more so when the Duke ungallantly rushed to the telegraph offices first to deny the engagement. A past diet of rich French foods and Russian caviar, plus all the strain of carrying on his strenuous role in Continental society, was proving too much for Uncle Ogden. At this time, when he was only in his mid-forties, hothouse grapes were a principal item on his daily menu.

'I hope your gowns get off by tomorrow's steamer,' May wrote to her sister Grace from Paris, 'and that you will be pleased with them. I have been so little at the dressmaker's since Ogden had that bad set-back and did not know anything of your order until Jean Worth sent me word to come to see your dresses before they went. Your two ball gowns are simply lovely—the colour is *new* and one has to get used to it. I think the little hat lovely and it looks like you. Chenille is the great rage. I have no less than three hats like that. I took the liberty of sending you a black hat which I think very chic and pretty—a little present for you. The bill goes with it, but I have paid it so that is all right.

'I wonder how you will like the costume Mlle. Smarty at Doucet's designed for you. It was really so plain when I saw it the other day I would not accept it. I found she had never shown it to Doucet, who immediately made changes, the embroidered gilet, braid, etc., which I think have made it very pretty. The colour is very nice and the style quite the latest. Everything in the way of walking costumes are made very simple and plain—I do hope you will not be disappointed!!

'And now a little about ourselves. Ogden is much better, almost over his dreadful illness. Is up and walking about the apartment but is still very weak. The doctor thinks he may go out next week if the weather permits—but what weather we are having.'

Then, in August, when Mother and Father had returned to Newport, Uncle Ogden suffered a fatal stroke aboard his yacht. A more fashionable demise could not be imagined, for his new twin-screw yacht the *Mayflower*, considered the world's most luxurious, was anchored at Cowes at the time, and the Prince of Wales, immediately upon hearing of his friend's illness, dispatched his personal physician to attend him until the end.

And so, at an early age, Aunt May became one of the richest widows in the world, maintaining her big New York chateau (although she was seldom in it), her Ochre Court at Newport (now a Catholic Seminary), and her villa on the Riviera near Nice. She seldom lacked suitors.

The same August that Uncle Ogden died, a valet of Richard T. Wilson's was arrested for stealing some family jewellery, and through this unhappy circumstance, the whole story of the anonymous letters of the time of Mother's wedding was, for the first time, aired in the New York Press. Portions of the letters were published, such as the revealing sentence, 'and that explains the fierce haste of the Wilsons to hasten the wedding when young Vanderbilt's father was supposed to be dying'.

For a while it was believed that Grandfather Wilson's English valet had managed to obtain some Metropolitan Club stationery and seals and had written the letters himself, but then suspicion shifted to a rejected suitor of Mother's. 'There are certain of the slanderous letters in the possession of the Wilson family which have never been published and which show the writer to be a man of education and refinement and a connoisseur of art,' stated one newspaper report. 'He used the language and forms of a society man and referred to occurrences and facts, especially in reference to the Wilson family history, that greatly antedate the time of the valet's arrival in the country and could not possibly have been known by him.'

The matter was dropped, unsolved, finally, although Grandfather Wilson offered $1,000 to anyone who could reveal the author of the letters. It is possible, of course, that they were written by a reporter simply to stir up newspaper circulation. But what a chain of heartbreak they caused!

It was also during the summer of 1897 that I received my first press notice, seven months before I was born! 'If the report be true,' hinted *Town Topics*, 'not many months will elapse before a baby who can bear the name of Vanderbilt directly will be welcomed.'

This news appeared following the birth of a baby boy to Aunt Gertrude Whitney, an event which returned Grandmother Vanderbilt precipitately from Lucerne, Switzerland, where Grandfather was still recuperating from his stroke. So concerned was she about his health, however, that she stayed in Newport only two weeks and hurried back abroad, without seeing either my father or mother.

'A bouncing baby boy was born in a bright, pretty room of a modest little brick house at No. 12 West 36th Street,' the New York *World* announced my arrival on April 30, 1898, during the second year of my parents' marriage. 'To all appearances, he looks like any other two-day-old, in flannels, snowy linen and dainty laces. When he thrust his chubby little fist towards the ceiling, his father laughed outright. . . . Society sees him only as a living question mark. Will he heal the breach between the families? If they are reconciled he will be worth many times his weight in gold.'

At that, I weighed a good deal—a hefty ten pounds, in fact.

Commented *Town Topics*: 'Someone once said that the Vanderbilt family can always be relied upon in times of dullness to furnish either news or a sensation of some kind. This remark has been justified within the past few days by the reported engagement of George W. Vanderbilt to Mrs. Edith Stuyvesant Dresser, and the birth of a long-expected son and heir to Mr. and Mrs. Cornelius Vanderbilt, Jr.' The society reporter then added ironically: 'I don't know why the arrival of a baby in this household should have caused the excitement it did on Sunday, for this arrival had been long discounted in society circles everywhere.'

If Father had hoped that the birth of the first grandchild to bear the Vanderbilt name would heal the great bitterness between himself and his parents, his hopes were soon dashed. Instead, his mother and father went directly from Switzerland to Paris to be on hand for Uncle George's wedding there, and soon all the members of the family on the senior side of the feud—the Sloanes and Whitneys and Shepards and Twombleys—sailed for France's capital. This event made the breach more evident than ever. Those remaining steadfast to my parents on this side of the ocean were the Wilsons, the Goelets, the Astors, and the Belmonts.

I was christened Cornelius Vanderbilt, the fifth male in our family to bear this distinguished name.

From England Aunt Belle wrote, 'I shall so love to be godmother to your little son and to take the responsibility of seeing that it is properly instructed in all beginner's matters. It is a great honour that you and Neily do me and I feel very pompous over being a godmother to a Vanderbilt! I am so thankful for all the good news I hear of its health. He seems a fine little fellow. Sister and little May give such amusing accounts of Neily in the nursery and how much he likes to carry little Neil, etc. I want to go to America to see darling Pappa and Mamma but I dread the hot, sticky summers at Newport.'

So apparently Aunt Belle did not come over for my christening. Nor did the senior Vanderbilts. At this time there were three living Cornelius Vanderbilts. Our friends solved the problem by calling Grandfather 'Cornelius' and my father 'Neily', while I was always plain 'Neil', as I still am today.

When I was only six weeks old, Mother popped me into a laundry basket and, along with my wet nurse, took me to France! Since that day I have made 150 Atlantic crossings. I've sailed the Pacific forty-six times and been around the world twelve. I can remember once, while crossing the flats of Siberia in a creaky old train, my travelling companion asking me, 'When is it going to start looking *faraway*?' To me, it never has.

'No wonder your friends call you Tumbleweed, my darling,' my Mother used to say. 'You get your wanderlust from me.'

'I hear that the latest inheritor of an honoured name—Cornelius Vanderbilt—is spoken of in the Vanderbilt family as "that Wilson baby",' a reporter wrote that summer from Newport. 'The general expectation was that a grandfather, however he might oppose a marriage, could not resist the soft clutch of baby fingers or the sweet appeal of baby lisps. But there are grandfathers and grandfathers, and the Vanderbilt family are as noted for their obstinacy as the Wilson family for shrewdness and tact. I believe, however, that the baby will conquer in the end, and enter into his millionaire heritage.'

Going through my mother's things the other day, of which there are truckloads (for she never threw anything away), I found a letter, dated July 14, 1898, written from Newport by Grandmother Wilson to her recently widowed daughter, my Aunt May Goelet. Apparently she had just put Aunt May's son Robert on a ship going abroad, for she writes: 'Darling daughter May: By the time this reaches you, dear Robert will be with you . . . I am sure he will be a comfort to you and a great deal of company. He was looking pale and rundown before he got through his examinations, but I hope the voyage will do him good.

'Your father has just sent me a telegram saying Santiago has surrendered. Glorious news. I hope and pray that the war may soon be over, for the suffering must be great beyond description. The yellow fever has broken out among our men, and the rainy season has commenced, which increased the discomforts to say nothing of the sickness.

'Getting away from the cry of "Extra, Extra", is a great relief. Newport is very quiet although there are more people here in cottages than ever before and many strange faces. Every house is taken. Grace and Neily have taken the Osgood house. It is too large and cumbersome for them, but the only one to be had except the Hadden house which has been shut up and they thought it was damp and very musty and dirty, and with all more *expensive*.

'*They were for some time undecided about whether they would obey the command to go away from here. When they finally thought it best to remain, all the houses were taken. Neily was firmly of the opinion that he could not go away and everyone said it was the most outrageous demand that had ever been made and it would do no good* [italics mine].

'They have gone to town for two days and then to Saratoga for a few days. The dear baby is growing and improving very fast. He is really a very pretty fresh healthy babe. I am keeping him here while they are away.

'Iris Astor returned on Saturday and came here today with a dinner invitation for Grace. She says that she had a delightful time in London, was going all day and night. Carrie and Orme are coming here on Saturday.

'I am delighted to hear that Baby May is enjoying herself. I do hope she will keep well and enjoy life. We are greatly interested in her and all that you have told us. I hope you will guide her affections in the best way for her happiness, if one could only know what way that was!

'Love to you all from your loving Mother.'

I can recall being called 'the Wilson baby'. When Mother took me to Bailey's Beach or into the shops, people would remark, 'My, doesn't he look like his Grandfather Wilson, though!' I don't remember anybody ever comparing me to any Vanderbilts.

That summer, while Colonel Teddy Roosevelt's Rough Riders were fighting in Cuba, another Vanderbilt romance blossomed. This was between my father's younger brother Alfred and the beautiful Elsie French. Commented the papers: 'It looks as if we should have another Vanderbilt engagement before long, if not a Vanderbilt wedding, for it is a sort of Punchinello's secret that young Alfred Vanderbilt, the second son of Cornelius, is engaged to that little beauty, Miss French, daughter of Mrs. Francis Ormond French, whose other daughter married the Hon. Hubert Eaton, of London, and who is in the smart Marlborough set and a reigning beauty. Young Alfred is not yet out of Yale, but like all the Vanderbilts, with the exception of his Uncle George, he is falling in love at an early age. As the Vanderbilts usually stick to their first love it looks as if the French-Vanderbilt alliance would go through all right. Miss French has a fine fortune in her own right and is of an excellent old family. There would probably be no parental objection to this marriage other than that the lovers are too young.'

When Father returned to New York from his European honeymoon, he decided to return to Yale to win his master's degree in mechanical engineering. This he accomplished, commuting each day to New Haven, and studying long hours every night at his in-law's house on Fifth Avenue. Then, the fall before I was born, he did an extraordinary thing. He swallowed his pride and presented himself at the employment desk of the family railroad to ask for a job. Chauncey Depew put him in the motive power and rolling stock department at what was termed a "moderate salary".

Some idea of the public esteem my father enjoyed during this period may be gathered from this *New York Times* article about his new job:

YOUNG VANDERBILT'S TASK

WORKING HIS WAY UP AS A MECHANICAL ENGINEER ON THE NEW YORK CENTRAL

SENT ON A WESTERN MISSION

CORNELIUS VANDERBILT'S OLDEST SON STRIVING TO WIN HIS FATHER'S FAVOUR BY HARD WORK—A NATURAL APTITUDE FOR MECHANICS

Cornelius Vanderbilt, Jr., the oldest son of the present head of the Vanderbilt family, is now in the West making an inspection of methods and conditions in the mechanical departments of the Lake Shore Railroad.

On his return to this city he will submit a report of his observations to President Callaway of the New York Central system, by whom he was specially assigned to this unusual mission. Since last fall young Vanderbilt has been a hard-working employe in the motive power and rolling stock department of the New York Central, at a salary which is characterized by his superior officers as 'very moderate'.

It was not upon the recommendation of his father or any other member of the Vanderbilt family that Cornelius Vanderbilt, Jr., was taken into the service of the New York Central Railroad. His personal request for work was considered upon his individual merits, and his assignment to the mechanical department was made in view of his known aptitude for that line of work, supported by the fact that he had taken a course of mechanical engineering at Yale College.

The estrangement between this young man and his father, in consequence of his refusal to comply with the parental wishes regarding a postponement of his marriage, has never been mended. Since the day the father and son parted, just prior to the prostration of the senior Vanderbilt by paralysis, the two have not met, and, so far as intimate friends of the family know, they have had no communication with each other. That parting was more than two years ago. Cornelius, Jr., married the girl of his choice, Miss Grace Wilson, and is now himself a father. Persons who know the young man well say that his affectionate regard for his father has never diminished, and that his voluntary abandonment of the ease and luxury which his own private means, as well as that of his wife, would enable him to enjoy, for the discipline and toil of a wage-earner, is inspired by a laudable purpose. Young Cornelius, it is said, is determined to show his father that he is not only able and willing to work, but that he has the capacity to become useful to the great system of railroads with which the name of his family is identified.

Some of the older officers of the New York Central—men who from life-long service naturally take a deep interest in all matters pertaining to the Vanderbilts—view the course of Cornelius Vanderbilt, Jr., with cordial approval. They say that the young man has set a hard task for himself, but they believe that he has sufficient of the Vanderbilt pluck and determination to carry it out.

'This young man intends to win back his father's favour by showing that there is something in him,' said a grey-haired official who has served successively under three generations of Vanderbilts. 'And you may depend upon it he will make his mark. He is a worker, and he appreciates the value of a thorough understanding of the details that makes the best executive. Unless I am greatly mistaken, this young Vanderbilt will be a great railroad executive before he dies.'

Some idea of the earnestness with which young Vanderbilt is engaging in his work may be gleaned from the statement that he was on duty almost every working day in July. Even the hot weather of that month failed to drive him away from his work. He is expected home from his Western trip in about ten days.

Just before he left on this trip, Father wrote to Mother at Newport: 'Dearest Grace, Your letter received. I saw your Father this morning about the bills and he did not seem *very* much surprised. He said for you to draw on him for all the bills and when they are all paid up he will sell enough of your securities—a portion of what you put away last year—to settle it. So go ahead and draw your checks and try and get them all paid. I did not sell any of my bonds but drew on your account $361.35 for Haff's, Veda's etc. bills and $150 for myself to go west with. Hope you will not be too lonely and get depressed as everything is really going all right.

'I have been to 12 West 36 and am having a key made for the library closet and have an appointment at 1 to meet a packer there to pack up the more important things and then take all to be stored. Except of course the 3 pieces in your room. Taylor will send you a list of houses.

'In haste, your devoted husband, C.'

'Another day and night!' he wrote her from Elkhart, Indiana. 'Such a busy time for your devoted C. This is the only 1st class shop for locomotion work on the line. You must be sick of shops and such talk in my letters. Your letter did not arrive today, very much to my disappointment, for I was counting on it when I came in from the visiting and am so sorry not to get it. I do hope to get 2 tomorrow. I wired you this evening for I want to hear how you are.

'I pray and trust you are well and Baby too. But you would have wired, were you not. And you have your Mother and Father, Belle and Robert to take care of you. Happy people!

'To return to the business talk. Tomorrow morning about 7 a.m. I shall get off at Englewood—part of Chicago—to see shops and shops and shops. Exactly what order to see them in I am not sure yet. But I hope to go through the Illinois steel works as I have letters.

'And I think that all the $1\frac{1}{2}$ days in the windy city will be nothing but a round of shop inspecting. You see I put on lots of airs on this trip and say this grandly and in quite a blasé way. But my head is a little turned, for I had all the 500 men working here kept at work another hour for me to get through seeing the locomotion shops tonight!

'Also had the wrecking train put in operation for me to see after dark (at 6.15). And had the crew of the wrecking car lift a full-size box car up off the track and show me how it worked. Each day I have lots of the tools that are not going put in operation for yours truly. You see what an awful snob and idiot I am to talk of this. I wonder if you have any idea of where Elkhart and Adrian and these other places are?

'We have a beautiful 'hunter's' moon and a delightful day as far as weather is concerned. And I go to look at the old man in the moon and think that he is looking at my dear little wife, too.

'I am so awfully sorry that you could not be with me on this sort of a trip. One is *so comfortable* and free. I must work hard and try to some day be able to take you about in this way. Such good food and I am getting very fat! Country air and the real changes are the best tonics in the world, at least for me.

'I do so wish you could travel comfortably in the regular way— I don't mean *you* personally—but one. The trouble is that as soon as one goes in the usual manner, it's not amusing at all; but one thinks it commonplace and dull and such poor country and so dirty, etc., instead of sort of a lark and interesting.

'Darling, good night to you and Baby. I'll soon be back now.

'Your ever the same and never changing husband, C.'

'Your letter cheered me up a great deal,' he wrote from Adrian, Michigan, 'for you seemed in much better spirits than your previous lines to me. Do be a good girl and not get worried or dreary while I'm away. But it's so hard on us both.

'Just returned from a Sunday evening service at a Baptist church in this little town. It was really nice. A simple talk from a good speaker and a hymn which seemed sincere and sung by all.

'In Adrian there are about 10,000 people. The L.S. and M.S. have a car shop here, so we are to see it in the morning early and then move on to the next and last stop.

'There is so much to learn about a Ry. It takes years and years to even learn in general the methods of one road. There are not so many people that try to understand more than one Dept. Dearest Wife, I hope you are not feeling very bad tonight and not lonely. Belle really must look after you, and I think I'll write her to tell her to be sure and see to you and take good care of my precious little Grace. I have written to you every day, so you should have a corresponding number of letters.'

'Louisville is quite a large place, 170,000 people, I think,' he wrote from Kentucky. 'It seems by moonlight to be pretty. Lots of trees and broad asphalt streets.

'I am so very happy to think that you are getting on so well and doing your best, poor dearest. I shall be glad to get back to dear you. Tonight I hope to dream of you. I did last night. Your devoted husband, C.'

A letter from Grandfather Wilson to his recently widowed daughter May that fall of 1898 explains how my parents came to move to 608 Fifth Avenue: 'We have all been much concerned about Gracie's getting settled for the winter and whether or not it would be wise on her part, in view of their family relations to the V's, for her to accept your sweet offer of your house and live in it. It was certainly most kind and sisterly of you to offer it to her which Robert told us you had authorized him to do for six thousand dollars. I have been and am still anxious to have them accept your offer and live in the house and I hope they will decide to do so within a few days. They have been afraid of the effect on their future standing with his family but I can not believe it will prejudice them or at least I would try it were I in their place anyway.

'I hear Senator Brice wants to rent your house but I hope you won't rent it as I think you would be adversely criticized if you were to let it so soon after Ogden's death to anyone except your sister. In my business affairs I hope I am making some progress towards selling some of my interests that would reduce the demands considerably upon my time and means. Our country seems to be very prosperous and if we do not elect a silver congress at our approaching November election and in that way upset the confidence of the money people of the country, I think we shall have a great prosperity for the next year or two.

'Tell dear May that I can hardly yet realize what a young lady she really is until I read of her visits to Ireland and elsewhere all alone. All who see her are loud in their terms of admiration of her ladylike and sweet and quiet manners, in all of which I have great satisfaction.

'I must now close darling daughter with my deepest and tenderest love for both yourself and dear, dear May.'

When Father returned from his railway-inspection trip, he and Mother moved into Aunt May's great red brick house on Fifth Avenue. At about Christmas time, Mother found that she was pregnant again, and so that summer they rented Westcliff, a cottage at Newport, to escape the city heat. Father also acquired two thirty-foot bowsprit racing yachts, the *Ilderim* and the *Veda*, in which he carried off several cups in the New York Yacht Club races.

'Dearest dearest dearest,' he wrote Mother the summer she was expecting her second child, 'by the time you are reading this, I probably am way up the Bay, the scene of my two victories and am reminded of what they teach us. That in nearly everything we may be down for a while—like last year's racing—but it does not last forever and is much pleasanter when victory comes.

'But my note is a lecture so far. A lecture to the 'Don't Worry' Circle of Snookhaven. Sweetie, Grace, don't look too pretty while I am away, and please write each day. Tho' it's not a long separation this time, thank goodness.

'If you want anything in town wire me and if you want to send word to me at my office, address Care Supt. Motive Power, N.Y.C. Ry. Grand Central Station. I do hope you will keep well and get stronger when I'm away.

'Yr. most devoted and loving husband, Cornelius.'

It was presumably also during this trip that Neily wrote the following note, which is written in pencil and undated: 'Dearest Grace, Just a short line to tell you not to cry; that I will soon, so soon return . . .

'Yr. Husband, the devoted old fellow, C.'

For some time Father had been interested in designing a new kind of locomotive firebox which would be attached to the boiler without stay bolts, a common cause of locomotive engine trouble. Such a firebox had been attempted in Germany, with unhappy results, but Father was convinced that a satisfactory one could be made. Finally, in August, 1899, Father donned a pair of overalls, climbed into the cab of his experimental locomotive, and drove it from West Albany to Syracuse. The trial run was an unqualified success. His new firebox, put into daily use on the Central's Mohawk Division, effected a saving to the railroad of several hundred thousand dollars a year. Almost immediately, the Baltimore and Ohio and the Missouri Pacific put in orders for the new cylindrical firebox, based upon Father's design. In railroad circles, he was hailed as a new 'genius' in locomotive engineering.

Not one single congratulatory word came from the cold marble recesses of the Breakers. Mother, meanwhile, was living but a few blocks away from her in-laws in a rented villa near Bailey's Beach. She was expecting her second child in September.

A letter from Grandfather Wilson that summer to his widowed daughter May illuminates the senior Vanderbilts' attitude: 'I am spending about half my time in Newport and the other half here [New York]. I came down yesterday leaving all well as usual. Newport is rather tame for me this year; not much doing except in the way of luncheons, dinners, etc. I think we have a greater mixture of everybody there this year than ever before. The place is very full and perhaps this time next month there will be the usual hurrah going on all around.

'We are thinking now where you will spend the summer and hope you may get comfortably and satisfactorily located. Don't you think you had better try and come over this fall if only for a few months? . . .

'You could stop with us at 511 or with Gracie if you preferred, although she will hardly be in condition to do much of anything in September, October and November. *There is no change whatever in the treatment of her by his family, they being as demon-like in their behaviour towards her as ever* [italics mine]. Her boy however is so charming and entertaining as to make up in a certain degree somewhat for the effects upon her of their outrageous conduct and then all the people sympathize with her although she does not go out to anything except luncheons.'

That summer, Grandfather Vanderbilt's health seemed definitely to be improving. He had remained in Newport, even going to a few parties and doing some entertaining. By September, he seemed so much improved that he began to be active again in his many business affairs.

On a Monday, September 11, 1899, he left Newport in the company of his wife and his daughter Gladys to return to New York to attend some meetings. He liked to sit in on sessions making decisions about his pet charities, such as the New York Home for Incurables, the Hospital for the Relief of the Ruptured and Crippled, the College of Physicians and Surgeons, and the Sloane Maternity Hospital. He also participated in the affairs of the General Theological Seminary and the Board of Domestic and Foreign Missions. And, of course, he was always available to the rector of St. Bartholomew's Episcopal Church, where he had first met his wife, Alice, and where he served as vestryman.

Grandfather arrived at his Fifth Avenue mansion at nine in the evening and went directly to bed. Grandmother Vanderbilt retired shortly afterwards in an adjoining room. At six the next morning she was awakened by his choking cries. 'Alice, Alice!' he called.

'I'm dying,' he murmured as she hurried into his room. Then, as she slipped her arm about his neck, he lost consciousness. Ten minutes later he was dead of a massive cerebral hemorrhage.

'Cornelius Vanderbilt [is] mourned by rich and poor alike,' remarked the *World*, which also noted that when news of the great railway king's death was received at Newport, flags were pulled to half-mast at the Reading Room, the Casino, and at Bailey's Beach.

'It might be Julius Cæsar who lies there,' remarked the coroner sadly upon leaving Grandfather's gold and red bedchamber in New York.

My father, his brother Reggie, and his two sisters at once left Newport by train. 'Young Cornelius looked haggard and plainly was very deeply affected,' a reporter observed when Father, for the first time since his marriage, stepped past the threshold of his parents' home.

'Darling Cornelius'—Mother wrote to Father from Newport: 'I know how awfully you are feeling but you are so brave for my sake, and I must be brave for you. It is too fearful and seems so sudden—but, Darling, we have the great, great consolation of knowing that we have done everything we believed to be right, and I feel that *he* will now see all that in the right way. I long to be with you and by your side now but I can't. Everything will be so hard for you.

'Would it not be better for you to go to 511 [the Wilson home]?

I think you had better stay there, as they are working at 608 and we forgot about this this morning. I am sending this by Papa. He and Mother were so kind and sweet and so grieved for you, darling.

'Mary Kieran is attending to me so nicely and she will see about my black clothes which of course I shall wear. My darling, I will be by you every minute in my thoughts. Any sympathy you can express from me, please do so.

'My brave and best love, your wife, Grace.'

The more sensational newspapers at once began speculating about whether or not my father had been disinherited. The whole history of his wedding was reviewed, including the story that he had struck his father, causing the first paralytic stroke.

Chapter Six

GRANDFATHER VANDERBILT'S closest friend and confidant was Chauncey Depew, lawyer, politician, and for many years president of the Vanderbilt railway, the New York Central. It was Grandfather's habit to walk back and forth from work with Depew, and in this manner they exchanged many confidences, which were not always of a legal nature.

At the time of Grandfather Vanderbilt's death, Mother was not on writing or speaking terms with her in-laws, but having a complaint to make, addressed it to Mr. Depew, knowing that he was a constant visitor at the big Vanderbilt palace on 51st Street.

'I enclose these clippings,' my mother wrote to Chauncey Depew, 'hoping that you, if possible, and my husband's people may try to correct these false statements about Cornelius. It seems too horrible that this story [Neily striking his father] should be circulated over the world at his hour of grief and forever afterward. The clippings are from the N. Y. Daily News and the Journal and World of September 12. Of small importance when under these *headings*, but unfortunately these articles are copied elsewhere. I am profoundly miserable over the great sorrow that has come to my husband.

'Believe me, sincerely, Grace Vanderbilt.'

Mother's second child was due in less than two weeks when, two days after Grandfather's death, she wrote to Father: 'Darling husband, The hours go so slowly without you and I am always thinking of your suffering so alone. Do try to be with your own people and put all the past aside—at least for these days of mourning. I am trying to be calm, as they tell me I *must*. Baby is a great comfort. He really seems to be trying to take care of his little Mother and to amuse her.

'Harriet has been so good—both she and Josephine are such splendid friends. I am going to use some of Josephine's black clothes until I can get mine. People seem *very* kind. I write you all these things to try to cheer you a little and take your thoughts from your own great affliction. If I could only be by you!'

'Do pray take care of yourself and don't get ill. I am getting along quite well. Mama does not leave me. Is there nothing I can do to show my grief and sympathy? Nothing about the day of the funeral?

'I suppose you will of course go to the grave yard—oh my beloved husband how much you are suffering. I pray you will feel some peace when you return to our little Cornelius and to my arms. Dear one, will you be here on Saturday?

'Good night. I am hoping you are not very, very uncomfortable at 608 [Mrs. Goelet's house].

'My darling write whenever you can. Your devoted wife, Grace.'

'The man was more than his money,' the Reverend David Greer, rector of fashionable St. Bartholomew's, eulogized Grandfather Vanderbilt. 'His wealth was regarded by him, not simply as something personal, but as a great and sacred trust which it was his duty to administer, not with a lavish carelessness, but with a wise and discriminating conscientiousness, for the benefit of his fellowmen.'

(Fortunately, Grandfather did not forget the rector in his will, leaving him a personal bequest of $50,000; his great friend Chauncey Depew got $200,000.)

But what had he left my father?

In Newport and New York speculation ran wild. Meanwhile Mother, who was approaching the end of her confinement, kept up a cheerful flow of letters from Newport to Father in New York. 'Darling—Here we are at Mamma's, Baby and I all comfortably settled and it does feel so very comfy, and quiet and bright,' she wrote on Monday evening, a week after Grandfather's death. 'I am glad to get here and just rest. Our house was *quite* topsy turvy before I left. Mrs. Thayer came and was *such* a dear about everything. Harry Lehr also came and was so funny I screamed with laughter—the first time in many days. His stories were mostly about Mrs. John Drexel and some *so wicked* but too 'drool' for words.

'I got this afternoon a very nice little letter from Mrs. Sloane. She sends you her love and very great sympathy and begs you to let her know the arrival of the little one.

'It's a most glorious night. A full clear moon, and not a breath of wind. Miss Jones arrived at 7.30. Poor little Baby is simply *covered* with spots, and I'm glad to get Miss Jones here. Romeo (her little brown dog) has been sent away! He is at Ochre Court!!

'I do so wonder what you are doing—and if it is hot, and uncomfortable, and if you are fairly well—??? Have you seen Journal and World of today— Do look at them. You are quoted in the World, and the Journal seems to know all about the three copies of the W [the will].

'I am writing because it's next best to talking to you!

'Your more than loving wife—your adoring Grace.'

'Dearest Cornelius,' Mother wrote on Tuesday, 'I had quite a good night but today is so disagreeable—warm and foggy and my poor feet are so hot and swollen. They look like elephants! This morning I went to Westcliff and, while there, who do you think came to see me, *Bella*. I found her *most charming* and sympathetic in manner!!! I was *exceedingly* nice to her, and asked her to come surely to see me in town. I have come to the conclusion that anyone you like is nice!

'I see the scum papers, such as World and Journal, persist in saying everything is very just, "so says Cornelius." But how they track your every movement—fancy finding out that you had not been at the office!

'How I wonder what you are doing. I have burnt the epistles you asked me to—I don't quite understand what you meant by saying "all this would cause a great deal of trouble." Of course it will but I don't exactly understand whether you have thought of new troubles or other ones. I'm sure it is hot in town today. Let me know how you are? I must drive now, darling, so adieu for today. Ever loving, Grace.'

On Wednesday morning Mother wrote again: 'Dearest Cornelius: I got your "special" letter only at 9.30, as I had left word that I did not wish to be wakened. And as I was awake, twisting and turning every second from 5 until 7 a.m., I was glad of a sound sleep from 7 till 9.30. I perfectly understand your not *writing things* and I think it is much better. I again cautioned Josephine yesterday when I went to see her. A cable just came from Yokohama to Cornelius Vanderbilt in cypher. I told them to forward it to 608, not knowing if it was for you or your mother.

'Today is pouring but anything is better than yesterday's fog and heat. Am going after this storm is over to take Baby and Miss Jones for a drive before he has his 12 o'clock sleep. He has at last got one of his 'stomach' teeth, so I suppose that accounts for the spots which are rather better today.

'Did Mary Kiernan arrive safely with all the servants and 'household effects'? I have simply not had one moment's bother about any of the moving—it's perfectly splendid for me, having her. I am sure the house looks and feels very nice and comfy but really I am rather enjoying my visit here to dear Mother.

'Papa writes he has not seen you, but I suppose you have good reasons. He is coming back here tomorrow and hopes to bring Robert. Adieu for this morning—I may write again before night— Kisses—!!! Your own Grace.'

'Darling Cornelius,' Grace wrote that evening, 'I am having some milk toast tonight in my own room—and this is my dinner. My legs have been so very swollen today that I am ordered to try what dieting will do. After luncheon today Mrs. Burdette came to see us, and was mystified by my bright manner, I am sure. She no doubt expected to find me in tears!

'Josephine drove with me and she said that no one should ever hear from her what I had told her. She says every one is discussing it and some have said to her that if you are cut off it will be *iniquitous* and she said, "Well, what would you consider cut off?" and they answered, "Why, five millions." She also had a long talk with old Edgerton Winthrop. And he also agreed that if it were true that you had been left very little it would be an outrage, but he would not for a moment believe any of those stories, as your father never could have done such a thing.

'I am glad you have seen some of your friends as it must be dreary beyond endurance in town for you now. My darling, I want to kiss you—so here is one—!

'A good night to you. Lovingly, Grace.

'Did you read Journal and World today?'

'Darling,' Mother began her letter on Thursday, 'I am beginning to feel that you *must come* and be with me. My patience is giving out. Shall you, do you think, be here tomorrow Friday? I am glad Mary Kiernan is looking after you. Before we know it she will be running everything, ourselves included!

'I can not guess who the person was that you saw last night but I have given up trying to guess at anything.

'Josephine Johnson has been here this morning. She says everyone says your mother is responsible for the state of affairs. And that she [Mrs. V.] is going abroad as soon as possible.

'Today is rainy and stormy. Baby has taken cold and does not seem very well.

'I had a nice letter this morning from Mrs. Pendleton. She is off to Lenox until Racing week when she hopes to see us. Why don't you tell Miss Kiernan and Felix they must find a good footman and have him there for you to inspect on Monday. I gave her all the addresses of the agencies. Dr. Flint is moving his family to town also on Sunday night.

'Must post this. Harriet is coming for a drive. Always lovingly, Grace.'

The other day, while visiting the Museum of the City of New York, I was shown, packed away in tissue paper in a trunk, two gowns given to that institution by the Vanderbilts. Strangely enough, they both belong to the same period.

The first, bought from Worth in Paris in 1898, belonged to my mother. It is a lovely thing of thick yellow satin, trimmed with chiffon the colour of Devonshire cream, with a train lined with silk and flounces of lace. Mother must have ordered the dress for the winter balls of early 1899; then found she was having another baby. The dress was carefully packed away and never worn— perhaps some slight change in style outmoded it. Eventually it was given to the museum.

Side by side with Mother's Worth evening gown is a turquoise-blue velvet ball gown with a four-foot-long train, heavily encrusted with pearls sewed into the shape of sea shells. This was a gown ordered by Grandmother Vanderbilt in her fifty-fifth year, before the sudden death of her husband put her in mourning for two years.

Two dresses never worn; a birth, a death, two women separated by a chasm deeper than either.

Two weeks after the death of Cornelius Vanderbilt, Sr., his widow returned to the Breakers with Reggie and Gladys to await the return of Alfred from the Orient. Until his return Grandfather's will would not be read.

On the same day that she boarded her private car, Father rushed back to Newport in response to a telegram from Mother.

A week later, my parents and I, accompanied by Mother's physician, Dr. Austin Flint, Jr., boarded the Fall River night boat for New York. The next morning we arrived at Aunt May's mansion at 608 Fifth Avenue: by midnight of that same day, my sister Grace was born.

'NEW VANDERBILT HEIRESS IS BORN AT MIDNIGHT,' the New York *World* heralded the arrival of my sister on September 25, 1899. 'This event may explain why Mrs. Cornelius Vanderbilt, Jr., was not present at her father-in-law's funeral,' the *World* goes on. 'She passed through the ordeal very well. Maybe now the young father's face will lose an air of suffering it has worn for so long, if the baby girl will bring members of the family together.'

Wrote Belle from the Avenue d'Iena in Paris: 'I was so glad to get your telegram about the dear little baby girl and so curious at the same time, for I do think it is so homey and nice to have a little girl— and I know you and Neily must be very happy over it. We all say its name will be Grace. I have just had Mama's letter, telling me how easily it came into the world. You see, I told you so. Oh, I do so long to see the little thing. As soon as you are able to write with a pencil, you will write, won't you, and tell me how you are and how you are standing all your troubles. Poor darling girl. I can't write much on your own subject until more news comes out . . .'

At last Alfred, who had been away on a round-the-world tour, returned home, and the Vanderbilt clan was summoned to Newport for the reading of Grandfather's will. The family gathered in the dark walnut and leather-panelled library of the Breakers.

Alfred was there, and pudgy Reggie. Gertrude Whitney and her twelve-year-old sister, Gladys, and, of course, Neily. Grandmother, then in her early fifties, without a grey hair in her unswept black tresses, sat very pale, swathed in black, in an immense red velvet refectory chair.

Father had now been married three years. During this time he and his wife had owned neither home nor furnishings but had moved, like nomads, from one rented place to another. They had undertaken no large-scale entertaining. They owned two modest-sized sailboats, and that was all. Withal, they appeared sublimely happy, and two Vanderbilt children had been born of their union. Grandfather had never announced publicly that he intended to disinherit his eldest son, and there was every reason to hope that Neily would be left considerably more than an equal share of his father's huge fortune. His diligence in pursuing his studies at Yale (where he had earned two graduate degrees), as well as his promising start as an inventor, could not have failed to impress his father. He had completed his recent inspection tours of the New York Central lines with considerable acumen and dispatch, still another indication to his father that he intended to assume with great seriousness the responsibilities inherent in the job of head of the House of Vanderbilt.

It seems appropriate to digress here for a moment to amplify a remark of my father's I heard many times—that every Vanderbilt son has rebelled like a tiger against his father.

The founder of our family, Cornelius Vanderbilt I, was called the Commodore, and he happens to be my great personal hero. A big, lusty man, with shrewd grey eyes slanting down at the corners from the bridge of an immensely long and prominent nose, the Commodore was a six-footer of incredible energy. His collection of cuss words, they say, has never been matched by any scow captain in New York harbour since the early nineteenth century. He enjoyed gambling and horses, so naturally spent a good deal of time at Saratoga, where he could be seen behind a pair of fast trotters. As he drove, he often sipped a small glass of gin and sugar. After siring twelve children by his first wife, he eloped at the age of seventy-five with a young belle from Mobile, who was surprisingly enough named Frank. This was only two years before his grandson, Willie K., married my Aunt Alva, who was also from Mobile.

The Commodore came from a long line of Dutch Van der Bilts who raised vegetables on Staten Island. He retained his Hollander frugality to the end of his days, refusing to carry a cigar-case because his friends might expect him to pass it around. 'When I take one cigar out of my pocket,' explained the Commodore, 'my friends don't know whether there are any left.'

When my great-great-grandfather was not yet seventeen, he

asked his mother to lend him $100 to buy a two-masted sailing barge to haul produce about New York Bay. She agreed to lend him the money on his birthday, a month away, if in that space of time he ploughed, harrowed, and planted eight acres of the family farm.

'Mother thought that she could get the best of me on that eight acre lot,' he related later, 'but I got some boys to help and we did the work, and it was well done, too, for Mother wouldn't allow any half way of doing it. I claimed my money, got it, hurried off, bought a boat, hoisted sail, and was the happiest boy in the world.'

By the time the summer was over, Cornelius owned not one but three ferries and gave his mother $1,000 in place of the $100 she had lent to him. During the War of 1812 he increased his earnings by supplying strategic supplies to military posts dotted about the harbour. To do this, he often worked continuously for twenty-four to thirty-six hours without sleeping, but he made enough to buy a fine schooner.

Within a few years the Commodore decided that steamboats, and not sailboats, offered the promise of large and quick returns. In 1849 he got a charter from the Nicaraguan government for a water route across the isthmus. In this way, he transported thousands of forty-niners from New York to California.

In the next eleven years, the Commodore made $10,000,000. It was not long before he sold out his vast fleet of steamboats and went into railroading, where he became America's first great railroad king. By this time he had sold his Staten Island home and moved into a Greek Revival mansion at 10 Washington Place, New York.

But although the address was correct, the aroma of the barnyard still clung to the feet of the Vanderbilts, in the opinion of New York society. Even when he ordered the construction of the *North Star*, a private steamship yacht 270 feet in length with *boiseries* of satin and rosewood in the drawing-room and a marble dining *salon*, the Stuyvesants and Schermerhorns managed to look unimpressed. 'We are sure that the English nobility and gentry will give the Commodore a reception commensurate with his rank as a merchant prince—one who goes abroad in a style not inferior to their own youthful sovereign,' glowed the New York *Illustrated News*. 'We predict a sensation at the arrival of this vessel in Europe, second to that of no arrival they have ever had from any quarter of the globe.'

Although the British greeted the Commodore coolly, the Russians did not. When the splendid *North Star* steamed into Kronshtadt, the Grand Duke Constantine sent one of the Czar's carriages to conduct the party to the Palace of Peterhof.

Meanwhile, at home, trouble was brewing for the Commodore. Until the time his yacht left New York harbour, he had been collecting twenty per cent on the gross receipts of his Nicaraguan canal route. On the day he departed, the payments ended. When he returned, months later, the Commodore's profanity turned the air about him purple. Then he dispatched a letter to the miscreants which reflects sublimely his particular business genius: 'Gentlemen: You have undertaken to cheat me. I won't sue you, for the law is too slow. I'll ruin you. C. Vanderbilt.'

And this he proceeded to do.

It has been said that the grand passions of the Commodore were railroads, boats, and horses, to which his son, William H., added art, great houses, and grand opera, and you might say that these still remain the special areas of Vanderbilt interest today. One has only to think of my cousin Harold, who for so many years defended the America Cup, and young Alfred Gwynne, the owner of Native Dancer and a president of the American Jockey Club, and my Aunt Gertrude Whitney, who gained international fame as a sculptress.

But, as these interests seem to pass through the generations, like the Vanderbilt hawklike nose and the downward-slanted eyes, so patterns of relationships between father and son seem to repeat themselves.

The Commodore's second son, Cornelius, caused his father such grief that he once confided to a friend, 'I'd give a hundred dollars not to have named him Corneel.' Young Corneel was an epileptic. As a boy of eighteen, he wanted to join the gold rush; his father commanded him to stay home. Corneel ran off anyway. When he returned, some months later, the Commodore had him locked up in the Bloomingdale Lunatic Asylum. Harry Clews, the famous Wall Street broker, said that although young Corneel was soon found sane and released from the asylum, he 'took the matter dreadfully to heart, and it had a melancholy and demoralizing effect upon all his future life'.

Young Corneel, who was addicted to gambling, frequently overspent his allowance. When his father refused to meet his faro debts, the young scion went to Horace Greeley, then the editor of the *New York Tribune*, and borrowed from him.

'Greeley, I hear you're lending Corneel money,' the Commodore finally confronted the editor in his dingy office.

'I have let him have some.'

'I give you fair warning,' roared the Commodore, 'that you need not look to me; I won't pay you.'

'Who the devil asked you?' the editor rejoined.

When Corneel wanted to marry, the Commodore called upon the young lady's parents to ask if she had many fine gowns or much jewellery. When the girl's father explained that he could not afford such things for his daughter, the Commodore replied: 'The reason I ask you is that if she did possess these articles of value, my son would either take them and pawn them or sell them, and throw away the proceeds at the gaming table. So I forewarn you and your daughter that I can't take any responsibility in this matter.'

Perhaps the old boy wasn't as hardhearted as he sounds. Once he pointed to a solid-gold model of his crack steamer, the *Cornelius Vanderbilt*, and remarked, 'I'd give that ship and her boilers, too [he pronounced it 'bilers'] to cure Corneel of his ailment.' Another time, he recounted all the misdeeds of his son to the girl Corneel had married. When he had finished, she remarked gently, 'Isn't it somewhat your fault?'

Although he made no reply, tears came to his eyes.

'The last time I saw young Corneel,' Henry Clews recalled, 'was at Long Branch where he took a drive with me one fine afternoon. He spoke feelingly about his wasted life, and concerning the many good friends who had come so often to his rescue, and had got him out of numerous holes into which, through misfortune, he had been thrown.

'Corneel, although always exclaiming against the old man's hardheartedness, had an intense admiration for his father's abilities and he was as sensitive as a sunflower when any other person would say a word to disparage the Commodore. While railing constantly at the parsimony of his father, he was as devoted a hero-worshipper of the Commodore as Thomas Carlyle ever was of the greatest of his heroes, and he never grew tired of talking of his achievements, with the history of which he was entirely familiar.'

'Let us,' observed Henry Clews, 'throw the mantle of charity over that tragic scene in the Glenham Hotel [where young Corneel committed suicide] and hope that his soul may have found rest which, in its poor afflicted body, it vainly sought here.'

It may be said that the entire Vanderbilt family threw a mantle over the unfortunate Corneel, for he is never mentioned or even counted. My grandfather called himself Cornelius Vanderbilt II just as if the Commodore's son had never existed.

The Commodore was equally critical of his eldest son, William H., from whom all the present Vanderbilts are descended. 'The old man is bound to have his way, and it is useless to oppose him,' William H. once commented, rather bitterly, while setting himself out to become a dutiful slave to his parent.

'Billy,' the Commodore remarked once to him from the deck of the *North Star*, 'I wish you would give up that smoking of yours; I'll give you ten thousand dollars if you'll do it.'

'You need not give me any money, Father,' the younger Vanderbilt replied, 'your wish is sufficient.' And he threw his lighted cigar into the Atlantic.

The Commodore then reached into his pocket and drew out a costly Havana, which he regretfully lit in the presence of his son.

William H. was trained as a book-keeper. In appearance he seemed utterly unadventurous, plodding, and meticulous, as he sat day after day in the bank on his high stool. When his salary reached nineteen dollars a week, he promptly took a wife, Maria Louisa Kissam, the daughter of a Brooklyn clergyman. The Commodore was not at all pleased, and refused to give the young couple a cent. When young William's health threatened to give way under the pressure of work, the Commodore's doctors persuaded him to set up his ailing son on a seventy-acre farm in Staten Island. So the book-keeper turned farmer.

When, several years later, William borrowed money to buy additional acreage, the old Commodore exploded.

'Billy, you don't amount to a row of pins,' he told him. 'You won't be able to do anything but bring disgrace upon yourself, your family and everybody connected with you. I've made up my mind to have nothing to do with you.'

For once the dutiful son defended himself. 'The farm required considerable investment,' he said, 'and I had no money. My object in life has always been to please you and I am profoundly grieved to see that I am unable to do so.'

Some time later, young William asked his father if he could buy the horse dung from the Commodore's Washington Square stables for fertilizer. 'I'll pay you four dollars a load,' he offered. His father, who knew that fertilizer was worth only two dollars a wagon load, agreed.

On the next afternoon the Commodore noticed at the dock a scow piled with horse manure. 'How many loads have you there, Bill?' he called.

'One load,' his son answered, snickering. 'One *scow*load.'

The Commodore was forced to admit his son was beginning to show the right instincts. But William was forty before his father opened up a career for him in railroading, making him vice-president of the New York and Harlem Railroad. 'This late recognition from his father gave William a dour and cynical outlook on life,' comments one of his biographers.

When the old Commodore died, in 1877, his fortune had reached the then unheard-of proportions of $105,000,000. For his widow and eight surviving daughters, the multimillionaire made modest bequests. But to his plodding, unspectacular son William he bequeathed approximately $90,000,000.

Shortly afterwards, William H. began the erection of his great mansion at 640 Fifth Avenue. Grace Wilson must have watched its construction as she strolled along the avenue, a white-gloved, long-legged girl of ten, with her French governess. Later this house was to become the scene of her greatest social triumphs.

When William H. died, the whole world was confounded by his riches. In spite of his timidity, he had doubled his patrimony! He left a fortune of over $200,000,000.

In 1885, the year of his death, few Americans were worth more than a million or two. Such a staggering fortune made the Lorillards, the Harrimans, even the Goulds and the Astors appear to be very small potatoes indeed.

'The ordinary mind,' wrote stockbroker Henry Clews, who was accustomed to see millions change hands on the ticker tape, 'fails to grasp the idea of such a vast amount of wealth. If converted into gold, it would have weighed five hundred tons, and it would have taken five hundred strong horses to draw it from the Grand Central Depot to the Sub Treasury in Wall Street.'

So intense was the interest fanned by my great-grandfather's demise, that his family feared body-snatchers might break into his tomb and hold his remains for ransom, as they had with A. T. Stewart, the great merchant, a few years before. Finally, after William H. had been laid to rest in the Vanderbilt eleven-acre mausoleum at New Dorp on Staten Island, they hired a watchman to guard it every night, punching a time clock at fifteen-minute intervals.

Although it was the custom in those days to leave the major share of one's estate to the eldest son, William H. divided the bulk of his vast fortune more or less equally between Cornelius II and Willie K. Some say that it was Alva, his Southern daughter-in-law, who inspired the old man's generosity towards his second son. At any rate, my grandfather, the older son, received $67,000,000, and Willie K. almost as much—$65,000,000.

When the sombre little group waited in the library of the Breakers to hear the reading of my grandfather's will in 1899, some of them must have speculated upon how many millions he had added to his inheritance. No one had ever displayed more pride in his family than had this upright Christian; surely he would provide for them all handsomely. Had he not built the Breakers as an immortal monument to the House of Vanderbilt, envisioning generation after generation of his descendants living within its granite walls?

So fearful had he been that fire might destroy this magnificent edifice that there was not one stick of timber in the place. Its heating plant was buried entirely underground, at a distance of several hundred yards from the house, in a boiler room the size of a ballroom, with twelve-foot ceilings. Heat was conducted to the Breakers by pipes running through a tunnel wide enough to accommodate a team of horses.

And so it was that the scion of the Cornelius Vanderbilt family, my father, waited with high hopes in the dusky gold and walnut splendour of his father's library to learn what inheritance would be his to carry on the great tradition of the family.

As the black-coated executors, with solemn faces, opened their gleaming leather portfolios and took out thick sheaves of legal papers, the fire in the hearth glowed under the white marble mantle which had graced a nobleman's chateau in sixteenth-century France.

'Little do I care for riches, and do not miss them,' its ancient script declared, 'since only wisdom prevails in the end.'

Chapter Seven

T HE tense moments ticked by as the Vanderbilt lawyers
gathered in one corner of the dark Breakers' library, con-
versing in low tones and glancing speculatively from time to
time from Neily to his brother Alfred.

That is the scene as I have always pictured it, with Father
nervously pacing up and down, his black tight-fitting London-
tailored suit accentuating the extreme thinness of his frame. He had
spent the morning racing up the Rhode Island coast in his swift
sloop, the *Ilderim*. But, although his face held the bronze burn of
sun and sea, his dark-blue eyes were shadowed and almost black
with suffering.

His vital father had died so young, at only fifty-six. Had he, his
son, been the cause of this premature demise? How terrible to recall
those scenes of anger between two who had once loved each other
so devotedly!

His mother sat remote and withdrawn, a tiny, immensely dignified figure in black, her plain features a frozen mask. Raven-haired
Gladys, just twelve, gazed at her brother with big pensive eyes as
she sat cross-legged on the floor.

Near her sat Gertrude, an elegantly angular woman in a black
Parisian gown, her long bony face very pale. With her usual sober
and composed expression, she waited for the lawyers to begin reading her father's will, one white unjewelled hand resting motionless on
the arm of a crimson velvet chair.

Young Reggie, then in his late teens, watched Neily curiously as
he paced restlessly up and down. This youngest Vanderbilt son was
quite tall, with a pouty, obstinate mouth and sleepy, heavy-lidded,
slanted 'Vanderbilt' eyes. Considered by his mother to be a 'nice'
boy, dutiful and well-mannered, Reggie spent much of his time with
her and his sisters.

He had not yet discovered the elegant gambling parlours of
Richard Canfield at Saratoga and in the East Forties, but already,

among the younger set, Reggie was acquiring the reputation of a young man who refused to be bored. Physical danger and fast violent sports appealed to him strongly; so did pretty girls. Like his brother Alfred, to whom he was very close, he was passionately interested in polo and horse-racing.

Alfred, just twenty-one, was the handsomest of the three brothers—lean, tall, and elegant, with a vivacious charm. He seemed to have no Vanderbilt conceit whatsoever and was often seen at his classes at Yale in an old and frayed blue sweater and a disreputable-looking soft felt hat. But he could also look the part of the dandy. Today, for the reading of his father's will, he wore immaculate white linen, a square-cut diamond stickpin in his four-in-hand, and Bond Street black.

When Alfred first entered Yale in 1895, he roomed in quarters with Neily over the arch in Vanderbilt Hall, and the two brothers, both tall and dark, quiet and unassuming, seemed much alike. But after Neily's graduation Alfred began to take more and more interest in proms and *débutante* parties, in polo and horse-racing. At his graduation he was voted 'the social light' of the Class of 1899. An easy-going kind of person, with the relaxed grace of an athlete, and no great student, he had so far shown little interest in becoming a power on Wall Street.

Despite the solemnity of this occasion, Alfred's blue eyes held their usual expression of bland good humour, I fancy, as he waited with a confident and assured air for the lawyers to get on with their business.

'I give and devise to my beloved wife Alice G. Vanderbilt, for and during the term of her natural life, my dwelling house on Fifth Avenue and Fifty-Seventh Street . . .' Now, at last, in sonorous tones, the senior member of the corps of Vanderbilt lawyers had begun reading the will.

They tell me Grandmother listened quietly as her husband's last testament listed all the properties, stables, household furniture, silver, and works of art which were to be hers.

'I except from this bequest the portrait and bust of my grandfather (the Commodore) and the portrait of my father, and the two portraits bequeathed to me in the will of my grandfather, all of which I give to my son'—the voice paused an imperceptible second, then continued—'Alfred,'

The Breakers and all its furnishings were also left to my grandmother, to be handed down after her to Alfred, Reginald, Gertrude,
and Gladys, or to their children. The vast Vanderbilt Oakland Farm,
in South Portsmouth, Rhode Island, was bequeathed to Alfred.

Alice . . . Alfred . . . Reginald . . . Gertrude . . . Gladys . . . over
and over their names were repeated. But there was no mention of
the eldest son, Cornelius. Finally, in the ninth clause of his will,
Grandfather directed that half a million dollars of a $5,000,000 trust
fund left him by William H. Vanderbilt be given to Neily.

Then Grandfather bequeathed $1,000,000 of his $72,500,000
fortune to his eldest son and namesake, stipulating that the gift was
in trust and the principal was not to be touched during my father's
lifetime.

The will went on for pages, naming charities and small be-
quests, but Father's name was not mentioned again.

Finally, as residuary legatee (and thereby also head of the
House), Alfred was named to inherit the bulk of the fortune.

Grandfather's widow and other children (except Neily) each got
approximately $7,000,000; until the estate was settled, there was no
telling how many more millions Alfred would get from the residue.

Father sat with his head bowed in his hands; from a great distance he heard the lawyer conclude, 'I have to this my last Will and
Testament set my hand and seal in the city of New York this 18th
day of June in 1896.'

With the mention of that date something must have clicked dully
in Father's mind, leaving him staring incredulously at the reader.
June eighteenth—that was four years ago—the very day he and
Grace had first planned to marry!

June 18, 1896 was a Thursday. On Tuesday of that memorable
week, Neily's father and mother had rushed down from Newport;
there had been long consultations with their lawyers; strained faces,
hushed voices. The next day Neily had agreed not to go through
with the wedding. That evening his parents were seen dining at the
Metropolitan Club in the best of spirits. Yet the very next morning,
Neily's father had signed this devastatingly vindictive will!

Nor had my grandfather, during the four years which intervened
between his signing of the will and his death, seen fit to restore a
single penny to his oldest son. The only significant codicil was
added in April, 1899, just a few months before Grandfather died,

when he bequeathed an additional $1,000,000 to Gertrude, whose husband, Harry Payne Whitney, eventually became worth, through his Standard Oil holdings, some $187,000,000.

Did Father know as far back as June, 1896, that he had been disinherited? And did he go ahead and marry my mother in spite of this? 'What a fool your father was,' William Randolph Hearst once remarked to me, 'to forfeit a fortune for a pretty face.'

Or had Father—as he always insisted—made some private agreement with the family, prior to his father's death, which gave him a rightful share of his inheritance? Newspapers immediately launched into this controversy.

When the terms of Grandfather's will became known to the public, Chauncey Depew announced that Alfred Vanderbilt was giving $6,000,000 of his inheritance to Father.

'When Alfred Vanderbilt returned he decided, from brotherly affection and for family harmony, to take out of his own inheritance and give to his brother Cornelius a sum sufficient to make the fortune of Cornelius the same as that of his brother and sisters. This has been accepted by Cornelius in same spirit,' announced Depew.

The next day, however, the New York *World's* first page announced: ' "There was an agreement that I should get at least $10,000,000"—Cornelius Vanderbilt, Jr.'

The article says: 'Cornelius Vanderbilt, at his home 608 Fifth Avenue, made this important statement to a *World* representative: "The agreement by which I received $6,000,000 from my brother's portion of the estate has been made to appear as a gift. It is no gift, but the result of a compact entered into before my father's demise. By this compact, I was to receive no less than $10,000,000." '

With this sensational news, Father became, according to the *World*, 'the most talked-about young man in the country'. And although Alfred spent a comparatively quiet day, a steady stream of people were reported to have called all day at 608 Fifth Avenue, where my parents were staying, 'manifestly inspired by a desire to express their sympathy'.

The following day Father granted another interview to a *World* reporter. 'Mr. Vanderbilt,' asked the newspaperman, 'were you quoted correctly in the *World* as saying that you were to receive not less than $10,000,000 under an agreement made before your father's death?'

'It is correct,' replied Mr. Vanderbilt. 'That agreement was made prior to my father's death—yes, prior to my father's death.'

'With whom did you make this agreement?'

'It was made between my brother Alfred and myself. The matter since then has been in the hands of my attorneys; they have full charge of my affairs.'

Father was then asked point-blank if there was a possibility of his contesting his father's will.

'He was then standing in the parlour, with his hands thrust in his trouser pockets and with one foot planted firmly on the seat of a red plush chair,' wrote the *World* reporter. 'He removed his foot from the chair, took his hands from his pockets, looked first at the ceiling and then at the floor, scratched his head, and, finally, with a deliberate determination that gave to the word almost the effect of a drawl, he replied, "PER-HAPS!" '

After that Father begged to be excused, and walked towards the stairway, referring the reporter to his lawyers.

'Mr. Vanderbilt seemed to be greatly disturbed,' the reporter noted. 'He looked as if there was something on his mind which he would like to divulge. When he spoke, his words were uttered with the utmost deliberation, but his whole demeanour indicated that he was labouring under an intense strain of suppressed emotion. He acted like one who wished very much to speak his mind freely, and who refrained from doing so only with great difficulty.

'His cheeks are hollow and his sunken eyes show clearly the traces of worry. Unlike the stout, healthy young man shown in his printed pictures, he is very thin and careworn.'

No public accounting was ever filed of the final settlement of Grandfather's will. But Father did not contest it. All the Vanderbilts signed waivers, and I found among the family papers a small slip of paper in Father's handwriting which says: 'October 25, 1899. A family settlement of property: (*a*) *to* me (CV) $500,000 immediately upon probate; (*b*) $6,000,000 less (*a*) when completed.'

This meant that with the $1,500,000 granted him in the will plus the $6,000,000 given him by Alfred, my father's total share was increased to $7,500,000. But twenty-one-year-old Alfred, as residuary legatee and head of the House, was left with $36,575,000.

Aunt Belle wrote to Grace at once from Paris: 'Darling Little

Sister: We have all on this side of the water been living with you in thoughts during these hard times that you have been through . . . I feel all trembling and quivering with the wickedness and injustice of it all and if I even begin to say anything only a volley of hatred will come out.

'Carrie and Orme will be our mouth-pieces and tell you what we have felt—and I suppose you will write to me yourself, or Neily will, what he proposes to do, and what he proposes to make of his future life. For surely this must be a definite crisis . . . Mamma wrote me nothing in connection with the Will, but Carrie will tell you what I feel. I really feel just as she does and I should listen to her and be guided a good deal by what she says.

'I expect, however, Neily will have taken his own line—and the right one—long before this reaches you. *It is the greatest wickedness* of the 19th century—when a son has been as good and upright and *pure* and *honourable* as Neily to brand him in the eyes of the world as an evil-doer, is the most iniquitous thing I have ever heard. I don't dare write at this distance, but I don't think there can any longer be a link between him and the others. Who *could* have so turned the heart of an ill man, stricken in mind—However I mustn't write until you tell me something. I shouldn't let a certain person now *pose* as trying to be kind to N. Having always been a stone before. I heard she sent a sympathetic telegram. Of course she will try to, in the eyes of the world, exonerate herself now.

'Carrie and Orme will soon be at home now and they will be a comfort to you except that Orme gets too violent. Carrie and I have been a great deal together and I must tell you that an entirely new feeling has sprung up between us. I have got to know *her* as herself, and I have got to really love her. I can't tell you what a soft sympathy I feel about her. She has let me see her real little sweet nature and I feel as if I had discovered something. I know this will make you smile, for you have always been so fond of her, but it has been a long time since I have felt so fascinated by a sort of delicate *amie* as I was by her when she was so sweet to me. I was awfully sorry when they went away, for we had been a great deal together. You must not smile at my writing you so enthusiastically. She's such a sweet little thing and so good and tries to make the boys good men and honorable. They are dear boys, too.

'Sister and Baby May are here—Sister not so very well, I don't think, after her Carlsbad cure. They have very good times with their little beaux and flirt abominably. Douglas Dawson is making up to Sister evidently, with the "bon motif" in view, and she is seeing a great deal of him, and encourages him I think too much for foreign ideas as the men get so *nasty* when they are refused over here, and she has no idea of marrying him!

'Prince H. d'Orleans is still making the court to Sister May but she will not hear of it and indeed in view of her future happiness it would be far from a good marriage. He has taken such an odd line in politics that he has turned every party and nation against him and you hear nothing but abuse of him on all sides. They have gone to dine and go to the play with him tonight.

'I'm afraid there is no chance of our being able to stop on here during the winter, as already Mungo is beginning to feel the first damp days of the autumn and his throat is relaxed and irritated. He is really so delicate nowadays. I must post this now, darling. Do please give the dear little sweet girl a soft kiss from me. How I should like to see her and dearest love to Neily and yourself from us. Belle.'

During all the furore caused by Grandfather's will, Father received many letters from strangers who, apologizing for their forwardness in addressing him, explained that their desire to express their sympathy and their admiration was so strong that they could not refrain from writing. Mother saved all these letters, which are filled with obviously sincere praise and good wishes.

'As a fellow citizen . . . I am proud of you . . .' one man wrote. 'The manner that you carried through your courtship and marriage of queenly Miss Wilson . . . showed true yankey pluck.' A woman who had married against 'Mamma's will', and never regretted it, told my father she considered him 'a *very honorable* gentleman for marrying a lady of [his] own choice'. Like many others, she wished Neily and Grace a long and happy life and invited them to her home. Another woman, writing that she had not been allowed to marry the man she loved and that not even the Vanderbilt fortune could induce her to accept another, assured Father that his name would be 'handed down for . . . generations as the noble, manly Vanderbilt who sacrificed millions for love'. Others wrote of the 'warm esteem' in which many held him, the injustice of his father's will, and the happiness that comes from love, not riches. Some expressed their hope that he would be restored to his rightful position as head of the Vanderbilt family.

There is no doubt that the whole fracas embittered my gentle father. Whether Uncle Alfred had made some previous agreement and then failed to keep his word, I do not know—but from the moment that the terms of the will became known, relations between the two brothers grew progressively colder.

Several months later, Alfred entered the treasurer's office of the New York Central as a clerk, in keeping with the Vanderbilt tradition of starting well at the bottom of the ladder. There is no indication that he spent much time at the office, however. Soon after he came into his vast inheritance, he became the first Newporter to own a private polo field and his blue-blooded horses were stabled under name plates of solid gold. He acquired, eventually, no less than four yachts and did not hesitate to pay $30,000 for one of the first automobiles, a ninety-horsepower Fiat. In England he became known as a famous whip by racing his team of celebrated greys from Twickenham to Barnes, easily outdistancing the English chestnuts.

At one time he undertook to gallop his tallyho by relay from New York to Philadelphia, and back again, a distance of over two hundred miles. Leaving the Holland House in New York City at six in the morning, he arrived in Philadelphia almost ten hours later. After a six-minute rest at the Bellevue Hotel, he climbed aboard the carriage with his valet for the return trip, which he completed in ten hours and ten minutes. A retinue of seventy-eight horses, staggered at relay posts between the two cities, was required for this twenty-hour jaunt.

On the same day that Alfred was ushered to his desk in the treasurer's office, Father quit his job with the New York Central, and never went back.

Grandmother Vanderbilt and Mother continued to ignore each other's existence. The fact that letters addressed simply to 'Mrs. Vanderbilt' were more often delivered to Mother than to the lonely dowager did nothing to soften the rancour between them. Alfred never came to our house, nor Reggie, nor Gladys, nor Gertrude. Mrs. Henry Clews, wife of the celebrated broker, sided with Grandmother in the family feud and was so dropped for ever from Mother's list. The Carnegies and the E. H. Harrimans, on the other hand, favoured the Wilsons, and for this Mother gave them a life-time of friendship. So the family breach was widened and deepened.

'We're the poor relations,' Mother used to say, with a small tinkling laugh. And compared with the other Vanderbilts, we were. Father's Uncle Fred, whose mansion is now a public museum at Hyde Park, N.Y., used to keep $3,000,000 rattling around in a *checking* account. His Uncle George owned 130,000 acres near Asheville, North Carolina, and a house with the largest roof in America. When Uncle Willie K. built Idle Hour, his Long Island villa, he included forty-five bathrooms. And then there was Mrs. Hamilton Twombly, daughter of William H. Vanderbilt, who lived to be in her nineties and was one of the frostiest *grandes dames* in society. She maintained a fleet of maroon-coloured Rolls Royces and until the time of her death, in 1953, kept a white-wigged foot-man whose major function was to open the front door of her hundred-room house in Convent, New Jersey.

A friend of mine was once invited to the Twombly establishment over Labour Day week-end. Early on Monday morning, as he tells the story, he was astonished to find that a valet had packed his bags and stacked them in a great front hall, along with all the other guests' luggage.

'Surely Mrs. Twombly doesn't expect us to leave today,' he ventured to remark to the butler. 'This is Labour Day, a legal holiday, and all our offices are closed.'

The butler bowed and retired to convey the message to his mistress. In a few moments he was back to announce regretfully, 'Begging your pardon, Sir, Mrs. Twombly says to tell you she has never heard of Labour Day.'

Immense wealth was so taken for granted by the Vanderbilts, and by many of their friends, that to Father it must have seemed the only normal state of affairs. No one thought it remarkable—before the days of income taxes—when the Pembroke Joneses 'set aside' $300,000 for entertainment at the start of every Newport season. And when in 1900 Grandfather Wilson's close friend Andrew Carnegie drew a personal salary from his steelworks of $23,000,000, no one in America's most social summer colony paused to consider what Frederick Lewis Allen later pointed out—that during that same year a steelworker in the Carnegie plants earned $450.

Although my father was not in Andrew Carnegie's category, his

$7,500,000, combined with Mother's personal income—all of it tax-free—meant that his penny-pinching days were over. There was money for a beautiful home, yachts, staffs of servants, luxurious travel, and all the other material comforts so necessary to my parents' sense of well-being.

In a letter to his daughter May, written early in the winter of 1900, Grandfather Wilson made no mention of the will or of the Vanderbilts, but showed considerable interest in the romances of his rich, widowed daughter. This letter reveals, I believe, the real match-maker in the Wilson family:

'Darling daughter May,' Richard T. Wilson wrote from 511 Fifth Avenue, 'Mother and myself have been to several dinners recently. One at the Gerrys a few days ago of forty guests and we had a dinner at Mrs. Astor's & dance there a few days before the dinner and we have some five or six other dinner engagements on hand & have invitations out for four dinners at home and we go to the opera on Mondays which makes up our lives.

'Orme and Carrie and their family are fairly well and also Neily and Gracie, but our little Neil is not well for the past day or two as he has a slight attack of tonsilitis.

'Robert came down a day or two ago and is looking very well and says he is getting on very well with his studies. He and Gracie have gone to the theatre tonight. We are all upset here in financial matters more or less by this dreadful English and Boer war. It really seems strange that it should affect our country as much as it does but it does interfere very greatly with our financial transactions in the marketing of securities and all such things as are called international financial transactions.

'I do not believe that we have written you since I received your letter advising of your decision that D.D. and I must tell you what Orme and Dick said one day downtown at the office. They asked me if you had made up your mind about D.D. I told them I thought you had and they both said they hoped you had decided not to accept: that you had too much to give for any one unless he had position and title and all other desirable things to give in return & when I told them of your decision, they both said you had acted wisely.

'Your dear little May I fear is an incalculable loser by the war, as you say there are no beaux left at home, and coming as it does at the very age when she should have the pleasures and enjoyments of her sweet young life it must make it very hard on her and I am so sorry as I do so much enjoy the accounts you write of your and her lives when they are as happy as they ought to be.

'We haven't heard much from Mungo and Belle very recently but suppose they are settled back in Paris and we do hope they keep well. I haven't told you a word yet about dear Dick's life. Well, he has become I fear almost a confirmed old bachelor. He does not seem to take much interest in society or in the young ladies.

'What has become of Miss Garrison? Do you ever see or hear anything about her? I don't think Dick thinks of her any longer as a sweetheart but I should like to know what has become of her. Miss Alice Blight is to go with Mother and myself to the opera next Monday and I suppose we may be able to get Dick to go with us but that will be all. Mother says you must not infer from what I have just said about Dick's going to the opera with us with Miss B that we want him to go further, for we do not.

'With my very best love to you and dear May, Father.'

The Miss Blight referred to in this letter was Alice Blight, a real beauty and a close friend of Mother's; she had been one of a handful of intimate friends present at Mother's luncheon party to announce her engagement to Neily back in June, 1896. She later married the British diplomat, Sir Gerald Lowther, who was one of the gay Edwardian set. Mother and Father subsequently saw a great deal of them in England.

In the summer following the settlement of the Vanderbilt will, Mother and Father went abroad. Overseas they met Senator Woollcott from Colorado and, as a result of many long talks, Father came to a really astonishing conclusion. He decided to enter politics.

And so one golden September day, soon after returning from abroad, Father donned his spats and bowler hat and, accompanied by Mother gorgeously arrayed in *feuille-morte* shades of taffeta, boarded a private car for Saratoga Springs to attend the New York Republican Convention.

Both the Wilson and Vanderbilt families had long been connected with this celebrated spa near Albany, but their interest had always been in horseflesh, not in politics. The magnificent old United States Hotel with its black-walnut staircases and suffocating upholstery, its acres of red carpet and miles of porches with green wicker rocking chairs, housed during the eighties and nineties all the best of New York society. Before the spa became so fashionable Richard T. Wilson, along with the noted turfsman, William Whitney (father of Harry Payne), had bought the Saratoga race track. But the Wilsons, apparently, soon deserted the rowdy spa for the gentler and more wholesome pleasures of Newport and the Homestead.

Saratoga was the spot where Broadway and Fifth Avenue met, where Lillian Russell exhibited her abundant curves on a gold-plated bicycle, and trailed into dinner at the old Unites States Hotel on the arm of Diamond Jim Brady, who wore on his bulky frame some 2,548 diamonds, including (so it was whispered) diamond underwear buttons.

Of all the fashionable spas in this country, Saratoga seems unique in that illicit liaisons were more or less countenanced, particularly in the thriving colony of hotel cottages.

'The cottages solved the problems of numerous lonesome Wall Street tycoons and Western copper kings,' remarked a late Saratogan. One oil millionaire is still remembered for having shared his cottage with no fewer than five lovely-looking secretaries simultaneously. Also surprising were the number of beautiful young nieces of obscure backgrounds who took up housekeeping for their elderly uncles.

Henry James, when he visited the great spa, was impressed both with the fragile beauty and sumptuous gowns of the belles lining the porch railings and with the inelegance of their escorts, who lounged back with their dirty boots off the floor, spitting plug tobacco into the hydrangea bushes.

'Horse society is nothing,' Mrs. Edward Hamilton Hough told Cleveland Amory with a disdainful sniff. 'It's anybody who owns a horse.'

Now I grew up in the days when many wealthy men had romances outside their homes and this was talked of quite openly. A lady well known in Newport said of her husband, 'Yes, I am his wife but I have an assistant down the street.'

I can remember my aunts and Mother discussing the subject on the lawn of Ochre Court in their stiffly starched organdie gowns and plumed hats. As the late afternoon sunshine threw soft, shifting shadows over their tranquil figures, they looked like Raphael Madonnas sitting there.

'Of course he has a mistress,' Aunt Belle remarked as matter-of-factly as though she were speaking of some gentleman's valet.

And Mother and Aunt May nodded calmly as though this were the most natural thing in the world.

Back in the early days of this century it seems there was a special protocol to be observed on the subject of mistresses. In Paris, for instance, when a man went driving with his *fille de joie* she always sat upon his left side, so that his associates could be guided accordingly and glance the other way. When he was driving with his wife, or a lady of spotless reputation, she sat upon his right. It was like the days of Claudius, when courtesans wore blond wigs to distinguish them from the patrician women of Rome.

Many European gentlemen kept their mistresses at Cannes, including a king who was said to have built an American actress' beautiful villa there. These same titled Europeans, visiting Newport, were amazed to see how few acknowledged *liaisons* existed in America's most social watering spot. This, it was explained, was because the women ran Newport and saw to it that all adventurers and adventuresses were rigorously excluded from the portals of the Casino or Bailey's, although a few actresses occasionally were smuggled into male parties at the Clambake Club.

But, whereas illicit affairs were countenanced in Newport only if they were conducted discreetly among the very best people, Saratoga, with its carriage-loads of women from the demimonde, blazing with diamonds and vivid with paint, was quite a different matter. Mother grew to dislike intensely this man's town, devoted to horseflesh, fast women, gambling, and drinking.

Father's arrival at the spa as a convention delegate was front-page copy for the *New York Times*:

CORNELIUS VANDERBILT FINDS POLITICS AN INTERESTING STUDY—MAY BE NAMED FOR CONGRESS

Saratoga, Sept 3. One of the central figures here is Cornelius Vanderbilt. He is a delegate from the Twenty-fourth New York District and there is a rumour current that he is to receive a Congressional nomination in New York.

There is nothing extraordinary about young Mr. Vanderbilt. To see him walking Broadway here no one would take him for a millionaire. He is spare of figure, dresses quietly, and his only article of attire to attract attention is a very wide brimmed Panama straw of the Fedora shape.

Mr. Vanderbilt is clean-shaven and very democratic. He was accompanied by Postmaster Cornelius Van Cott, and when a Times reporter spoke to Mr. Vanderbilt about politics, Mr. Van Cott said: 'Ask him about railroads. That is something he is posted on.'

But the reporter wanted Mr. Vanderbilt's opinion about politics, and in his answer to his questions, he said:

'I find politics most interesting. The political field offers great opportunities for practical information of value. I am not an office seeker. I have a penchant for politics, and when I was asked to be a delegate, I gladly acquiesced.'

'Do you propose to take an active part in politics?' he was asked.

'Yes,' he replied, 'I think that is the duty of every American.'

In response to another question, Mr. Vanderbilt said: 'I have not thought of office-holding, yet I should not be averse to representing a constituency in Congress or in any other legislative body. But I am not seeking any office. I simply want to do my duty as a citizen. I find politics most interesting and I like to mingle with the men who frame and make the laws. I don't care to say much on this subject. I am only a novice. I read a good deal and have my own opinions about matters, and, while what I say may have very little weight, I am at all times at the service of my country.'

'Would you like to go to Congress?' he was asked.

'Certainly,' he answered, 'but it is not for me to pass upon that sort of question. If called, I shall respond.'

It is hard to imagine anyone talking in such stilted phrases. Certainly I never heard my father speak like that. But I suppose the reporter felt that all gentlemen used five-dollar words, and wrote it up that way. The fact remains that my father always had a very strong sense of public duty.

Many years later, Father told me about that Republican Convention of 1900. Senator Chauncey Depew was there—thin and weedy, with prominent cheekbones and shrewd eyes. He had been chief attorney and president of the New York Central lines for many years before he entered the Senate. His reputation was made as an after-dinner speaker, for he was a spellbinder, but his particular genius lay in string-pulling. About him the liberal editor of the *New York Post*, Oswald Garrison Villard, once unkindly wrote, 'Possibly no man in American life did more to debase the politics of his state than Chauncey Depew during his long service as political manager of the New York Central Railroad.'

Senator Depew let my father cool his heels for several days during that 1900 convention while he looked him over very carefully. The celebrated attorney of the New York Central had once boasted that Grandfather Vanderbilt had kept no secrets from him. More than anyone else outside the family, Depew must have known the history of the tragic feud between my grandfather and father. Perhaps he decided that although my father's name would be magic at the polls—for he was an immensely popular young man—his moral courage and independence were not quite the qualities the party was looking for.

One afternoon Father was summoned into one of those historic smoke-filled back rooms. One of the politicians gathered there took a big Corona out of his mouth and said: 'Well, young Vanderbilt, if you want to go into the state legislature, we can put you there. It will cost you a hundred thousand dollars.'

And he gave the others a broad wink.

Father could feel the back of his neck getting hot, but he replied evenly, 'And how much to go to Congress?'

'Oh, I guess about three hundred thousand,' said one of the boys, glancing at Senator Depew, who said nothing.

'Three hundred thousand dollars!' repeated my father.

'To become a member of the lower house,' the spokesman added patronizingly.

'And the United States Senate?'

'Half a million.'

My father walked up and down without looking at anyone. Finally he said mildly, 'Look, my name happens to be Vanderbilt but I'm not a Rockefeller, you know.'

The political bosses roared with laughter. So Father walked out of the room. He said this was the first and last time he was even remotely interested in a political job.

.   .   .   .   .

Grace Graham Wilson before her marriage to Neily

Neily's father, Cornelius
Vanderbilt II

'Alice of the Breakers', Neily's mother
(the author's grandmother)

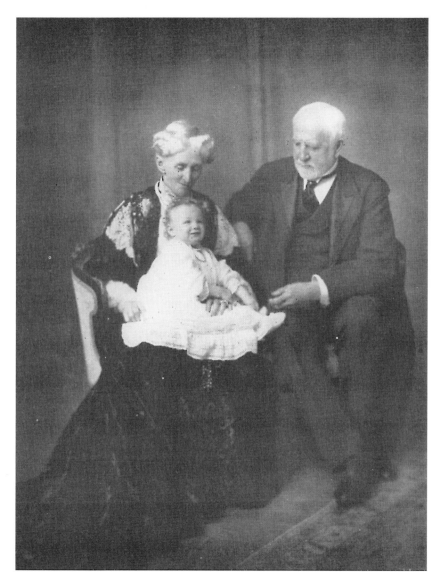

The author with his maternal grandparents, Mr. and Mrs. Richard T. Wilson

Neily and Grace watching a polo match at Newport just before their marriage

Neily and Grace on their honeymoon in Europe

Grace and Neil (the author)

*Mrs. Grace Wilson Vanderbilt,
'Queen of the Golden Age'.
wearing over a million dollars
worth of diamonds*

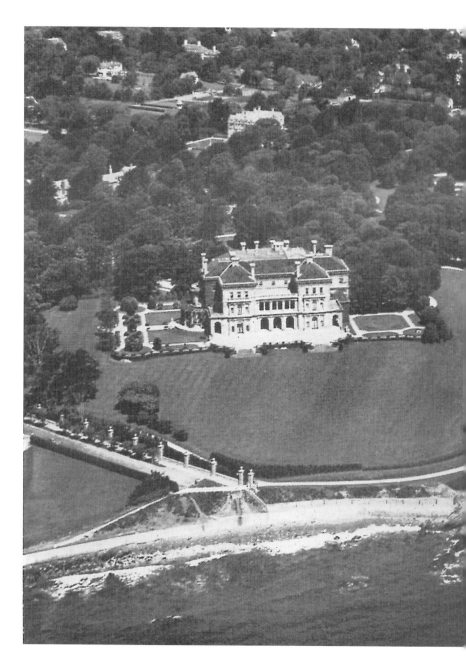

*The Breakers and, two villas away, Ochre Court, the
home of Grace's eldest sister, Mrs. Ogden Goelet*

Guests at Beaulieu enjoying the view from the ocean terrace

Grace, Neil and their father on a drive

*Kaiser Wilhelm II and
Mrs. Vanderbilt on the*
North Star *at Kiel*

The Vanderbilt yacht
North Star

*Theodore Roosevelt, Admiral 'Fighting Bob' Evans, (Commodore)
Cornelius Vanderbilt, Mrs. Vanderbilt, and some friends on the*
North Star

Neil and Grace on the sea wall at Beaulieu

*The Vanderbilts' Sunday parade leaving the New York
residence of Neily's family*

*Prince Henry of Prussia, the Kaiser's brother, and Neily, who
brought his new Packard over to him on the* North Star

Neily and Grace in later years

The Vanderbilt family—Grace, the General, Mrs. Vanderbilt and Private Vanderbilt at Beaulieu in 1918

640 Fifth Avenue had seventy rooms

*Grace Vanderbilt and Alice Roosevelt Longworth, 'T.R.'s' tempestuous
daughter, were great friends*

Grace Vanderbilt in the library at 640 Fifth Avenue, where she held court every afternoon (in 1940)

Grace Vanderbilt's most famous pose, in her later years, when press photographers tried to snap her

That fall Father rented an office at 30 Pine Street and set himself up as a consulting engineer. In his spare time he worked on his railroad inventions, of which he patented more than thirty. I can recall his office very well—a two-storied room with some ten thousand scientific books stacked in shelves to the ceiling, which Father's assistant reached by climbing a librarian's ladder. My sister Grace and I loved to race up and down this ladder, making Father terribly nervous.

Father was known to be 'in' with the smarter, younger element on Wall Street, and soon became a member of the boards of directors of important corporations, including railroads, banks, and insurance companies. He was only expected to attend a few board of directors' meetings a year, but Father did much more than this, always insisting upon familiarizing himself with the detailed conduct of each corporation. Meanwhile, on his many trips abroad with Mother, he had been studying the underground railway systems of London and Paris. He was convinced that such a system would be feasible in Manhattan, but since that island consisted largely of solid rock, the problems of construction were formidable.

Nevertheless, he allied himself with August Belmont ('the only Belmont who was worth a tinker's damn,' according to Mother) in the organization of the Interborough Rapid Transit Company and became consulting engineer in the building of the first New York subway.

'We had a rapid transit meeting today,' Father wrote from the Knickerbocker Club in April, 1901, to Mother who was at Hot Springs, Virginia. 'I am sending you clippings from last week's Railroad Gazette. What do you think of it? You see, as I told you, Vauclain made use of a lot of my ideas in his "future loco"! The parts marked in red ink show my thoughts marked respectively. (1), (2) and (3)!!! and in the part on the present Vanderbilt boiler he (Vauclain) gives me full credit for my "extraordinary" invention! The short piece is an editorial and is still more satisfactory. So you see I have the right to be pleased.

'I saw E. H. Harriman today. He said he had not yet concluded his negotiations for his car but that if he found similar points in both we should not work at cross purposes! He is to let me know when he is ready with closing up his patent rights. I think from his talk he would like some sort of a coming together of our plans perhaps!

'I shopped at Tiffany's and bought a little gold watch for Sonny's birthday and arranged with my Secretary to pay your bills. The foreign ones sum up about $13,000. Fortunately the B and O has had a further rise and little O'Neill is about $40,000 richer than he was two weeks ago. Of course I had this on inside information and will soon sell out of that stock.

'Yesterday and today I have been feeling much better physically which I attribute to my morning rides and stricter way of living. I need the exercise. About going abroad, I wish we could for the spring but you can see when I am doing so well and have so many interests in locos and cars etc. that it is hard for me to arrange.

'Whenever I think of your new ring I am pleased, for it is the sort of thing you *should* have and what I enjoy giving you.

'I am so glad you and the children are feeling better and wish I could have been there with you.

'I am going down in the regular car and the private car is to be ready for us on Sunday night. Your devoted C.'

While Father was busy with his new career, Mother had been searching for a town house, and she and Father finally settled upon a large brownstone at 677 Fifth which belonged to the Belmont family. While it was being done over and furnished, we moved into a charming old house on Washington Square with white shutters and a white picket fence. I was almost two, and Grace three or four months, when Mother, with the Vanderbilt name to back her and under the tutelage of her two well-connected and wealthy sisters, began to study the exacting art of becoming a society leader.

Chapter Eight

MOTHER, the sweetest, most loyal, and steadfast of friends, seldom forgave an enemy. So when, five years after her much-discussed marriage, she gave her first major party, she fastidiously avoided inviting any of her husband's people or any of the senior Mrs. Vanderbilt's friends who had taken sides against the Wilsons.

Probably at no other time in American history were parties both as sumptuous and as frivolous as at the turn of this century. James Hazen Hyde, heir to the Equitable Assurance fortune and a great friend of Uncle Alfred's, hired Sherry's for one evening and, at the cost of some $200,000, turned its upper ballroom into a scene from the garden of Versailles. Statues imported from France were ranged about the walls and framed in thousands of orchids. Rose petals covered the floor of the supper room. After dinner, the actress Gabrielle Rejane, a great favourite in Paris, who had been brought to New York for this single evening, recited a few verses. The party made newspaper headlines, and the resulting public outcry led to an investigation of the Equitable's affairs and to Hyde's exile. Characteristically, he chose to live at Versailles.

The Bradley Martins, old and good friends of Mother's, also fell foul of public opinion by the senseless extravagance of their parties, and finally moved abroad permanently. 'I did not know your mother too well,' young Bradley Martin wrote me recently. 'The reason, no doubt, was that my family rented a deer forest in Scotland and from then on we spent less and less time in this country.'

The public also resented Harry Lehr's famous 'dog dinner', at which his friends' dogs, waited on by footmen at an elaborate dinner table, were fed chicken and *pâté de foie gras*. The famous restaurateur Delmonico, harangued by patrons on all sides who wanted him to give 'the most superlative dinner ever given, regardless of cost', came up with such monstrous ideas as truffled ice cream. And the most famous stag party of the day featured a dinner served to white-tied guests on horseback in a New York hotel ballroom. They ended the evening, I believe, playing polo.

Mother's first large entertainment, in the winter of 1901, when she was thirty-one, was a sumptuous but tasteful dinner party at Sherry's. I have a copy of the menu before me and, studying it, I can see how Mother's conception of a good dinner changed as she became more experienced as a hostess. I don't see how her 166 guests ate their way through this perfect mountain of food. Perhaps, like Mother, they took tiny sips of water and morsels of food and concentrated on the conversation, which would have run to such amiable subjects as the planning of country-seats, the picking out of 'specimen' fern-leaved maples, where to acquire the best high-stepping horses, and, of course, plans for European travel in the spring.

So Mrs. Astor, wearing spangled purple velvet and diamonds; Grandmother Wilson in green brocaded silk and pearls; Mrs. Stuyvesant Fish in white net over white, trimmed with silver; Mrs. Ogden Mills in mauve with pearls; and Mother in pale-green velvet with her cabochon emeralds, chatted softly with their male partners as they enjoyed:

Oysters

Consommé de tortue

Hors d'oeuvres

Striped bass with cream sauce

Cucumbers

Saddle of lamb

Green peas   *New potatoes*

Terrapin

Chaud-froid de caneton

Broiled chicken

Jellied ham

Salad

Sponge cake with rum sauce

Glacé aux marrons

Petits fours   *Fruits*

Coffee

Champagne   *Apollinaris*

After this leisurely repast, lasting an hour and a half, the guests descended to a ballroom on Sherry's second floor, where Craig

Wadsworth and Mother led the cotillion. The favours for the women included metal clocks in jewelled settings and suède pocket-books with clasps of turquoise and sapphire; the men received leather stamp cases, mounted in silver, and jewelled orders. A second supper was served following the cotillion.

The party was considered a great success, and *Harper's Bazaar* published a picture of Mother in her ball gown, with a caption that said she was 'a great favourite in a large circle of friends . . . very prominent socially in the best society circles in New York'.

Mrs. Cornelius Vanderbilt, Sr., the magazine went on to say, although considered 'the social head' of the family, was still in mourning and 'it will be some time before the Vanderbilt mansion at 57 and Fifth is thrown open for any large social entertainment'.

After Grandfather Vanderbilt died, Grandmother and little Gladys (then twelve) almost literally shut themselves in their rooms for a year, seeing no one and going nowhere. After twelve months of black crêpe, they wore black and white for another six months, and shades of lavender for six months after that.

'It does one good to retire from the world for long periods of quiet,' stoutly insists my Aunt Gladys, the Countess Széchényi. 'Today—except for a few old New York families—nobody mourns anyone, or seems to miss them. They just rush on.'

As Grandmother came from a large family of Gwynnes in Cincinnati, and as there seemed to be countless Vanderbilts dying off, this elder member of the clan was, according to my aunt, 'seldom if ever out of mourning'.

In the summer of 1901, we acquired a beautiful summer villa in Newport on fashionable Bellevue Avenue, only a few doors down from the Breakers on the sea cliffs. It was this villa which was to play such a dominant part in Mother's role as a society leader. Mrs. Astor was directly responsible. For years she had been feuding with Mrs. William Waldorf Astor, who lived next door to her. Since each insisted upon her mail being addressed simply 'Mrs. Astor' and since both lived on Bellevue Avenue, the poor mail-carrier's life was a miserable one. After years of this, Mrs. William Waldorf Astor gave up the fight and moved permanently to England. We moved into her vacated villa.

Beaulieu, as Mother named the place, meaning in French 'beautiful place', sits on a broad cliff shaded by magnificent copper beeches and surrounded by eight and a half acres of fine green turf, sculptured hedges, and gardens. Built in 1850 for the Peruvian Minister, Señor de Barreda, it was painted yellow, but Mother soon had it sandblasted back to its original pale-pink brick. Square in shape, and three stories high, its slate Mansard roof has dormer windows looking out in four directions, and its immense white veranda almost completely encircles the ground floor of the house.

The house contains sixteen bedrooms and thirteen bathrooms (including some servants' rooms), while over the stables are ten more servants' rooms. A six-roomed gatehouse and generous-sized greenhouses stand near a high pink brick wall along Bellevue Avenue.

While from the outside Beaulieu has a kind of massive dignity, we always found it an extremely livable house—so much that it was in the family more or less continuously for fifty-three years. Most of the rooms are square and well-proportioned, none of them overwhelming in size, with large french windows which open on the piazza.

Mother's colour schemes were considered quite radical back at the turn of the century. Red is supposed to denote cruelty and is in any case a difficult colour to use effectively, but Mother combined red so cleverly with muted pale-grey walls and carpets and faded pearly damasks that it seemed interesting rather than startling. She introduced okra-green, pale-peach, and coffee-and-cream shades at a time when most American homes were bright emerald green, brilliant yellow, and hard pink—'birthday-cake colours', she called them disdainfully. She favoured the Louis XV period in furniture, using only authentic pieces that she picked up in small shops in Paris. Some of them were so good that they had graced the *salles du roi* at Versailles. All the woodwork, the fireplace mantles, the wall panels painted by Fragonard or Boucher, and the satin *boiseries* came from Europe, looking faded and centuries old, and that is just the way Mother kept them. She never regilded and seldom reupholstered. A three-hundred-year-old chair *looked* that old, even to its frayed seat and chipped gold leaf. And when she combined new materials with old, such as carpets and curtains, they were delicate and faded-looking, too. The effect was very relaxing and at the same time comfortable. Beaulieu was never the kind of place where you hesitated to sit down or use an ash-tray.

The drawing room had oyster-white walls panelled with gold motif and eight Fragonard French oils, crystal candelabra on the white marble fireplace, and window draperies of brilliant American-beauty satin. Scattered about the room were small dark-red damask screens which cut off draughts and formed small conversation groups of the gilt-and-satin chairs and sofas.

When I think of this room now, and it seems to me that it was never empty, I hear the echo of some words Edith Wharton penned back at the turn of the century. Mrs. Wharton lived for years in Newport, and it might very well have been Mother of whom she wrote: 'What is there in the atmosphere of some women's houses that makes them so enchanting? Why is it that those women alone know how to put the awkward at ease, check the familiar, smile a little at the overknowing, and yet encourage naturalness in all? The difference of the atmosphere is felt on the very threshold—the flowers grow differently in their vases, the lamps and easy chairs have found a clever way of coming together, the books on the table are the very ones that one is longing to get hold of. The most perilous coquetry may not be in a woman's way of arranging her dress but in her way of arranging her drawing-room.'

My childhood days at Beaulieu are among the happiest I can remember. It was the one place where I could put down roots, for otherwise we seemed always to be travelling.

In those days I had curly mouse-blond hair that hung to my shoulders. At Beaulieu my sister and I slept in a big, sunny, rose-papered nursery on the third floor with our English nurse, Anna Coxhead. She was very British, very stern, and we obeyed her much better than we did Mother. We also had a French nurserymaid, whom we called Zette; she was gay and affectionate and we adored her.

Up at seven, to the wild singing of birds in Mother's conservatory, we took sponge baths five days a week, for Mother, like the English, thought daily baths harmful. After breakfast we were some-times allowed into Mother's room for a few minutes if she was not sleeping or not too busy planning a party.

Mother's bedroom suite was on the second floor, facing the ocean and adjoining Father's. Her bedroom was very large, with pale-grey walls and carpet and subdued chintzes. Beside her bed was a telephone with sixteen push buttons, each labelled with a name—Mr. Vanderbilt's Room, Italian, English, Pink, Yellow, West, and so on. Another push-button arrangement beside the telephone had buttons for the butler, the housekeeper, and her personal maid.

The telephones were all the old-fashioned type, just as the bathtubs at Beaulieu at that time were made of tin, and set in dark mahogany frames. Mother always hung the large part of the telephone receiver up, and the servants were always changing it around again.

Mother often had a fire in her bedroom and beside the fireplace slept her little brown dog (she had a long succession of these) in a little canopied wooden box with silk brocade cushions. Her dogs were all champion rae pinschers, purchased in Germany, where they were well known as the favoured breed of Emperor Wilhelm. I used to feel that the dog was the only comfortable visitor in Mother's room, for most of the chairs were spindly wooden French antiques with straight, unpadded backs. Naturally, this did not bother Mother, as she was always in bed. She rarely rose before noon or one o'clock, and this, I believe, was the secret of her truly remarkable vitality.

Mother was one of the first people in this country to have built-in cupboards—with racks for parasols (of which she had dozens, of every possible fabric and colour), racks for shoes, for handbags, and for hats. In her bathroom a French print on the wall opened up cleverly to become a three-way mirror, and the toilet was covered with French wicker. The towel racks had hot water flowing through them to keep her towels warm, and the fixtures were gold-plated, with crystal handles.

It seemed to me that while my sister and I visited in Mother's room the telephone never stopped its shrill ringing. Mother had several phone numbers, both public and private, as well as a complicated set of signals which her secretary rang on the house phone from downstairs. 'No, no, I don't want to talk to her,' Mother would instruct the secretary, and then, as that poor lady was making excuses for her, Mother would push in a button to listen and sometimes even interrupt the conversation with 'Mrs. Fish! How delightful of you to call!'

As I rose to go, Mother would signal to her maid to line up my chair in its precise position against the wall. She could never bear to see anything in the room even an inch out of place.

At ten o'clock, Zette in her black uniform and apron and Anna Coxhead with her white hair in an immense swoop on top of her head, went with us to Bailey's Beach in the pony cart. In those days, we owned a *calèche* (for state occasions, receptions, and garden parties), two broughams (named after their inventor, Lord Brougham), two victorias, Father's Irish jaunting cart (in which one sat sideways), his Irish dogcart, and his black, polished phaeton, Mother's wicker phaeton, two Brewster station wagons, the carryall to take servants to the boat landing or to church, two pony carts, an express wagon for trunks and heavy equipment, and two sulkies. All together there were seventeen vehicles, to which Father soon added Packards and Stanley Steamers, which in those days cost between $10,000 and $15,000 each. We had thirty horses, some of them riding horses, for we all rode, and fifteen stable boys and grooms, as well as a coachman. The latter was a person of considerable importance, ranking just below the English butler and the French chef.

We often carried a picnic lunch to the beach with our nurses and remained there until three o'clock, when we returned for our naps. Even then we were not alone, for Nana or Zette napped in the same room, or sat mending our clothes.

At five o'clock I was dressed in a white sailor suit. This was the precious hour of the day when Mother, looking like some ethereal goddess in her floating gown, sat behind the great silver tea service on the piazza. To the left, one could see Aunt Alva's great Marble Palace, empty most of the time since her marriage to O. H. P. Belmont; while beyond it loomed the impressive bulk of the Breakers. Father always called his mother's place the Rock, as if he were speaking of Alcatraz.

Grouped about my parents on the palm-filled veranda on fine afternoons, one could find the cream of Newport society. Climbers were always trying to break into Mother's charmed clique; Mother dealt with them politely, but decisively. If the butler came out to announce someone she didn't care to see, Mother would tell him

graciously, 'Please say that Mrs. Vanderbilt regrets that Mrs. B——
is not on her calling list this afternoon.'

Mother could be very cold and stuffy when she chose, but with
her friends she was unaffectedly natural and delightful. Nor were
her closest friends always society people. Once, at Hot Springs, she
made the acquaintance of the local parish priest in this small Virginia
town, and invited him to New York to dinner and the opera. The
dazzled man was put upon her right hand, above several diplomats
and admirals, and treated with the deference due the Pope. My
Southern relative Aunt Flew also ranked above all the important
dowagers and was invariably put on Father's right.

Mother was always attracted to the 'doers' in life, not the
'looker-on-ers'. She especially admired Theodore Roosevelt, whose
zest for living matched her own. She often quoted a saying of his,
'You must rise up, Grace, and strike out.' His vivacious daughter
Alice, although younger than Mother, became a special friend of
hers, and when Mother visited Washington she often stayed in the
White House, where she and Alice stayed up half the night, gossiping and, so I have been told, giggling like schoolgirls.

Once they had a big row while Alice Roosevelt was at Beaulieu,
and Mother refused to speak to her until, at teatime, the President's
daughter came crawling across the piazza on her hands and knees,
like a contrite puppy. Then Mother's lovely tinkling laugh pealed
out, and she went over to the irrepressible Alice, helped her to her
feet, and embraced and kissed her.

Sometimes, if I was very lucky, there would be a lull in the
constant coming and going of guests. Father would go off to the
men's reading room in Newport or for a sail before dinner, and I
would have my beloved mother all to myself. Then I sat very close,
drinking in the fragrance and beauty of her, and clinging to her
hand, while she teased and joked with me until Zette arrived to take
me in to supper. And if Mother's particular friends came to tea, such
as the ravishing Langhorne sisters from Virginia, or Mrs. Ogden
Mills, or resorters Frederick Prince and Lispenard Stewart, she
would send them into the dining-room where my sister and I ate our
supper cereal at the vast waxed mahogany table.

Alice Roosevelt, who eventually married Nicholas Longworth,
says that my sister and I seemed 'terribly repressed' as children.
And, coming from the kind of household she did at Sagamore Hill,

she doubtless would have found us that way. There was no such thing as self-expression in our young lives. We were taught never to exhibit strong emotion, never to laugh or cry too loud; always to rise when a lady entered or left a room and never to sit down in a carriage until all the ladies were seated. We never broke into adult conversations, nor did we speak unless first spoken to. I bowed and Sister curtsied to our elders.

I guess there are worse systems of education than the cultivation of perfect manners.

The only times I can remember being allowed to yell and scream and act silly were when Mother hired a Fifth Avenue bus and took a bevy of kids, sometimes fifty of us, to the circus or rodeo at the Hippodrome. And sometimes she took us to Coney Island for the day, and none of us acted younger or gayer than she did.

After supper at Beaulieu, when we had repeated our prayers to Nana and were permitted a peck on her leathery cheek, Grace and I sometimes sneaked down to the second floor to watch the preparations for a party.

The dining-room table at Beaulieu seated only thirty-six, so that Mother had to use considerable ingenuity and many small tables set up on the piazza and in the octagonal hall to accommodate a really large party. And when she had what she called 'a young people's table' out on the porch, she was always careful to include a few white-haired dowagers and gentlemen!

Mother generally had two large dinner parties a week and a ball at least once each month. On 'party' days, as much as a hundred pounds of fresh lobster would arrive in the basement kitchens; footmen would stagger upstairs with wooden crates of champagne from the wine vault; and—if our own greenhouses were depleted—dozens of long-stemmed American Beauty roses were delivered by carriage from Aunt May's Ochre Court.

How we loved to peek through the dark oaken banisters at the arriving guests! They smiled and waved to us as they went in to dinner; the small stone fountain splashed near the conservatory, where dozens of bright-plumaged birds and canaries were singing and calling; from the music-room came the strains of a Hungarian gypsy orchestra.

Father went in first with the lady who was guest of honour on his arm; all the others followed by twos, and lastly Mother on the arm of the male guest of honour. She used a special kind of rinse on her hair, brewed from a tea blended for Queen Victoria, and under the blazing candlelight of the hall chandelier her hair looked as gold as her Worth *lamé* gown. She smiled at us over her shoulder and raised her hand. From her slender wrist dangled a gold bracelet with five golden charms; only a few of us knew that each charm contained a tiny gold key to her five jewel boxes.

I can recall Mother's taking me for a drive at Newport and, quite unexpectedly, having the coachman stop by an ancient graveyard. She and I wandered, hand in hand, among the tombstones as she read aloud the names and verses. Then, when we had climbed back into the carriage, she told me gravely, 'All those people in there thought themselves quite some pumpkins, darling, in their day and age. But who remembers them now? When you grow up, you'll find that life is often very difficult. So have all the good times you possibly can, just so long as you don't hurt other people.'

Several times we repeated our visit to this old graveyard. As a result, I have no fear of cemeteries; in fact, walking across the grassy mounds brings back the sensation of Mother's cool slim hand in mine and the rustle and perfume of her gown, the sound of her smooth, warm, delightful voice.

Another incident which stands out vividly in my mind is my seeing a domestic in Newport hanging out clothes as my Mother and I drove by. 'Whatever is that lady doing?' I asked.

Mother smiled and laid a gentle restraining hand on my arm. 'That's not a lady, darling, that's a *woman.*' And she went on to explain that a lady was someone who showed perfect breeding always, who wore silk stockings and silk gloves, and who never, never turned her hand to menial tasks. This, of course, was the prevailing attitude among the gentility of Mother's day.

Father's code was a little different. 'A gentleman can do anything,' he told me, 'even shine his own boots, providing he does it well.'

How disgruntled he could be when Jimmy Van Alen exhibited a better tennis stroke than mine or young Harriman beat me at swimming! And I was often outclassed, for I was tall, excessively thin, and lacking in the sense of timing that makes an athlete.

Once when I stepped into a dinghy tied to the dock, I jumped in too quickly, and the craft upset. Instead of pulling me out of the water, Father put his foot on top of the overturned boat, forcing me to swim underwater until, gasping and thoroughly terrified, I managed to reach the surface. My father also had a way of tossing me overboard in water over my head to teach me swimming. I think that Father, who was ordinarily the epitome of gentleness, had been subjected to the same tortures in his youth and actually thought he was acting in my best interests—that such rough tactics would 'make a man' of me.

As a child I had a particularly vivid imagination, and this led to much disagreeableness with my scientifically minded father.

One summer evening when our family was dining alone together, I began telling my parents about my experiences crabbing that afternoon with my tutor.

'And suddenly,' I said, 'a large eagle flew over our heads, carrying a young lamb in its talons.'

My father looked up incredulously, then slowly put down his fork.

'Where are American eagles found, son?' he asked me kindly.

'In the Rocky Mountains,' I replied promptly.

'Have you ever heard of an eagle being seen at Newport?'

'It was a vulture,' I improvised rapidly. 'A horrible black gruesome creature, carrying a young calf.'

Mother burst out laughing, but Father's face contorted with anger. 'Go and stand in that corner,' he commanded. 'There will be no supper for you tonight. How dare you lie like that!'

And I could not explain to him that I was not lying, that I had seen a large bird with something in its claws. Without a word I slipped over to the corner and sulked—famished, resentful, convinced that I had the most unreasonable parent in the world.

The summer of 1901 Father joined the Twelfth Regiment of the New York National Guard. Starting as a second lieutenant, he began his slow rise through the ranks of this valorous regiment.

It goes without saying that Father made a perfect officer—fearless, conscientious, devoted to duty. He was stern, but scrupulously fair, and the men in the ranks both loved and respected him. I'm told that when they were sick, or got into scrapes, or needed money, Father frequently called his carriage and drove into Hell's Kitchen to visit them personally.

Father rode in all the big parades, and as we sat at a big open window at 677 Fifth Avenue, opposite St. Thomas', cheering and waving flags, we could see a ripple of interest in the crowds below as he came by, and hear the people remark, 'It's Vanderbilt!' And I would tingle with pride at the elegantly erect equestrian in a blue scarlet-lined cape who was my father.

'It takes brains, money, and infinite tact to stay afloat in society,' Ward McAllister observed in making up his original list of New York's Four Hundred.

'I know of no art, profession, or work for women more taxing on mental resources than being a leader of society,' my indefatigable Great-aunt Alva once remarked with a sigh.

'Never before in Newport's history have the lines between the smart set and the others been more closely drawn,' a society reporter wrote in the summer of 1901. 'A few women seem to lead the concourse like sheep and there is an almost riotous struggle of getting in and keeping other people out. Everyone is waiting to see if they will be asked to one of Mrs. Astor's dinners, the acme of social success. On the other hand, there is the hostess who, despite an unlimited supply of money and the backing of three influential women, seems to have met with nothing but disaster from the very commencement of her campaign. She is almost forced to go into the highways and byways to gather in her guests.'

With Mother, it was all so simple.

One brisk morning in February, 1902, the German Kaiser's imperial yacht, the *Hohenzollern*, anchored in New York's harbour. Presently a plump, mild-looking gentleman stepped into a small Navy launch with a rear-admiral of the U.S. Fleet. 'Prince Henry is a real good fellow,' the admiral told reporters later. 'He is more like an American than any other foreigner I've ever met.'

To welcome Prince Henry, brother of the German Kaiser, New York stood on its ear. J. P. Morgan gave the royal visitor a three-hour luncheon at Sherry's with terrapin and champagne. The only guests, Morgan announced, were to be captains of American industry, personally chosen by J. P. himself, and as he had been snubbed by many a society millionaire in his day, so he rapidly passed over a multitude of hopefuls.

Society retaliated by staging a gala opera performance at the

Metropolitan for the Prussian Prince. Every seat in the orchestra and the Diamond Horseshoe was filled, creating a brilliant display, although the balconies—where seats were selling for thirty dollars apiece—were more than half empty. The Prince found the music dull and left long before the completion of the programme, but not before he personally dropped into Mother's box to pay his respects.

'The visit of Prince Henry to the box of Mrs. Cornelius Vanderbilt on Tuesday evening at the gala performance and his marked attention to her have been matters of current discussion since that event,' the *New York Times* remarked on its front page the next day. 'The recognition was so marked and the singling out of this young matron so obvious that it took many by surprise.'

Town Topics the next day remarked: 'Prince Henry's visit gave young Mrs. Cornelius Vanderbilt a chance for a *coup d'état*. When it was learned that she was the woman chosen to entertain the Kaiser's brother, the query arose, 'How ever did she manage it?' It is an open secret that Mrs. Astor aspired to entertain His Royal Highness and had postponed going abroad in order that she might participate in the festivities. In fact, she never dreamed that she would be 'euchred' by any of the Wilsons, who have been her special protégées. But Mrs. CV played her little game in a very simple way. She wrote the sweetest of letters, so the story goes, to Dr. von Holleben, the German Ambassador at Washington. It was only a little letter, asking for advice, and such a letter as, under the circumstances, was perfectly proper. Mrs. Vanderbilt had been very kindly treated by the Imperial family in Potsdam some years ago, when she was the guest of Mrs. Goelet. She was entertained by the Kaiser and Kaiserin and she had met Prince Henry and his family. She only wanted to show to the Kaiser her appreciation. This was very natural and very graceful.

'Dr. Von Holleben cabled the contents of the letter to his Imperial Master. Emperor William was delighted. He remembered the beautiful young American woman, and now that she is a Vanderbilt—a name that has great weight abroad, where it stands for untold riches and power—she fitted in with his plans. He sent her an Imperial cablegram—a very great honor for an American woman—requesting her to ask Prince Henry to dinner, as he wished his brother to dine with a representative American family.

'Much has been said about the Wilson tact, and here is an example of it. It was precisely what a woman of good breeding would do, yet how few would have thought of it! The mere honor of entertaining Prince Henry . . . is a trifle. The real triumph is that Mrs. CV has become *the* Mrs. Vanderbilt. She is recognized as the head of the family by the Kaiser. It is her branch of the Vanderbilt family which is to carry out its traditions. Mrs. Alfred Vanderbilt may hurry back from Palm Beach, and Mrs. Vanderbilt Senior may storm and fret in her 57th Street mansion. Young Mrs. Cornelius, in the few years of her married life, has not only won over Willie K. and other members of the family, but she has succeeded beyond cavil in establishing herself as the representative of the most powerful family in America.

'Mrs. Astor will sail before the dinner takes place.'

The battle, which perhaps strikes us nowadays as somewhat of a tempest in a teapot, was not yet over, however. 'On the evening of the gala performance at the Metropolitan Opera House, Mrs. Ogden Mills sat in great glory and diamonds on the opposite side of the house from Mrs. Cornelius Vanderbilt,' reported a later issue of *Town Topics*. 'She had heard all about that clever woman's adroit play, which gave her the Prince. 'Teenie' Mills was too astute a bridge player to let Grace Vanderbilt get all the picture cards. She did a little byplay herself, and with the aid of a most influential person, and by representations to the Kaiser that the singling out of one woman in New York to the exclusion of others would make some very unpleasant complications, she has secured the Prince for breakfast—and that one day before the date of the proposed Cornelius Vanderbilt dinner.'

The winter night that Mother had the Prince to dinner she ordered a red carpet laid from the vestibule down the front steps and over the sidewalk to Fifth Avenue with a huge canvas marquee erected over it. Father waited outside, surrounded by policemen stationed to control the crowds, until Prince Henry's carriage arrived, as is customary when welcoming royalty.

My father and the Prince, both passionately interested in automobiling and yacht racing, became fast friends at once. It's a pity Henry was born the second son, for he was as urbane and charming as his older brother, the Kaiser, was arrogant and overbearing.

At dinner, Mother sat between His Royal Highness and the

German Ambassador. Father was seated between Mrs. Ogden Mills and the Countess Grey. Father often said that a host had no fun at his own parties, since he was always stuck with the important dowagers. Occasionally, Father would sneak downstairs just before the guests arrived, when Mother was busy dressing, and switch around the gold-inked place cards. When the guests filed in, and Mother found the tottering, black-wigged Mrs. Astor down with the nobodies at the far end of the table, and a ravishing *débutante* next to Father, the light of battle really glittered for an instant in those extraordinary green eyes.

The guest list for this particular dinner—which I have before me—is loaded with foreign diplomats, admirals (Prince Henry, who would have made a happy English country squire, served instead as an admiral of his brother's navy), and the upper crust of New York society. But not a single Vanderbilt, aside from my father and mother, was there.

Munsey's magazine termed Mother's dinner 'as brilliant, as costly, as cosmopolitan as any the world could produce'. It was the only dinner party the Prince attended in America. About the same group of guests went to Mrs. Mills's breakfast and Mother's affair, and then took off *en masse* for Boston in their private railway cars to witness the wedding of my bachelor uncle Dick to Marion Mason, daughter of a fashionable Back Bay doctor.

Grandmother Wilson, now seventy-three, was becoming increasingly feeble, but she had lost neither her zest for people nor her capacity to be shocked by them. To the end she remained a great lady of irreproachable rectitude, yet with a sweet and lovable character. We dined at the Wilsons' almost every Sunday after church; then Grandfather would take Grace and me around the corner to Huyler's to get a great chocolate soda. I remember him best in a spotless white waistcoat and Prince Albert coat with satin lapels, wearing high shoes and dark-grey spats. He was an immensely big man, with a nose which looked as though it might have been flattened at some time, back in his romantic Rhett Butler days in the South, before he became a dignified pillar of finance.

I am reminded of a story Aunt Flew's daughter once told me about him. 'I was about ten years old and had just come back from an afternoon at the zoo,' she said, 'and Mr. Wilson asked me what animal I had liked best. I replied, "I like the tigers, but I didn't want to say so out loud, because of the lions' feelings." While everyone laughed, R. T. Wilson looked at me gravely and remarked, "The quality of tact is all a woman ever needs to be a success. Never forget that." '

'You can attract more flies with honey than with vinegar', was one of Mother's favourite maxims, which I'm sure she got from her father. If Mother felt that a person disliked her (and many did at the beginning) she would put herself out to be so agreeable and charming ('pussy purring' we called this strategy of hers) that the enemy was almost always won over.

One of the cardinal rules in Newport for the newcomer was never to outdress, outjewel, or outentertain any of the ruling dowager queens. Now, however, Mrs. Astor's mind was failing, and everyone waited to see where her crown would fall.

One cool July day, in the summer following her *coup d'état* with Prince Henry, Mother was pouring tea before the fire in our library at Beaulieu. She sat on a pale-yellow sofa before one of the $50,000 Gobelin tapestries she brought up from the New York house each summer. At one side of the wall hanging was a bell for the butler, and on the other side of the room (so that she wouldn't confuse the two) another bell which rang an alarm in the Newport police station. All the big villas on Bellevue Avenue had this alarm system; fortunately, Mother never had occasion to use ours.

'I think I'll have the *Wild Rose* come to Beaulieu,' Mother announced brightly. 'It's a marvellous play. I know every tune by heart,' and she started to hum 'Cupid is the Captain'.

Father set down his teacup on a library table, neatly stacked with the latest copies of *Tatler*, *Punch*, and the *English Review*.

'But it's still playing in New York!' he protested.

'Yes, I know,' she said, putting three lumps of sugar in her teacup. 'Won't it be fun, though! I'm so tired of amateur theatricals and clambakes and picnics and costume balls. This will be something absolutely new and different.' And she began to sing in her sweet soprano 'They Were All Doing the Same', the hit tune of the Broadway musical they were discussing.

'Oh, come now,' said Father, 'why not the *Götterdämmerung*? Grand opera in July would really be new.'

'August,' Mother replied, ignoring the sarcasm. 'End of August, I think. It's the last party of the season that's best remembered.'

I think that if Mother had not decided to become The Hostess of her day, she could have been a great impresario. In many ways she was an indecisive person—she used to call this a Wilson trait—and before she made up her mind what dress to wear, or what dinner service to use, or whether she should have her hair washed any particular day, she drove her employees to distraction. And not only did she have trouble making up her mind, but she was always changing it.

'There'll be six for dinner,' she would inform Masse, our French chef, when he appeared with the day's menu outside her bedroom door.

And then she would come home from the polo matches with twenty.

Or, having ordered her supper served at eight o'clock in her room, the footmen laden with trays would pass her, tripping down the stairs. 'I'll be back in an hour or so,' she'd carol in that delightfully musical voice of hers.

This indecisiveness of hers was somehow communicated to me. 'If I ask the Peruvian Minister and ex-Senator Green and that English cabinet minister to dine—Lord What's-His-Name,' she would write in her exuberant handwriting to me at boarding school, 'whomever shall I put on my right?' And although I knew that Mother knew perfectly well the protocol involved, the question would haunt me for days and keep me awake at night, deciding. To some extent, Mother made up her own rules, for to her a Prime Minister or Senator or Secretary of State never lost his status, no matter what adversity befell him.

I have often thought that Mother asked people's advice as a subtle kind of flattery, knowing all along precisely what she intended to do. No one who was not a born executive could have staged the show she put on at Beaulieu in August of 1902.

'The great party of our century,' pronounced the social historian, Wayne Andrews. 'The Fête of Roses', Newport still calls it. And even the blasé city editors at their newspaper desks in New York were impressed: the day following the affair they awarded one column to President Theodore Roosevelt's political tour and four and a half columns to Mother.

She termed her fête an 'at home' and sent out only two hundred invitations. Even Mrs. Ogden Mills would hardly have dared to trim her guest list so close. Remarked the oldest inhabitant of social Newport the evening of the party: 'The Vanderbilt guest list is a victory in vacuums. Nobody is here who ought not to be.'

Mother greeted her guests on the lawn, standing in a little green circle of light, looking like a portrait by Gainsborough in her *mousseline de soie* pale-green and white gown and a huge plumed black picture hat. With the costume she wore her cabochon emeralds and diamond stomacher. Directly behind her on the lawn of Beaulieu stretched a midway some 275 feet long, enclosed in turkey-red calico and blazing with red calcium lights, looking, as one guest observed, 'like a funnel of fire'. At the entrance to the midway stood a large jar of orchids and a Persian rug.

Moving down the midway across a brilliant red velvet carpet which entirely covered the lawn, the guests paused at various booths —wheels of fortune, Punch and Judy, strength-testing machines, Negro troupes, and dancing girls. At the end of the midway was society's clown, Harry Lehr, in a false moustache, with reserved seats for the Broadway musical comedy *The Wild Rose*. The pasteboard tickets were exact replicas of the ones sold at the Knickerbocker box office in New York, except that they said Beaulieu Theatre.

For an hour and a half the guests amused themselves at games of chance—Prince Hohenlohe at the fish pond, Sir Philip Burne-Jones shooting wooden ducks, the beautiful Duchess of Marlborough (Father's cousin) extending a pale white hand to a swarthy gypsy fortune-teller. Then on the stroke of midnight, the flaming red tunnel was deserted as the guests moved into a huge wooden theatre on the lawn. Here all was dim and cool, with garlands of pale-yellow and white flowers about the great crimson velvet stage curtain. From the rear of the theatre came the dull boom of waves thrashing against the stone cliff far below.

The Broadway star of the show, Irene Bentley, came down the middle aisle, and Father gallantly helped her up over the row of calcium footlights. She disappeared behind the curtain. The audience leaned forward with eager chattering expectancy. The orchestra struck up in the pit, the curtain slowly rose.

Mother was too wise to subject her guests to a three-hour show commencing at midnight. Instead, she had only the prettiest chorus girls on the stage, the snappiest tunes. The abbreviated performance took just an hour and was greeted with thunderous applause.

'The most interesting feature of this entertainment,' observed the magazine *Theater* afterwards, 'was the deliberate effort made by both Mr. Vanderbilt and his wife to make the occasion for the actors and actresses take the form of a personal compliment to them. The bouquets were handed over the footlights by Mr. Vanderbilt personally. After the performance Mrs. Vanderbilt thanked the members of *The Wild Rose* on the stage, made pretty compliments to the composer and librettist, and in every way extended to them the most graceful cordiality of feeling. . . . From the time the company arrived at Beaulieu until they left in the early morning, they were made to feel that they were welcome guests of the Vanderbilts.'

'My, I didn't know women could be so good-looking,' one of the chorus girls remarked, according to a *World* reporter.

'And the men are good-looking enough to require chaperons, too,' retorted another.

'How much money is there in the house?' comedian Eddie Foy quizzed facetiously, squinting through an opening in the *portières*.

'About 'steen billions,' actor Albert Hart replied.

At the end of the performance, supper was served to our guests in the house and on the piazza, made fragrant with thousands of American Beauty roses. The cast enjoyed the same food, but under a special tent at the end of the midway. 'Naturally enough, these supper tables became known as Bohemia,' commented *Theater*, 'and the guests strolled into this ever-fascinating atmosphere and mingled there with the prima donnas, the comedians, and the chorus. Under the combined fire of experienced chorus eyes, Mr. Vanderbilt finally fled precipitately behind a Japanese vase.'

During the supper at one in the morning an army of workmen transformed Beaulieu Theatre into a ballroom, and a hundred couples danced the cotillion to the music of two orchestras. Mother led the German with stockbroker Henry Bull. During the dancing, hundreds of costly favours were distributed—such as silver French horns, silver atomizers and cigarette cases, automatic dancing dolls and monkeys. The sun was up before the last guest rose from the breakfast tables and bid his host and hostess adieu.

'The theater and Midway required two gangs of carpenters working night and day for five days,' remarked the *Times*; 'the electricians worked for weeks arranging the illuminations, and the florists were compelled to work night and day for several days to complete their task. In addition there was the closing of the Knickerbocker Theater for two days and the transportation of the entire opera company to Newport for a "one stand" performance.'

My Aunt Flew tells how proudly Father stood by his beautiful wife's side that evening. 'Isn't she wonderful?' he kept saying. That her idea of an 'at home' should consist of a combined carnival, Broadway show, ball, dinner, and sunrise breakfast for two hundred, at a cost of that many thousands of dollars, did not, at this time, seriously agitate him.

'I have never even dreamt of such luxury!' the Czar's cousin, Grand Duke Boris, swore to Harry Lehr that evening. 'Is this really America, or have I landed on some enchanted isle? Such an outpouring of riches! It is like walking on gold. We have nothing to equal it in Russia.'

And he took the opportunity to invite my mother and father to dine at the Imperial Palace at Peterhof, should their travels carry them into that remote corner of the globe.

In October, my English Uncle Mungo received the appointment everyone in the Wilson family had been waiting and hoping for— the Ambassadorship to Washington. When the Cunarder, the *Campania*, docked in New York, the Herberts with their small sons, Michael and Sidney, accompanied by fifty-three pieces of luggage, descended into the arms of Grandfather Wilson and my overjoyed Mother. 'Mrs. Ogden Goelet is to remain in New York this winter,' *Town Topics* commented, 'and will occupy the same opera box, which belongs to the Goelet estate, as she did last season. This will add to the prominence of the Wilson family on that side of the house. Both she and Mrs. Cornelius Vanderbilt intend to entertain a great deal, and Lady Herbert will be in New York almost as much as in Washington.'

The prediction was true, but it was not the opera and dinner parties which brought my Aunt Belle so often to New York that winter season. It was my Father.

While Mother had been planning and giving her superb parties, Father had been putting in long exhausting hours on original research. An article of his in the *North American Review* that December, entitled 'Electricity as a Motive Power on Trunk Lines' was widely discussed in engineering circles and brought him much critical acclaim.

Then, quite suddenly, his health broke. A severe cold drove him to bed; before a week had passed, his illness was diagnosed as typhoid.

How many times I heard Mother recount that desperate siege! His fever went to 103, then 104, and remained unchanged for days. Frantic with worry, Mother refused to leave his bedside in spite of the entreaties of the three trained nurses and four doctors who were attending him. Night after night she sponged Father's burning head with alcohol, helped wrap him in rubber sheets, and covered him with ice blocks. When his delirious raving grew worse, she telephoned the Mayor and asked that something be done about the noise in the street. Within an hour, straw and tanbark had been spread over the cobblestones to deaden the clatter of horses' hoofs.

This was a custom Mother had learned about in England, where it was done to soothe the nerves of fashionable women in confinement—thus the old expression 'She's in straw', denoting an imminent delivery.

The *New York Times* laid the cause of Father's illness to overwork. 'For months he has allowed himself very little rest, considering the demands of his work,' a front-page story said, 'and has even denied himself the athletic recreation enjoyed by his brothers.'

When it became known that Father had typhoid (the disease which killed his older brother, Bill), a steady stream of carriages lined up at our door as friends anxiously inquired for news. Aunt May moved into our house to be near Mother, as did a Wilson lady cousin.

Grandmother Vanderbilt and Gladys were vacationing in Europe and, although they were in touch with Father's doctors by cable, they did not return to New York, as day after day his life hung in the balance. For twenty-one consecutive days, a fever of 104 racked his thin frame, reducing him to a handful of skin and bone and a wild black beard.

'There was no such thing as the wireless telegraph on the big ocean liners in those days,' my Aunt Gladys has explained it. 'Mother and I couldn't bring ourselves to get on a boat, knowing

that we would have no news of Neily for a week.' A strange explanation of Grandmother's strange behaviour!

I have always understood that Father caught typhoid while on
training manœuvres with the National Guard. 'If only I'd been
drinking Scotch instead of water, this wouldn't have happened,' he
managed to quip to Mother.

So great was the strain on her that her honey-blonde hair turned
white. It remained that way the rest of her life, for Mother disapproved strongly of bleaches and dyes. She also acquired a lifelong
mistrust of the medical profession.

The French have a belief that if you wrap your toes in cotton
treated with camphor and then dip your feet in a bowl of hot water,
you can cure a cold. Mother would sit in her bathroom like this and
sneeze into innumerable handkerchiefs and somehow manage to
break a cold out of her head or chest in this strange way. She did not
believe in hospitals or surgery, rarely took medicines, and insisted
that good health was purely a state of mind.

So when Father developed peritonitis after three weeks of
typhoid, Mother—who was in a highly distrait state—blamed his
plight on his doctors.

The nineteenth of December, 1902, was a bitterly cold day, with
high north winds. Father's four doctors stood shifts beside his bed
all day. Grandfather Wilson arrived at noon and stayed with Mother
until four o'clock. When he left, he told reporters, 'He's still
conscious. We're hoping the boy will pull through it.'

Mother's brother Orme and her nephew and niece, Robert and
May Goelet, came. Finally Aunt Belle rushed up from the British
Embassy in Washington.

When the Reverend Ernest Stires, rector of St. Thomas', arrived,
the crowds collected on the sidewalk thought the end had come, but
he reassured them that he had come voluntarily to inquire after
the condition of his young parishioner, of whom he was 'very
fond'.

The only Vanderbilts who called were one of Father's aunts,
Mrs. Sloane, and his Uncle Willie K. The newspapers said that
Father's brother Alfred was in the city at the Knickerbocker Club
'ready to go to his brother's bedside if the worst should come'.

At seven that evening, a special Vanderbilt car arrived at Grand
Central, attached to the end of a regular train. In it were my Aunt

Elsie, Alfred's bride, his brother Reginald, and Reginald's fiancée. Uncle Alfred met them and took them to a hotel.

The next day, the *New York Times*, on its front page, announced that if my father lived through the day, it was believed he would recover. Reporters stationed on my parents' doorstep reported that women of all classes, many of them in the poorest kind of clothing, came to ring the doorbell tearfully to inquire if it were true that Father had died.

'The patient's temperature was up to 105 all day, but his mind remained perfectly clear,' reported the *Times*. 'Mrs. Vanderbilt sent word to St. Thomas' Church requesting that prayers be offered for her husband, and was informed that what she was asking for had been done for several days. The rumour that Mrs. Vanderbilt had broken down under the strain of her husband's illness was declared to be false.'

At four o'clock, it was reported, Willie K. drove up in his maroon-coloured carriage; in the evening Father's sister Gertrude telephoned twice.

Wrote the *Times* reporter: 'Reginald Vanderbilt, accompanied by his fiancée, Miss Neilson, drove up to the residence, read the bulletin (issued hourly by father's doctors), left his card, and drove away again.'

I don't believe that Uncle Alfred ever came at all.

Then, miraculously, Father began to mend. His doctors, who could do little but sit and wait, saw the symptoms of peritonitis gradually subside as Mother kept her steadfast and devoted vigil.

A month later, when Father was still very weak, Grandmother and Aunt Gladys returned from Europe. A member of their party, when queried at the dock about a possible reconciliation between Mrs. Vanderbilt and her son and daughter-in-law, answered, 'No comment.' Reporters observed that Grandmother went straightway to her own mansion at 57th Street.

Chapter Nine

WHEN Mother began the deceptively simple career of party giving, I do not believe that her social aspirations extended beyond giving a handful of diehard Vanderbilts their comeuppance. The notion that she could become the premier hostess of America I do not believe ever seriously entered her head.

On the other hand, she was so eminently well qualified for the job that it was almost impossible for her to escape Mrs. Astor's crown.

'Mrs. Cornelius Vanderbilt knows not only *how* to do things but *why* she does them,' *Munsey's* magazine complimented my mother after her first few major parties. 'It is her talent, her skill, her *savoir faire* as a woman that captivate . . . She has at her tongue's tip what the French call *l'art de bien dire*. Above all, she is essentially a talented woman . . .'

Right from the beginning, Mother had definite ideas about entertaining and often deplored the brash tactics of Newport's most dynamic queen, the irrepressible Mrs. Stuyvesant Fish.

Cleveland Amory has left a memorable picture of this lady. As he points out, Mamie Fish was not beautiful, but she generated a considerable amount of what was known then as 'come hither'. 'It doesn't make any difference what you decide to do in life, but you must do it better than anyone else,' she declared. She decided to become Newport's leading hostess in order to 'liven things up'. Heartily bored with the two- and three-hour dinners of that day, Mrs. Fish had guests served in fifty, forty, and finally thirty minutes flat. Some of them have told me that the zeal of her footmen in rushing through eight courses was such that it was necessary to hold on to a plate with one hand while using a fork with the other.

Mrs. Fish was the first fashionable hostess to invite celebrities to her home—anyone who could 'hold a fork', as she used to say. Mrs. Astor had let down the bars for Edith Wharton and Isadora Duncan, but Mamie Fish tried John L. Sullivan and Marie Dressler. To all, so I have been told, she was equally insulting.

There is a story that, at her opening party of the season one year, she looked down the table, sweeping the guests with a glance. 'Here you all are again,' she yawned. 'Older faces and younger clothes.'

She is also credited, too, with this exchange with Harry Lehr, soon after he had married an extremely rich Philadelphian. A group at Mrs. Fish's house were entertaining themselves by trying to guess each other's favourite flower. 'I know yours, Mamie,' Lehr remarked to the hostess. 'The climbing rose.'

'And yours, pet,' retorted Mrs. Fish, 'is the marigold.'

Attractive-looking men with the necessary social graces often played a kind of gigolo role to Newport's rich and lonely widows. Mrs. John Drexel had a male secretary who was her constant companion. One day a relative of hers rushed up to Mrs. Fish saying: 'Have you seen Cousin Alice? I've looked everywhere in the house.'

'No,' replied Mamie. 'Have you tried under the secretary?'

'I heard what you said at Tessie Oelrich's last night,' Alva Vanderbilt once fumed at her. 'You can't deny it, Mamie, because Tessie told me herself. You told everybody I looked like a frog.'

'No, no,' protested Mrs. Fish. 'Not a frog! A toad, my pet, a toad!'

My mother could not abide Mamie and her breezy, brash, cruel wit, her breaking with the traditions of the past. It was Mrs. Fish, she always claimed, who created the nucleus of what later became café society. Yet, upon one occasion at least, she had to admire the deft way in which Mamie Fish could handle a delicate situation.

One evening, at the end of one of Mrs. Fish's balls, a young lady's maid was found in the dressing-rooms with no young lady to accompany home. Determinedly Mrs. Fish shooed all her guests out the door. Later, the young lady, who had been out driving alone with a gentleman, returned. Mamie cut her off her list for ever, but she never revealed the girl's identity.

Mother modelled her hospitality upon Mrs. Astor's, of whom Ward McAllister wrote: 'When you entered her house, her reassuring smile, her exquisitely gracious and unpretending manner of receiving, placed you at your ease and made you feel welcome. She had the power that all women should strive to obtain, the power of attaching men to her, and keeping them attached, calling forth a loyalty of devotion such as one yields to a sovereign whose subjects are only too happy to be subjects.'

At the beginning, Mother's careful adherence to social protocol may have grown out of a desire to outdo her mother-in-law, who was known to be a stickler for rules and propriety. Before long, however, the rigid forms and stilted patterns of gentility—which all too often lack all heart or meaning—came to assume a larger and larger part in Mother's life.

I could never comprehend, for instance, why we should spend every glorious summer afternoon at Newport showering the colony with our calling cards when we had already nodded and spoken to our friends several times since breakfast.

Yet punctually on the dot of three Mother expected my father, sister, and me to join the splendid dress parade of carriages on Bellevue Avenue. How vividly I can recall the tedium of those occasions when, proceeding at a snail's pace in a shiny black victoria and clutching our hateful card cases in spotless white gloves, we accompanied Mother on this sacred ritual. At each imposing entrance, a Vanderbilt footman would step off the carriage and deliver our cards to the front door. We seldom alighted ourselves, as it was considered a *faux pas* to be found at home—everyone was out dropping cards at everybody else's house.

For two hours in the velvet-upholstered carriage we were not allowed to lounge, or slump, or cross our legs. My cards, at the age of nine, read 'Master Cornelius Vanderbilt, Junr.' Nor would Mother ever tolerate my changing the English abbreviation of 'Junior' to the American 'Jr.'

Father's boredom on these expeditions matched my own. However, he soon developed the habit of disappearing to his boats or club just before the calling hour began. Mother left several of his cards, anyway, with the corner turned down to indicate that he was in Newport and available for parties, a favour for which he did not thank her.

While Mother was being mentioned everywhere as the successor to Mrs. Astor as queen of society in Newport and New York, her young niece, May Goelet, was having a gay social whirl abroad.

Aunt May's only daughter was twenty-four and not yet married but, as a gay, attractive, rich American related to the powerful Vanderbilt, Astor, and Herbert clans and as heiress to the Goelet fortune, she did not lack for beaux. In the winter of 1902, she wrote to my mother from Bad Homburg: 'I can't begin to tell you what fun I had in London. It simply was glorious. You know how fond I am of dancing and all my old partners were so kind to me, and I made several new ones.

'To go back, though. I must give an account of my proposals. Well, first Lord Shaftesbury popped almost as soon as he returned to London. He came one afternoon. Mamma happened to leave the room for a few minutes and off he went—like a pistol. I told him it was quite ridiculous as he had only known me three weeks and he couldn't possibly know his own mind—and besides I knew nothing of him nor his past beyond the fact that when he was 21 he had been devoted to Lady N—— which he said was true but that was all over long ago—and he was certain he knew his own mind. I like him very much only I have no intention of marrying him or anyone else at present.

'Mamma is terribly afraid I will accept Lord Shaftesbury, though! The Duke of Roxburghe is the man that everyone says I am engaged to. I didn't see him at all at first as he never goes to balls, but at a dinner at Mrs. James' he came and talked to me and the following night we met at Lady Curzon's where we were dining. Such a nice dinner. Lord Castlereagh took me in (the Londonderry boy) and we talked together afterwards so I didn't have a chance of saying a word to the Duke.

'Mrs. Benson is crazy to make a match between Captain Holford and myself! And Lord Grey who married Captain Holford's other sister is very anxious to arrange it too. The Prince said to Lord Grey, "It's quite time George (Captain H.) was getting married. I know just the right person for him—a charming girl, Miss Goelet. It really must be arranged."

'Now the funny part is that Capt. Holford has never said a word for himself. He wants to find out, you see, if we are willing before he commits himself in the least. Dorchester House, of course, would be delightful and I believe he has two charming places in the country. Unfortunately, the dear man has no title, though a very good position—and I am sure he would make a very good husband.

'Well, the next offer was from George Cornwallis-West, Princess Pless' brother. Such a dear, attractive, good-looking boy, and quite the best dancer in London. Anyway he fancies himself very much in love with me. So foolish of him. I am so sorry about it—but what can one do? I like him ever so much as a friend —but why they have always to wish for something more, I can't imagine—.

'Here we are at Homburg. The Duke of Buccleuch and Lord Herbert Scott plus Lady Winborne and Ivor Guest are all here, too, and we dine every night together. Lord Herbert bores me out of my senses, though *please* don't mention it, as Mamma fairly adores him. Ivor Guest is such a conceited donkey I really can't stand him and he detests me equally in return. Colonel Davidson arrived last night— he is really nice. Do you remember Alice Blight had a tremendous mash on him once at Cannes? Colonel Paget is here. I can't make out in the least how affairs stand between him and the Mater. I heard in London that he was very devoted to Lady Essex again! This morning was the first time he has been near us and that was because Mamma sent for him saying she had to see him concerning the little boat—— [word indecipherable].

'I was so sorry to leave London, that is to have the season over. The last night, Friday, we went to Lady Savile's dance. It was quite a surprise party—only arranged the night before—and everybody helped her to send out the invitations. It was quite one of the best dances of the year. We stayed until 4 a.m. and I don't think I have ever enjoyed myself so much before!

'Do you know I am wonderfully lucky. I have never had to stand out a single dance for want of a partner and generally am engaged 4 and 5 deep. Don't think I am boasting in the least. I am only so happy over my good luck. . . .

'You must forgive this dreadful scrawl, but my arm is very stiff, for, as there is nothing to do here, I have taken to golf, with the happy result of digging up a great deal of earth and losing my temper freely. Do come abroad. I'm so longing to see you, darling— with a great many messages of love to the family and young Cornelius, ever your loving May.'

Mother was indeed going abroad—and in a manner befitting a queen. For Father had purchased one of the world's most luxurious ocean-going yachts. He named it the *North Star*, after the famous yacht which once belonged to Commodore Cornelius Vanderbilt, the founder of the Vanderbilt fortune.

When Father bought this steam yacht in 1903, its luxuriousness put him at once in a class with yacht owners like King Edward VII, Emperor Wilhelm, and J. P. Morgan. Until the First World War, the palatial vessels belonging to these gentlemen—the *Victoria and Albert*, the *Hohenzollern*, Morgan's *Corsair*, and Father's *North Star* —were perhaps the most famous in the world. Their owners became, naturally, the arbiters and leaders of international yachting, and lived aboard with a ritual and spit and polish which made our pilgrimages around the world (to a child's mind at least) something less than pleasure trips. 'You can do business with anybody,' J. P. Morgan was fond of saying, 'but you can only sail with a gentleman.'

The *North Star* was a one-stacker, gleaming white, with a beautiful curving bowsprit like the old-time clippers. Her immense length —233 feet—and wide beam—about thirty feet—made her an exceedingly roomy yacht. Our drawing-room, for instance, was twenty-six feet long; the dining-room, thirty feet; the seven big staterooms, each fifteen feet square. She carried, as well, quarters for a crew of forty.

The *North Star* was Father's special province, and Mother's initials were not allowed on anything. All the linens and the dinnerware were monogrammed CV; and the crew wore silver buttons on their jackets engraved with N.Y.Y.C. (New York Yacht Club).

Father fought a continual battle to keep the ship from becoming 'too chintzy' in Mother's hands; he wanted it very nautical and masculine. Nevertheless, when the ship's outfitting was finally complete, many of its cabins had silk walls and silk screens, wastebaskets of wicker lined with pink silk, and even silk window blinds, made in France. The chairs were overstuffed Italian imports of Genoa red velvet which Mother had covered in beautiful pale French hand-screened prints. The handrails were ropes of velvet, and everywhere, on fragile rosewood tables, stood Chinese porcelain vases, Imari bowls, heavy crystal flower vases, and tortoise-shell cigarette boxes, filled with Turkish cigarettes that bore the blue and white pennant of the *North Star* with its two crossed Vs.

The *North Star* had two separate china sets: white and gilt Copeland with a pink band and Father's monogram, for dinner and breakfast; and a flower-decorated Copeland set, for tea and coffee.

There were twenty-nine teacups and thirty-seven coffee-cups, and woe to the steward who got them mixed up! In the dinner set, for formal entertaining, were 108 dinner plates!

I know all these figures exactly because I have her a complete inventory of everything on the *North Star*, prepared by Wylie and Lochhead, Ltd., of Glasgow.

The linens of the *North Star* were also monogrammed CV; the blankets were all French, bound in silk, and the sheets—there were 107—were of the finest Irish linen. Even the toilets had pale silk covers.

Father saw to it that the library was stocked with books he liked —such as H. G. Wells, Rudyard Kipling, Robert Louis Stevenson, and Conan Doyle—and on stormy days he read to us Kipling's *Just So Stories* and *Ivanhoe* and Verne's *Twenty Thousand Leagues under the Sea*. He allowed Mother to hang a few French prints here and there, but mostly the walls were decorated with old etchings and oils of yachts and frigates and famous sea battles. The galleys contained eight different kinds of crystal champagne and wine and liqueur glasses. The yacht's wine room was well stocked with cases of Grand Vin d'Ay 1889, Margeaux claret, and Grand Marnier, as well as quantities of top Scotch and Irish whisky for Father's yachting friends. In those days, Father himself drank little but beer, which he took at lunch and dinner in a tall silver tankard with a glass bottom, emblazoned with the crest of the New York Yacht Club.

Father loved all the special ritual of yachting. When we boarded our steam launch at the dock, Father went first, Mother next, then my sister, and finally myself. The boatswain would be standing to one side with the boat hook, one sailor would be running the motor, and two more would be standing stiffly at attention. As Father stepped in, they would salute.

When we reached the *North Star*, Father stepped aboard first. On deck Captain Timpson and our crew again saluted.

Father was also very precise about the kind of clothing we wore on his ship. With his yachting costume, he wore a dark-blue captain's cap, but the moment he stepped ashore he exchanged this for an ordinary yellow straw hat. Grace and I wore white duck sailor suits—trousers for me, a pleated skirt for her—and expensive English sailor hats, with a broad black ribbon and 'S. Y. North Star' printed in gold in front.

The wind was always blowing these hats off our heads, and once Captain Timpson scolded us and said how would it look if the whole crew lost their hats. We thought it would look very funny; so as the yacht was steaming out of Plymouth harbour, Grace and I went up to the afterdeck of the *North Star* and skimmed not only our own hats but all the sailors' hats we could find into the water.

The *North Star* shuddered to a sudden stop and a motor-boat was launched to circle back to grapple for the tiny bobbing hats. For this I got a good caning, but to my vast chagrin Grace only lost the chance to go ashore at our next port.

Mother had no great love for yachting, and she often suffered from acute seasickness; but from the very beginning she did everything she could to encourage Father's love for this sport of kings. It was fine for his health, it made him happy, and she also perceived how this hobby could be put to good practical use. Mother believed (so she told me) that if Father became good friends with various foreign monarchs their countries might buy Father's inventions. Now this may sound terribly naïve, but in those days monarchs really ran their kingdoms. And the royalty payments and patent sales from the inventions my father sold in England, Germany, Spain, and other European countries more than compensated for the cost of the upkeep of the *North Star*.

For our maiden voyage abroad in the *North Star* in the spring of 1903, my parents invited Mr. and Mrs. Edmund Baylies (he was Mother's attorney) and Aunt May and her daughter. The Goelets were then yachtless, Aunt May having bequeathed her late husband's *Mayflower* to the presidents of the United States. This is the same *Mayflower* which was used, until recently, for presidential pleasure cruises.

After this initial crossing, Father kept the *North Star* in England, and we crossed the Atlantic in the big British or German liners. This was partly a matter of economy, for if any yacht was kept in American waters for more than a few months it fell under American registry and the seamen's wages were upped considerably.

I never knew Father to cross the Atlantic in a French or an Italian ship; he said that in case of shipwreck the crews on these liners were always the first to the lifeboats. He was careful never to lock his stateroom door on any train or ship. In case of wreck or fire, he said, the steel plates would buckle and one would never be able to unlock the door. So instead of shooting the bolt he propped a

suitcase in front of his unlocked door to keep it closed. I find myself doing the same!

Since both King Edward VII and Emperor Wilhelm of Germany
were in Italy to visit the Pope that spring of 1903, and all the
fashionable people of Europe there with them, the *North Star* also
steamed into the Bay of Naples, where the royal fleet was anchored.
In a long letter to Aunt May written in Mother's bold and dashing
hand, those faraway days glow again with excitement and colour.

'Darling Sister May,' Mother wrote from the Grand Hotel in
Rome, on May 1, 1903: 'Our trip from Cannes to Naples was a very
rough one, but we were quite repaid for our suffering when we
steamed into the Bay of Naples last Saturday afternoon [April 25].
It was a most inspiring sight. A large fleet of great, grey men of war
in the outer harbours and when we rounded the breakwater we came
into the midst of many more great battleships surrounding and
guarding the King of England's yacht. Bands were playing, people
singing, flags waving, hundreds of small boats and launches darting
about. And it was altogether one of the most wonderful scenes I've
ever beheld. Mt. Vesuvius was puffing great black clouds of smoke
like a great chimney!

'At five o'clock we tied up to the port alongside the Narada. I
sent Hedworth a little note saying we had just arrived. He sent back
word that he would call *immediately*. So a few minutes later he came
in the royal launch and made us a long visit, returning to the yacht
just in time for a men's dinner on board. He took Neily off to write
in the King's book, and said "I know the King wants to see you." At
8.30 a note came from Mr. Walker saying he had a box for the gala
performance at the opera that night and asking us to come. We went!
And had such fun. It was a splendid box. We arrived late and the
moment we came in the King saw us! Hedworth came round to see
us and was a perfect dear. He said the King wished Neily and me to
come on board the next morning, Sunday, for service. I said we
should be delighted.

'After Hedworth went back to the Royal box, Seymour came and
made us a little visit and I assure you everyone in the house looked
at us, with great interest, seeing all the King's party in our box. And
the *dear* King himself couldn't keep his eyes off our box!! I wore
my jewels, which I afterward heard from many people were much
admired. The next morning early Hedworth wrote saying the King

thought I might feel shy being the only woman on board the yacht for service so he asked me to bring the rest of our party which consisted of Alice and Mr. Crane. He also asked us to come at 10.45 as the King wished to speak to us before service.

'Punctually we arrived on board and were met by Seymour and Hedworth. The King was still breakfasting but in a few minutes he appeared and really, Sister, I cannot describe to you the charming impression he created upon us all. So majestic, so wise, so strong and yet so gentle, so considerate. He has grown very *broad* and stout since I've seen him but it is most becoming, and he looked so fresh and rested and well. He said, "I haven't seen you since your marriage which is about seven years now, and how are your sisters? I haven't seen Mrs. Goelet in a long time. She is not going to be married?" "Oh, no, Sir, I do not think she will ever marry again."

' "No," he said, "I do not think she ever will. I do not think so," and then he looked as if he were thinking of Ogden, but he said: "Miss Goelet. She must marry." I said, "Yes, when she finds the right one," which made him laugh. He then (or rather it was before this) said: "How wonderfully well your brother-in-law, Mungo, has been doing. That man Bowen, Mrs. Vanderbilt, was a dreadful man and Mungo has done splendidly." I added that I had heard that no one but Mungo could have managed to get on with Bowen (these were Smalley's words to me) and the King seized upon it, and was delighted. He said, "That is just it. No one else but Mungo could have done all this and it is entirely due to his ability that it has been settled so well and I am very pleased. When are the Herberts coming over? And your sister is such a success over there, too. Where is Mrs. Goelet now?" etc. Then he said, "Your husband, Neily, was just outside on deck. I met him too before you were married."

'So I motioned for Neily to approach, and he shook hands and was so nice to him. Then he said how-do-you-do to Alice and Mr. Crane and we went into a part of the ship which had been arranged like a chapel. All the sailors sat facing us. I sat directly next to the King and Alice sat by me. And all the others behind us. It was a simple service but beautiful and impressive. The King singing and answering all the responses loudly, as did also the sailors. Afterwards the King said, "They sing very nicely, my sailors."

'It seemed so funny to sit by the King when they prayed for His Gracious Majesty. I answered a loud and fervent Amen and felt it so much. He is so charming when one sees him like that one can honestly *pray* for him. After the service he walked off a little distance with me from the others and began a long conversation. . . .

'We talked of the Emperor and he remembered presenting me to the Emperor at the Osborne! He asked if Prince Henry's visit had really been very popular. I said I believed it had pleased the people and he said, "Yes, but they were not taken in by it—they saw through it" and seemed much amused and also a *little bit jealous*, I thought, and liked it when I laughed over it with him!! . . .

'He kept on chatting so pleasantly and so long that I began to get nervous as there were admirals upon admirals (Italian) arriving all the while and I also knew he was going to lunch early with Lord Rosebery. So in a pause in the conversation I gently said, "Shall we be going now, your Majesty?" He seemed to pull himself together and he said, "Well, yes, perhaps it would be better as I have to receive these admirals." The admirals having been waiting, trembling in their boots, all this while.

'He said, "I hope to see you in Rome, etc.," and off we all went. Oh, I forgot to say that he said, "Don't you think your husband would like to see my physician while he is here?" He had spoken of Neily's illness etc. I also told him that I wanted him to know that all our family difficulties had been settled. He said: "I am very glad. Very glad indeed." And then he looked angry and said: "It was so wrong of them. So outrageous. I am glad that it is all over."

'I could have thrown my arms round his neck and kissed and thanked him. He seemed so to mean what he said, and to feel it. Well, we spent a very pleasant Sunday and Monday afternoon we came up to Rome, arriving here at 8.30 at night. I can not describe my impressions of Rome. Everything is more beautiful than I had conceived it to be. I have not been able to do much sightseeing yet as we have been kept very busy socially. The Meyers have been most kind about arranging things for us. . . .

'Tuesday night we went by special invitation to the gala opera. It was a most brilliant sight and we had an excellent box, or rather seats in a box as everyone was crowded like sardines and there were no other strangers, except ourselves, outside the corps diplomatic. The King and Queen of Italy and King Edward, as he is called here, and Duke d'Aosta and Count de Turin all sat together in the front of the box. Duke d'Abruzzi and others behind. Then the ladies in waiting etc. etc. There were lots of lovely women in the house and they all looked very chic and attractive.

'As soon as the King entered he looked around the house and again spied us out. He then pointed me out to the other royalties (all this I heard from one of the other ladies in waiting, the beautiful one who used to be Vittoria Collonna—I forget her married name). And he said how charming I was. And they all said I had the most beautiful jewels in the house that night. This same lady in waiting said the King of England had told them before this that at Naples I had looked so lovely at the opera! Is it not kind of him to recommend me to the Italian King and Queen?

'I hear that all the Italian papers speak of me and my jewels. I wore my tiara, my emerald collar, my pearls with the emerald piece Belle gave me, my diamond fringe across the front of my gown (they admire that extravagantly) and my other emerald piece, all this with my yellow and silver gown looked very pretty. Alice looked lovely with white flowers in her hair. We had a splendid time.

'Coming out of the opera I met the Duchess of Sutherland and she rushed up to me and was so nice. The next night we went to the British Embassy reception, arriving very late, 11.45, just as the King was starting away. He stopped and again began quite a conversation, keeping carriages and everything waiting, and he looked dead with fatigue, but his face lighted up and he said: "I saw you, looking lovely, last night at the opera. Be sure to come to England this season etc. etc."

'Everyone was astonished as they said he had snubbed old Countess Graville who threw herself upon him as he was trying to leave. I also heard that Lady Herbert prostrated herself before him, kissing his hand and saying, "Oh, I can't thank you for all your kindness to my boy." They say he looked so bored but answered her civilly—but the other one was too much and he merely bowed stiffly and passed on by! . . .

'On Sunday the Emperor is to be received by the Pope and on Monday His Holiness is giving us a private audience!!! Neily says he can't be here as all this has tired him physically and he has gone back to the yacht to bring it from Naples up to Civita Vecchia where I shall join him on Wednesday. Alice and I stay until then. Neily has enjoyed it all very much and has been much liked. They all seem to know about him and his inventions.

'Marconi arrived here last night and the town went wild. They took the horses out of his carriage and pulled it through the streets. He came here and we saw him at dinner. He saw us and rushed up to us. Everyone is much interested in him so it was great fun. He came aboard and talked after dinner. I have just met him in the hall and he said he had just had an audience with the King and Queen and tonight he is to meet the Emperor. . . .

'Everyone is much impressed by the way the Emperor does everything. They say he wrote directly himself to the Pope saying he could call at such and such an hour, date and day and the Pope answered in person. He, the Emperor, has sent his carriages and horses on here. But not so with the King of England. He got here and then did not know how to get to the Pope. He could not drive there in the Quirinal or Royal carriages, as they would not be allowed to enter the Pope's domain so there was a great question. Finally it was settled by his using the Embassy carriages and starting from there. He, of course, was staying with the Italian King and Queen.

'Only think I have written these twelve pages and have not told you any of my impressions of Rome. I have been to the Forum and the Coliseum and I was simply rendered speechless by both. Also St. Peter's and the Vatican. I feel much too tiny and insignificant to express my opinion. It is all so wonderful, so grand, so splendid and it makes me feel that another and much superior race of people must have existed in those days. To die and never to have seen Rome seems a life that has been lived in vain. Since seeing it, I feel there can not be anything else on earth that compares to it. It looks so gay and lovely now with all the decorations which today have the German flags instead of the English. I will write again after the arrival of the Emperor.

'Did I tell you old Grand Duke Michael sent me his photo? Dearest Sister, would you mind immediately sending this on to darling Mother and Father as I can't write all this twice.

'Ever your most loving and devoted sister, Grace.'

On our initial trip abroad that summer on the *North Star*, I was only five, and my sister three, but as we repeated the voyage almost every summer until the First World War, I had many occasions to remember Emperor Wilhelm very well.

He seemed a big, virile, handsome man with a large moustache, waxed to a ferocious stiffness. I thought him extremely conceited and quite a show-off as he rattled on to Father in his thick German accent about jibs and spinnaker booms and tables of scantlings. He seemed determined to show my parents he was just as good a yachtsman as King Edward VII of England, of whom he often seemed envious. Father listened politely and managed to control his annoyance when the Kaiser scoffed at the slowness of our steam yacht, which took eleven days to cross the Atlantic.

Usually on our visits to the German royal yacht, the *Hohenzollern*, Sister and I wore white leggings, shoes, and coats. Little Grace clutched an ermine muff and on her curly brown head wore an immense feathered bonnet with a large rose in front. With her big blue eyes and round pink cheeks she looked just like a French doll. My shoulder-length curls brushed an ermine collar, and I had a white sailor hat with an ermine band.

On one occasion, my mother had been chatting on the *Hohenzollern* deck with the Kaiserin, exchanging petit-point patterns, and now that the prescribed twenty minutes for a royal visit was finished, she rose gracefully to go. I stepped back out of the way, and my foot somehow became entangled in my long coat. As I started to topple backwards near the edge of the deck, the Kaiser sprang forward and caught me in his arms.

Years later, after the First World War, I tramped through the woods of Doorn, Holland, to interview the exiled German Kaiser. I found him on top of a haystack collecting eggs. When I had introduced myself, and asked for a statement, he looked me over petulantly and remarked, 'Had I let you fall overboard that day at Kiel, you would not be intruding upon my privacy now.'

'The Empress of Germany must weigh at least sixty pounds more than her husband. She is as big as our former wet nurse,' I wrote irreverently in my daily log on the *North Star*.

'The Kaiser,' added my sister after we had dined aboard the imperial yacht, 'cuts turkey better than our cook at Newport. But it takes him longer. Because of his crippled right hand, he cuts the bird with his left. He serves himself first and the moment he finishes eating, the footmen take away everyone's plates. We felt hungry after dinner and Neil said he wished he could ask for a glass of milk.'

Mother seemed to get along fine with the arrogant Kaiser; indeed, she once remarked that she had never met a man she didn't like.

On the Fourth of July of 1903, Father and Mother gave a

banquet on board the *North Star* in honour of the Kaiser and Kaiserin. Prince Henry also came and renewed his acquaintance with my parents, who had entertained him the previous winter in New York. His wife, Irene, sister of the Russian Czarina, was a lovely, charming person. She took to Mother immediately. The letter she wrote Mother the following summer shows how quickly their friendship blossomed:

'Dear Mrs. Vanderbilt—Could you have seen the joy the arrival of the Golliwogg cards gave the children & their mother this morning, I think you would have smiled. Heads close together reading the names and laughing at the pictures and each clutching at them with excitement. It is really very dear and kind of you, & I thank you a thousand times for them—such a pretty case too. I hope that your little ones are quite well, & that your dear little boy has quite recovered from his illness. My sister wrote to me from Peterhof to say how sorry she was not to have been able to see you, but it was quite impossible just then she told me.

'I hope your whole trip has been successful, & that you are satisfied as to your husband's health too. Your coming to Kiel was really such a pleasure, & I shall often think of it. Pray remember me to Mr. and Mrs. Baylies, as well as to your niece Miss Goelet and Mr. Vanderbilt.

'The Prince is still away. Yours very sincerely, Irene, Princess Henry of Prussia.'

As a small boy, I was very susceptible to coughs and colds and attacks of flu; Mother, too, caught cold easily and therefore slept with a ruffled nightcap on her head, under a perfect mountain of blankets, with all the windows closed. She worried a great deal about my health, and I believe that is one reason why she took me everywhere with her. Sometimes we crossed the Atlantic as many as six times a year.

'THE VANDERBILTS ROYALTY'S GUESTS', the *Times* headlined our visit to Russia that summer. At Peterhof, Mother was formally presented to the Empress Alexandra, a haughty, aristocratic-looking beauty who dressed habitually in violet and whose half-demented infatuation with the monk Rasputin was the talk of the world. Her husband, Czar Nicholas II, bore a striking resemblance to my father. They were both tall and spare, with dark moustaches and black pointed vandykes. (Father, who had been clean-shaven up until the time of his typhoid attack, had now adopted this most becoming beard.) Like Father, the Czar was partial to yachting costumes and gold-headed canes. When Father went ashore at St. Petersburg, he was at first astonished by the number of peasants who traipsed respectfully at his heels. Finally, someone who spoke English inquired if he were the Czar.

'No, no,' replied Father, aghast. 'I'm an American travelling with his family.'

While we were in Russia, I attended for several weeks the school of the Czarevitches, but picked up no Russian that I have ever been able to remember. The Grand Duke Boris entertained my parents with a dinner at the Imperial Palace, as he had promised, and in return we gave the royal family a banquet on the *North Star*. But what Father talked about most was an exhibition of superb marksmanship—Cossacks on white Arabian steeds standing up in their stirrups and shooting from the hip at a full gallop. He never forgot about this, and when I reached the age of twelve, he engaged a special riding master to give me lessons.

Mother made such a hit with the Russian imperial family that by the following spring the Grand Duchess Anastasie was telegraphing her at Cannes: 'Could we dine with you Friday next, our party consisting of my son daughter, Duke Duchess Cumberland, two daughters, one lady, one gentleman. Anastasie.'

To invite oneself and eight guests to lunch or dinner is not as surprising as it sounds. Indeed, it is a great honour, since royalty traditionally designates not only the time and place and guest list of any party, but also the hostess.

At the beginning of August—with the *North Star's* bath pipes still filled with the greenish water of the Baltic—another pennant was hoisted on her foremast, the pennant of His Britannic Majesty, who seldom failed to preside over the Cowes Regatta.

An hour later, a white-bearded, powerful-chested man with yellowed flannel trousers, creased not in the middle but on the side, settled his broad frame into a green wicker chair on the deck of the *North Star*. With him was his beautiful and understanding wife, Queen Alexandra, who was known to possess the world's most perfect shoulders and bosom for the display of jewels.

King Edward was a suave and worldly sophisticate who was never too regal to bounce us on his knee and regale us with stories about Mrs. O'Leary's cow (which, having only foreign governesses, we had never heard about). His voice was a deep baritone, and as he talked, gusts of laughter shook his great frame. He was like a fresh, tangy sea breeze in the Court of St. James after the dreary widow-hood of his mother, Queen Victoria. Americans interested him, especially beautiful American women, and he had an avid curiosity about American slang and customs. Still, he was always a king. My mother once told me that when an American forgot herself so much as to say to him 'Look here, my good man——' he interrupted her with 'But my good lady, I am *not* your good man.'

Father and King Edward often rode horseback together on the Isle of Wight and talked of boats and racing sloops and yachting. Of the two of them, Father seemed much more British and correct. I can recall his telling me that once during a country weekend at Wilton House he came upon the King alone in the library painting his heel with black ink to disguise a hole in his sock. Father was horribly embarrassed and tried to pretend that he had seen nothing, and was further shocked when the King lightheartedly told about the episode at dinner.

Whenever Father was invited aboard the King's two-stacker, the *Victoria and Albert*, he was careful to change into an old shiny serge jacket and yellowed flannel pants. Otherwise he knew his new yachting clothes would move the royal entourage to tease him unmercifully.

But formal occasions aboard the royal yacht were quite a different matter.

THE MASTER OF THE HOUSEHOLD
HAS RECEIVED THEIR MAJESTIES' COMMAND
TO INVITE
MR. AND MRS. VANDERBILT TO DINNER
ON BOARD H.M. YACHT VICTORIA AND ALBERT
AT 8.30 O'CLOCK.

GENTLEMEN: SHORT COAT, WHITE WAISTCOAT
BLACK TIE OR YACHTING DRESS

LADIES: HIGH GOWN

Mother's stateroom on the *North Star* had pale-grey silk walls and pale flowered silk curtains which matched her bed coverlet. The room was lighted softly with French ormolu candelabra; the furniture was Louis XV. I had just come from Father's private laboratory up on the foredeck, with its smell of Father's Turkish cigarettes, burned chemicals, and scarred tables covered with dis-assembled mechanical gadgets. I can remember the thick, luxurious feel of Mother's carpet under my feet as I first knocked, then ventured shyly in.

'Come in,' Mother carolled from her dressing-table. 'Oh, it's you, Neil darling.'

Sophie, her German maid, had laid out on the bed a white satin gown with a long train. On the dressing-table lay Mother's white *glacé* gloves and a great heap of jewellery, including her diamond tiara. I could see that Mother was headed for a very important affair.

'How are you, darling?' she asked vaguely, her eyes on her reflection in the mirror.

I was feeling very sore and resentful indeed, my backside still aching from the caning Father had just administered. 'Father spanked me,' I told Mother, leaning over to kiss her smooth cheek. She smelled delicious.

Mother made small comforting sounds of sympathy. 'Sophie, I simply can't decide . . .' She held up her famous diamond fringe, which was three inches long and hung from shoulder to shoulder across her bosom. 'Perhaps the pearls and emeralds . . .'

'Mother,' I began, 'I need a new bicycle. Mine's all banged up.'

That's what the punishment had been about. Father, stepping out of his laboratory unexpectedly, had run into me riding my bicycle about the deck. 'Get off that bicycle at once!' he had ordered. 'Do you want to maim someone for life?'

'No, sir,' I replied, losing control of the thing and crashing into the rail.

'Come into my laboratory immediately,' Father directed.

The bicycle came out of the encounter with only a bent spoke or two, but it was important to get back at Father.

'May I have a new bicycle, Mother dear?' I repeated.

'Of course, darling,' she said, giving me for the first time her radiant smile and full attention. 'Tomorrow afternoon when we go ashore for tea, we'll buy you one—the biggest, most beautiful one in the store.'

'And a red drum?' I pressed her. 'And a real fur monkey that winds up and dances?'

Mother laughed, and it was like the sound of tiny silver and gold bells. 'We'll see, we'll see,' she told me fondly, and I knew that I had won. 'Now run along, angel, like a good boy. Mother's dining with the King and Queen tonight.'

And her green eyes sparkled like the emeralds in Sophie's plump white hands.

Ahead of me the afternoon presented a grey, empty vista of boredom and loneliness. Dragging my heels, I reluctantly started to leave, moving so slowly that Sophie with a rush of stiff, rattling petticoats and baleful German imprecations finally chased me from the room.

Often these few brief moments with Mother were all I had all day, for she seldom ventured from her cabin except to disappear on the steam launch for tea or a garden party ashore. At first, Father always accompanied her. But in later years he found excuses to stay aboard, smoking cigarettes feverishly as he worked away at his designing board.

Mother disapproved of smoking, and one of my earliest memories of Father is seeing him trapped in the act of smoking in her boudoir in New York. As we heard her footsteps approaching, Father extinguished the stub and looked about for some place to hide it. He finally tucked it behind one of the damask tiebacks for the curtains, and scuffed the spilled ashes into her pale carpet. If anyone dared to do this to his rugs on the *North Star*, I noticed he was furious.

Father returned home alone in the middle of August, while we remained with Mother at Bad Nauheim and then went to our usual suite at the Hôtel de Crillon in Paris. To fill my days while she was involved in fittings with her dressmakers, Mother let me buy all the little brass trains I could find on the Rue de la Paix. Then I would lie on my stomach on the Persian carpet in our suite and pretend that its designs were tracks. I would run the little trains up and down the carpet, shouting out conductor's commands in French and German, and trying to imitate the squeaky little whistles of foreign trains.

When this palled, our nurse took my sister and me to the

Tuileries gardens. In London, we stayed at Claridge's, and in Berlin we put up at the Adlon on Unter den Linden, which is now in the Russian zone. In Rome, we stayed at the Grand or the Hassler; in Cannes, on the French Riviera, my parents liked the Carlton. Father had a lot of business affairs in Geneva, and while there we stayed at the Hotel Beau Rivage.

'I like to lead a well-rounded life,' was an expression Mother used all the time. By this she meant that she liked to be in various parts of the world when the social season was on.

When I had established myself in a very different kind of life from my parents', I said to her, 'I consider a well-rounded life to be spending some time in a cabin in the Northwest woods, and then going to the beaches of Florida, and then maybe travelling to the Orient.'

But Mother never understood any of this. Not only did her life revolve about the social sphere but the sphere moved with her, you might say, at least in this country. The season officially 'began' when she opened Beaulieu at Newport, and when she decided to take the cure at Hot Springs, other women scrambled to get there at the same time. They even tried to get reservations on the same train; and everywhere, across the country, women copied what Mother thought, wore, and did.

Mother liked virile men and feminine women. She had absolutely no use for women who went to college or had a career or worked for 'causes'. She saw her own particular role in life as a kind of catalyst between people. When some distinguished foreigner arrived from abroad, he would say to Mother, 'I want to meet Mr. B,' and Mother would arrange for them to be together at her next dinner party. When Taft and Teddy Roosevelt fell out, it was at a party of Mother's that they first shook hands again. Father sometimes became furious at Mother for inviting to his home his worst business enemy—yet, often as not, over a few brandies by the fire, after an excellent dinner, peace would be made. Eventually, Mother saw herself as a kind of international peace ambassador.

'How long remain? What are your next plans? Best compliments, Anastasie,' the Czar's sister wired my parents at Kiel the next summer.

'Dear Mr. Cornelius Vanderbilt,' reads a note from the Admiral of the *Hohenzollern* in August, 1904: 'H.M. the German Emperor wishes me to ask you if it will be convenient for you and Mrs. Vanderbilt to accept his coming for lunch on board your yacht tomorrow at one o'clock accompanied by three or four gentlemen.'

The same summer the Kaiser's brother, Prince Henry, wrote: 'My dear Mrs. Vanderbilt, At last I have been able to procure a small photograph of the "Orion" under sail, taken during one of the races this year. It is not a very good photo, as it is not distinct, however you will be able to distinguish my racing flag & I hope you will accept and keep it as a souvenir of our various trips on board the good old boat. Perhaps the photo may find a place on board the 'North Star'.

'Till now we have enjoyed most glorious, hot summer weather, quite unusual in this part of the country. His Majesty [Wilhelm] still being away in Norway, I have not yet had a chance of speaking to him about his new yacht, but as Mr. Vanderbilt kindly told me that the designers were somewhat hard to deal with, I want to inform H.M. of this fact . . .

'Hoping that you and the children have not suffered all the way home & to be remembered to Mr. Vanderbilt, pray believe me, my dear Mrs. Vanderbilt, Yrs, always most sincerely, Henry Pr of Prussia.

'P.S. The Princess sends many fond messages!'

And as we sailed for home, he cabled our ship: 'Eckernfoerde. Mrs. Cornelius Vanderbilt. Kaiser Wilhelm II. Devoted thanks letter & charming photos. Hope children well. Bon voyage to you and Mr. Vanderbilt. Speedy and safe return home. Hope you will both come again. Will write to Newport. Princess sends fond messages. Henry.'

Shortly after we returned home from our initial voyage in the *North Star*, Princess Irene of Prussia wrote Mother a particularly warm and affectionate letter addressed simply to Mrs. Cornelius Vanderbilt, Newport. The mailman delivered the royal-crested letter to the Breakers, where apparently Grandmother digested its contents before sending it over to Beaulieu, for penciled on the outside it says: 'Sorry. Opened by mistake. A. V.'

Cousin May Goelet finally made up her mind between her many ardent titled suitors and, in one of society's most fashionable weddings, became the Duchess of Roxburghe. The young Duke of Roxburghe was slim, dark, and handsome. Mother was particularly fond of a picture of him in an ermine cloak, wearing a gold-hilted sword, with a page holding on a white satin pillow his diamond coronet.

After her marriage, Cousin May moved into an immense and truly enchanting Scottish castle near Kelso, with acres of turrets and dungeons, creaking drawbridges, and mossy towers, surrounded by thousands of acres of forests and hunting grounds. It was known as Floors Castle (pronounced Flewers), and of all the splendid English castles and country places Mother knew well, including Blenheim and Wilton House, Floors was by all odds her favourite.

In the winter following Cousin May's spectacular marriage, the Count Boni de Castellane, who married the American heiress Anna Gould, visited Washington, D.C., and in his memoirs mentions the 'sumptuous' dinner given for him by Sir Michael and Lady Herbert. Unfortunately the Ambassador's health could not stand the Washington climate, and after holding his post for only a year he was forced to resign and retire to Davos, Switzerland. There in a very short space of time Uncle Mungo succumbed to the tuberculosis which he had fought so gallantly and cheerfully for so many years. He left a heartbroken and still beautiful widow of thirty-eight. Tragically enough, she soon found that both her sons, Sidney and Michael, also suffered from the same dread disease.

Meanwhile, my own health had been giving my parents increasing concern and finally they decided to put me into a typical Dickensian English school called The Priory, at Malvern, in middle England.

During the five months I spent at The Priory in 1904 Father was cruising about Europe in the *North Star* with Richard Crane (the midwestern plumbing magnate), Tom Keck, and George A. Cormack, all great friends of his from the New York Yacht Club. Mother thought they exercised a bad influence on Father, especially in the matter of drinking, but there was little she could do about it. After watching the arrival of the American yachts at Lizard in the transatlantic race for the Kaiser's Cup, the group went to the Kiel races and then to Norway. Before returning to New York they stopped at Glasgow in Scotland, where two months earlier Father had ordered a model of the *North Star*. According to the *New York Times*, it required a dozen men to complete the model, which cost over $10,000. Marvellously exact in every detail, the little model was loaded on the *North Star* for the trip to New York. Father presented it to the New York Yacht Club, where it can still be seen today.

In October, 1904, the family was reunited at Newport, where we stayed until time for Mother's semi-annual trek to Hot Springs, Virginia. While she was gone, the Newport staff would close up Beaulieu, filling several van loads with household effects, and then open up the New York house. When everything had been un-shrouded from its muslin covers and mothballs and put back into place, Mother would return. I have seldom known a better executive.

The cool, early fall days in Newport were ecstatically happy ones for me, for then the fatiguing whirl of parties was ended, and Mother spent the golden late summer hours with us. I can remember picking blueberries with her, and the rich, warm, chocolaty smell her fudge made as we stirred up a batch in the great basement kitchen with its enormous racks of shiny copper pots and pans. At bedtimes she had time to read us the Psalms, many of which she knew by heart, and sometimes she sang in her very sweet treble old Southern lullabies. After dinner, she frequently played the piano while Father sang 'Onward Christian Soldiers', his favourite hymn.

I can still see Father's lean dark frame stretched out on the nursery floor as he fussed with my electric trains, and I remember his delight when Cousin Consuelo sent us a small Blenheim spaniel from her English place, that we called Cricket. And on Sunday mornings, Sister and I were allowed to read the comic strip 'Little Nemo', on Father's bed.

Whether at Beaulieu, or on the *North Star*, or in New York, Father's bedrooms looked the same—filled with complicated-look-ing weather gadgets, ship models, ropes tied in sailor knots, and old Dutch and English ship prints. At Newport, his bedroom walls were painted tan with a rust-coloured trim; his fireplace was black marble. Mother had searched and searched for the handsome hand-screened linen nautical print which covered his single bed and matched the tall screen between it and the windows.

Sometimes the whole family would go crabbing, taking along some servants to build a bonfire on the beach and to carry Mother's special crab dressing. It was made of mayonnaise and Roquefort cheese with lots of Worcestershire and ketchup—we all loved it. Often we caught as many as fifty crabs and roasted them over the fire, then cracked them apart and ate them hot with the rich pink sauce.

When we went on a family picnic, there was no such nonsense as sitting on the ground and using paper plates and napkins. Instead, a carriage went ahead to the picnic site with two footmen, a maid, and one or two grooms. These servants set up a table under the trees with a white linen cloth and some of our best silverware and crystal. When we arrived on horseback, everything would be ready. The food was carried in English wicker baskets and consisted of cold *consommé*, in thermos bottles, and ham or chicken sandwiches on bread which was sliced very, very thin. Tomato and lettuce salad with olive oil and vinegar dressing, French rolls, many kinds of delicious flaky French pastry prepared by our chef, and apples, pears, nectarines, and peaches. Often we had clotted cream spread on bread and topped with home-made strawberry jam.

Mother wore an English habit, with a tall hat and blue veil, and rode side-saddle. She had done a great deal of fox-hunting in England as a young girl, and rode very well. I wore very long and puffed-out brown whipcord breeches, made by Tautz in London. My leather boots, which came to the knee, were from Peale's of England. With this I wore a black ribbed jacket, very tight-fitting, with a foulard or white stock about my neck.

Father was an excellent rider and seldom missed his early morning canter. In New York, we often rode together around the reservoir in Central Park, the cops touching their hats respectfully as we passed.

This was a busy, happy, productive period in Father's life. He was following the efforts of the Wright brothers, and even went along on one of their early flights. Marconi on his yacht the *Electra* and Father on the *North Star* spent days exchanging wireless messages across the Baltic Sea. His New York subways were an unqualified success, and his close personal friendship with many of the crowned heads of Europe must have done much to sweeten the bitter fact of his ostracism from the Vanderbilt family.

'A bunch of big fellows—a Commodore, a President, an Admiral—' Mother scrawled in her expressive hand across the bottom of a snapshot of Father (then Commodore of the New York Yacht Club) on the deck of the *North Star* with a Navy admiral and President Theodore Roosevelt.

Grandfather Vanderbilt had been dead for eight years now. Aunt Elsie came occasionally to tea, but her husband, my Uncle Alfred, had never crossed our threshold. When Father and he met in public, they nodded coldly, but did not speak.

Once in a great while, Father took my sister Grace and me to the Breakers for tea. Mother never went along on these occasions. I can remember how terrifyingly huge and cold the Breakers struck me as a child, with its high throne chairs and suits of armour. The music *salon* seemed as vast as an auditorium and as lifeless as a museum. Grandmother greeted us stiffly, seated on a high-backed red velvet chair. She asked a lot of perfunctory questions about our lessons, but hardly seemed to listen to our whispered answers. At the end of the visit, she and Father drank tea while a footman in a white wig brought us children French vanilla ice cream with the thickest, richest, creamiest chocolate sauce I have ever tasted. Afterwards, as we shook hands politely and turned to leave, the food lay cold in the pit of my stomach, like the cold little chill about my heart.

Grandmother was very fond of some of her daughters-in-law and showed them great generosity. When Reggie married Gloria Morgan, his second wife, Grandmother asked them to lunch with her at the Ambassador Hotel. During the meal she inquired, 'Has Gloria received her pearls yet?'

'Now, Mother,' pleaded Reggie, 'you know I would love to give Gloria pearls, but I do not intend buying her a cheap necklace, and I cannot afford the kind I would like.'

'Please bring me a pair of scissors,' the dowager summoned the *maître d'hôtel*. She then snipped off a third, or about $70,000 worth of the rope around her neck.

'There you are, Gloria,' she said fondly to her new daughter-in-law. 'All Vanderbilt women have pearls.'

Mother never did receive a wedding present from her, but when Alfred married Elsie French, Grandmother sent the bride a diamond diadem.

In the fall of 1907, Aunt Gladys, father's youngest sister, became engaged to a member of the old Hungarian nobility, Count Lâszló Széchényi. Remarked a Vienna court official to a *New York Times* reporter: 'Miss Vanderbilt will be received at court at Budapest, but not in Vienna, unless the Emperor should dispense with the proof of nobility with respect to sixteen of her ancestors, which otherwise she would be required by Austrian court etiquette to furnish.

'Such a concession is sometimes made, and very likely it would be made in the case we are speaking of, out of consideration for the social standing of Count Széchényi and the importance of the Vanderbilt family.'

Aunt Gladys had been a girl of ten when her father disinherited her brother. Now she was twenty-one and, from having spent so much time abroad, was as cosmopolitan in viewpoint as my mother. Her gentle nature shrank from any kind of discord; she was the first of Father's family to become fast friends with Mother.

'Dear Grace,' she wrote from the Rue de Varenne in Paris on the first of September, 1907. 'Neily may already have told you of my engagement to Lâszló Széchényi but I want you to hear about it from me, too. It is not to be announced until October 3rd so please be *very* careful and not tell a single soul, for we should feel dreadfully if it got out before that day.

'I hope that you will still be at Newport when we arrive about the 25th and that I shall surely see you there.

'With love, and please destroy this letter! Affectionately, Gladys.'

It was typical of Mother that not only did she *not* destroy the letter, but I'm sure revealed the news by a multitude of sly hints and insinuations. Mother was hopeless at keeping secrets.

A month later, Gladys and her dapper, moustached fiancé, wearing the uniform of his Hussar regiment, arrived at the Breakers. Father went over to a small family dinner honouring his sister and the Count. I understand that my Mother was also invited but, as usual, flatly refused to enter her mother-in-law's house.

By this time, Grandmother Vanderbilt's social prestige was nil, while Mother's social star had soared to the zenith. Now it was my mother's 'list' which was all-important, for she wielded enough influence to cut dead with impunity whomever she chose. Her first dinner party at Sherry's, to which no Vanderbilts were invited, established her as a promising new social leader; with her charming capture of Prince Henry, the Kaiser's brother, she became *the* representative of the wealthy Vanderbilt clan.

Her diamond and emerald jewellery, gifts from Father and her two sisters, were the talk of two continents. The guest list of her fabulous Fête of Roses made other hostesses swoon with envy. With the acquisition of the *North Star*, one of the world's most luxurious private yachts, my parents reached a degree of intimacy with royal racing circles unprecedented by any Americans. The marriage of Mother's niece, May Goelet, to the Duke of Roxburghe strengthened my parents' already strong ties with the Court of St. James, as did the appointment of Uncle Mungo to the post of British Ambassador to the United States.

If Grandmother Vanderbilt had once secretly longed to wave society's sceptre, the tragic events of her life had long since dulled such ambitions and erased all traces of humour or gaiety in her sombre, plain-featured face.

As she grew older, I suspect that her fierce family pride burned even brighter and that she longed to see the Vanderbilt clan as firmly joined as the great granite and marble walls of the Breakers, the monument her husband had built to posterity.

For eleven years she had shunned my mother, and hardly communicated with my father, even when he was nearly dying of typhoid. Now the reasons for her hatred, whatever they had been at the beginning, must have seemed less important than the unity of the family to which she had given a lifetime of devotion.

Perhaps, too, it was her elation over her sixth and youngest child's engagement, which brought a distinguished foreign title into her family at last, that thawed for an instant the icy reserve about her lonely heart.

'We should all have luncheon together tomorrow somewhere,' Grandmother announced happily at the end of the dinner honouring the Hungarian count, her future son-in-law.

Father and his sister Gladys had been talking together at one corner of the room. Now Father unexpectedly spoke up.

'Why not at Beaulieu?' he said.

An electric silence fell. Everyone looked at Grandmother, expecting a cold refusal.

Instead, to my father's amazement, she accepted humbly, in a tone of full surrender. 'Very well. If Grace will not come to me'— she paused and seemed to continue with difficulty—'then I shall go to her.'

Chapter Ten

I WAS nine years old by the time Grandmother Vanderbilt first came to our house for dinner.

She arrived alone, a petite, straight-backed figure in black velvet with festoons of white matched pearls which began at her throat and dangled down almost to her knees.

Gerald, our portly English butler, escorted her to the drawing-room. 'Mrs. Vanderbilt,' he announced quietly, and withdrew. There was nothing in his expression to indicate the triumphant end of eleven years of bitter and unyielding intrafamily warfare.

Of course I had often wondered about the strange feud. When I asked Mother why Grandmother Vanderbilt never came to our house, not even for tea, Mother explained that Grandfather Vanderbilt and Grandfather Wilson had been business rivals. Her clever, resourceful father had outmanœuvred the chairman of the board of the New York Central Railroad in a business deal; for this, she said, the Vanderbilts could never forgive the Wilsons. We maintained this polite fiction, my Mother and I, long after I learned it was not true.

To me, the secret of the senior Vanderbilts' resentment of my mother is still a profound enigma. But I can well understand Mother's rancour. I have often marvelled at the feminine capacity to adjust to the inevitable heartaches of life. A woman can be deceived, cheated, neglected, or betrayed, and still manage to preserve a warm and magnanimous heart. But there is one slight she can seldom forgive or forget, and that is the social snub.

Most men fail to understand this. When Grandmother Vanderbilt entered our drawing-room for the first time, Father jumped to his feet with an expression of touching joy. His thin, sensitive hands were trembling as he clasped to him that cold-looking, indomitable little figure so elegantly dressed and bejewelled. Tenderly he drew his estranged parent over to where Mother sat beneath her richly glowing tapestries.

Mother smiled and extended her hand with a graceful regal motion. Thus she received at her box in the Diamond Horseshoe, when important social figures trooped dutifully in to pay their respects during the *entr'actes*. Never, never, did she go to *them*.

Mother had finally forced my proud grandmother to her knees, but Father's sister Gertrude still remained aloof. The angular young *débutante* was now a striking-looking woman with great style and a kind of cold, brilliant charm. I remember that her husband, Harry Payne Whitney, sometimes affected high-collared Russian blouses of amethyst silk. He was stunningly handsome, with a head like an Adonis, and was one of the few men in this country who could lay his hands upon $5,000,000 in cash within an hour. Two attractive children, Sonny and Flora, had been born to the Whitneys. They were about the same age as my sister and I, and lived but a few doors from us at Newport, but we were forbidden by my mother ever to have anything to do with them.

The only Vanderbilt Mother seemed to entertain any fondness for was Gladys (which my aunt pronounced Glay-dis). Father's youngest sister used to be a wholesome-looking girl who wore tub frocks and glasses. But now that she had become a member of the highest Hungarian nobility, the Countess proceeded to become a hostess of the utmost chic and distinction. Withal, she maintained a quiet, steady affection for her family, and as the years went by she came to lean upon my father more and more. Between them blossomed a late-flowering but very sweet and deep affection.

And so after long years of estrangement, Grandmother and Aunt Gladys decided to become related to my mother. All three of these ladies lived according to a set of social rules, prohibitions, and taboos as complicated and inexorable as the laws of the Medes and the Persians. The highest cultivation of manners, they believed, enabled one to conceal from the world one's true feelings.

So each was prepared to go through the outward forms of family harmony—the exchange of gifts, notes of sympathy, flowers, card dropping, and all the rest of a strictly prescribed routine. Never again was the Vanderbilt feud a subject for speculation in the yellow press, to my father's intense relief. Yet one look at my mother's face as she greeted my grandmother that evening long ago, and I sensed, child-like, that her smile was the flash of sun on the surface of a glacier.

As I think back to my grandmother, I am struck once again by her truly extraordinary self-discipline. 'We cannot always control the desires of others,' she sometimes remarked, sadly, 'but,' and her beady Indian eyes (as Mother called them) glowed with determination, 'most certainly we can control our own.'

I was told that she suffered from the obsession that every unmarried female in the United States yearned to marry one of her sons and that no trick was too scurrilous, no deceit too shocking, to propel these hopefuls towards their goal.

To her, the sublime pinnacle of social success was to attain the title of Mrs. Vanderbilt.

Ironically enough, of all the daughters-in-law Grandmother eventually acquired, none of them, except my mother, even remotely filled the requirements of a great social leader. Yet Grandmother stubbornly refused to admit this.

Her son Reggie seemed her particular favourite, possibly because he was for ever in hot water. At the time of his second marriage, Reggie was so afflicted with insomnia that he and his young bride, Gloria, kept open house for their friends until four or five o'clock in the morning.

Reggie found formal society a profound and crushing bore populated by dolts and dullards. Yet, fantastically enough, I can remember a family dinner when Grandmother Vanderbilt turned to his wife during a pause in the conversation and said, 'When I am gone, my dear Gloria, *you* will be Mrs. Vanderbilt.'

Gloria, then in her twenties, looked her surprise. Mother broke in crisply. 'Nonsense, Neily is older than Reggie. When that day comes, then *I* shall be Mrs. Vanderbilt.'

Grandmother, with a noncommittal expression, dug into her grapefruit.

'Really,' my gentle father remarked, aghast. 'Must we quarrel about such a ridiculous subject? You are all Mrs. Vanderbilts here.'

But of course he was aware, as we all were, that to be Mrs. Cornelius Vanderbilt or Mrs. Alfred or Reginald Vanderbilt was a far cry from that sublimely lonely pinnacle—*the* Mrs. Vanderbilt.

Aunt Gloria wrote in her memoirs that there seemed to be no point of contact between Reggie and Neily, adding that the younger brother found my father ridiculously stilted, formal, and pompous. The beautiful Gloria, on the other hand, found my father 'an extremely shy and charming man who, had he been allowed to lead his own life, would have led it quite differently'.

But Father was a Vanderbilt. He had been reared by his parents in the firm belief that they were America's aristocracy, embodying in their lives and actions all that was fine, honourable, and Christian. Theirs was a sacred God-given trust to maintain these standards.

My sister and I were brought up like European royalty; indeed my mother grew to think of herself as a kind of American royalty. 'Dear, poor Marie Antoinette,' she once remarked. 'I feel so sorry for her. If the revolution ever came to this country, I would be the first to go.'

Father, too, believed in his special destiny, but—unlike his two pleasure-loving brothers—he coupled his intense family pride with a deep sense of public service. As his father before him had busied himself with the affairs of the church, missions, the crippled, and the sick, Father gave generously of his time, money, and attention to organizations like the Salvation Army, the Seamen's Institute, and the National Guard.

He also served on the boards of some twenty corporations, and at one time joined the rosters of more gentlemen's clubs than any other society person in New York. These included the ultra-exclusive Brook Club, the Piping Rock Club near Oyster Bay, the Turf and Field, and the Meadowbrook—at one time, at Mother's insistence, he belonged to as many as twenty-five different clubs.

Father was also named by the Reverend Charles Wilbur Nicholls at the turn of the century as one of the 'ultrafashionable' men of New York.

I can still remember the simply amazing number of coats my Father owned—a fur-lined top coat for the opera; an Inverness (also fur-lined); a chesterfield in black; a long, loose sack overcoat, silk-faced, for spring and early autumn; a double-breasted Newmarket coat; a single-breasted Prince Henry coat; a Strand coat; rain and steamer coats; yachting suits; a double-breasted ulster; homespun golf jackets; and a short covert coat for in-between seasons.

'Your Father is waiting in the grand foyer, Master Neil,' a foot-man, puffing from his climb up four flights of stairs, announced to me at the door of my bedroom. This was on the top floor of our Fifth Avenue brownstone, next to the servants' rooms. Unlike

Mother's and Father's rooms and the guest suites downstairs, which were furnished with great lavishness, my room had straight metal furniture, painted white, and simple muslin curtains. In the middle of the room stood a single bed with a white coverlet. It was all I needed, for I was never, under any circumstances, allowed to invite friends overnight.

It was September, 1913, and Father and I were about to travel together to Concord, New Hampshire, where I would enter his beloved alma mater, St. Paul's preparatory school. Mother was still at Bad Kissingen in Germany, taking the cure. After this, she would go to Interlaken, Switzerland for a 'nach cure', or aftercure, or 'cure of the cure'. Then Paris. We did not expect to see her again until Christmas.

I turned to my old English Nanny, Miss Coxhead, and gave her a final embrace, feeling the swift blind sting of tears. 'Work hard, Master Neil,' she admonished, 'and write often. You will like St. Paul's, I fancy. Just like Eton and Harrow. they say it is. A real gentlemen's school,' she finished proudly.

The tears came harder as she adjusted my tweed visor cap. As I turned to go, I caught sight in the mirror of a tall, painfully thin, narrow-shouldered boy, all arms and legs, in an English-cut suit bereft of the deceit of shoulder-padding, with the pants too long, the sleeves too short, and the jacket too tight, in the English school-boy tradition.

I rushed down the stairway two steps at a time, the footman struggling after with my bags. Below, on the ground floor, six footmen in maroon livery stood at attention in the foyer to bid me adieu. Indeed, our hard-pressed English butler often complained that our family lived with more pomp and circumstance than many of the crowned heads of Europe.

Father—tall, handsome, and debonair, with his black-pointed vandyke beard—stood drawing on his thick French suède gloves. He wore a pleated white shirt, stiff high collar, dark-grey spats and derby, and carried a gold-headed cane.

I kept my head down, afraid he would see my tears and find them unbecoming. Instead, a kindly smile transformed his usually grave expression, and he slung one arm in a comradely fashion about my shoulders. He looked happy and excited, as if this journey back into his past meant a great deal to him.

Fifth Avenue was thronged with narrow, high-topped automobiles, which by then had almost displaced the horse and carriage. Our chauffeur crept along at a sedate pace—not long before Father had been arrested on Madison Avenue for speeding at twenty-four miles an hour. He had actually been led into court by a policeman— a fantastic experience for a Vanderbilt.

Now the cops on the corners of the great avenue smiled and respectfully touched their caps as our black limousine came past. 'Morning, Captain,' they sang out to my National Guardsman father. Father, unsmiling, acknowledged the salute with a military nod.

At the depot I was surprised to discover that our private car was not there. This was a special Pullman for our exclusive use, with a dining- and living-room, bedrooms for us, and galley bunks for three or four servants. Mother was for ever trying to 'chintzy things up', as Father put it, but in this she failed; for as far back as I can remember the car was decorated with green felt and plain wicker chairs.

'This way, sonny,' Father urged me into an ordinary Pullman car. We pushed our way through strangers to reach our double compartment, Father's valet disappearing into the room next door.

'Sit down, sonny.' Father indicated a chair. I did so, still surprised. It was the first time in my fifteen years that I had ever travelled on a regular railway car.

'No doubt you will see lots of your classmates on this train,' Father said with a smile. 'It's a special train for St. Paul's.'

This, then, was the reason we were not travelling in our private car.

Father took out a gold cigarette-case and lit a custom-made Turkish cigarette bearing the crossed gold insignia of the New York Yacht Club and his own private yacht signal.

'I designed this yacht signal while I was at St. Paul's,' Father remarked, regarding the cigarette. 'Two crossed V's—you see? I flew it on my very first sailboat. Father gave it to me as a birthday surprise.'

He appeared lost in sad reflection for a moment.

'Someday, when you're a bit older, I'll get you a sailboat. Now then, I know you'll like St. Paul's, sonny.' He smiled encouragingly.

'The instructors are splendid, and the scholastic standards very high.'

I sighed, turning my head away. I was well aware that Father during all his years at St. Paul's had stood in the top ten of his class, even above that serious young man John D. Rockefeller, Jr.

'Of course, you'll have lots of sports,' Father went on, 'rowing, hockey, baseball, football—cricket—you'll like that. And ice-skating and sledding—it gets way below zero at Concord sometimes, plenty of snow and ice.'

I winced. Sports never really appealed to me and, like my mother, I could not endure extreme cold and was for ever succumbing to the sniffles when subjected to it.

Presently, with the help of Father's valet, we dressed for dinner. It did not matter to Father that we were eating in a public diner; one always dressed for this occasion. I thought I detected a few snickers as we strolled into the crowded dining-car full of business-suited New Englanders and noisy small boys. The steward, however, snapped to attention immediately and ushered us past a long line of waiting people. 'Good evening, Mr. Vanderbilt,' he greeted my father. 'This way, sir.'

Railroad people usually managed to recognize my father. The history of his quarrel with his father, the thousands of miles he had travelled on inspection trips over the lines of which he was a director, the many times he drove long freight trains, testing one or another of his inventions, had made him a legendary figure in their eyes.

'Look at the limey,' I heard a boy remark loudly across the aisle. 'And *listen* to him,' he hooted, imitating the broad English 'a' I had been taught to use since childhood, 'I cawn't make up my mind, Fawther, what to have for *dinnah*.'

Snickers greeted this humorous sally, and I blushed to the roots of my hair.

Father appeared not to have heard them. 'I was talking with Mr. Guggenheim the other day,' he continued (Father and Mother seldom used first names no matter how intimate the acquaintance), 'and he was saying that if you should aim for Yale or M.I.T.—I would prefer to have you study engineering at Yale, naturally—he would be glad to consider you for a position with their mining interests in South America.'

'Yes, Father,' I answered dutifully. 'How kind of Mr. Guggenheim.'

Mother, I knew, wanted me to be a banker, like her father R. T. Wilson. Or else a stockbroker—these two positions having the highest cachet in society's book. It seemed impossible to explain that the only thing I had ever wanted to be was a journalist. Their distaste for this profession was so pronounced that I had long ago given up even mentioning it. Not until years later, when I was working for William Randolph Hearst, did I have any inkling of why my parents resented the American press so bitterly.

As our train wound through the flame- and russet-coloured mountains of New England that September day of 1913, Father decided the time had come to tell me the facts of life.

It seems incredible that any boy of fifteen could have been as uninformed as I was. But until this time my state of ignorance had been quite deliberately fostered by my parents, my nurses, my tutors, and scores of other ever-present adults. Indeed, I had hardly enjoyed an unescorted moment since I was born.

I can imagine the paralysing effect of my innocent, then disbelieving, then shocked blue eyes riveted upon my parent. He stammered, mopped his forehead, and gazed with distress out of the train window as his voice dropped lower and lower and finally, in despair, ceased altogether. This was the first and last time he ever talked to me about sex.

'My dear wife,' Father wrote to Mother during one of her prolonged cures abroad at Bad Nauheim: 'I arrived back from the inspection trip yesterday, quite tired out by six days and nights on the train with no rest "ashore" and very much in need of a bath. I was told of the enclosed outrageous article in "Town Topics" of last Thursday, so I am sending it to you. Isn't it perfectly scandalous? I hear that the lady is still abroad and that she is expected back this week. She has been away since about the time you sailed and you *must* know how foolish the whole thing is. I am more than sorry to have to bother you with it, but it is only right that you should know.

'Am really too disturbed but of course you know how ridiculous it is and so does anyone who knows anything about things in New York. Please don't mind it too much. Don't overdo in Paris about clothes and shopping and lose the good of the sun and rest. As ever, C.'

Enclosed in Father's letter was a clipping from *Town Topics* about a certain handsome multimillionaire and a certain 'much-married' lady with 'limpid black eyes' and 'alabaster shoulders' who had been 'one of the prettiest *débutantes* in New York.' The item —using no names—described an indiscreet romance which, it said, had all society tongues wagging.

In his next letter to Mother Father wrote: 'Your letter depressed me more than I can say and I am so very sorry that you felt (for I hope you still do not feel) so frightfully depressed. I fear my sending you that horrible clipping won't help cheer you up, either. This week "Town Topics" had nothing at all. I consulted DeLancey [?] Nicholl about it and found there was nothing of course legally libellous in it. I told him that any denial would make it worse, but how long the *not being mentioned* will last, I don't know, as they are such a scoundrelly lot of unprincipled people connected with that paper.'

Now the tattle sheet *Town Topics* was edited by a certain Colonel Mann, whose forte was not libel but blackmail. His reporters mingled with the butlers and chambermaids of the rich, but in general his best spies were the hangers-on who never quite managed to crash society's magic circle and who were full of spite and bile towards those who had snubbed them. Mother, naturally, had many such enemies.

To avoid libel suits, Editor Mann presented unpleasant gossip anonymously (as he did in Father's case), but this always pained him, for he would much rather be paid to have the news suppressed. Thus, when he was finally brought to public trial, it was discovered that he had blackmailed J. P. Morgan to the tune of $2,500, had taken Collis B. Huntington for $5,000, and had managed to gouge from Father's gay and cosmopolitan uncle, Willie K. Vanderbilt, Sr., a whopping $25,000.

It was inevitable that my brilliant father, so darkly handsome, scion of such a powerful and wealthy clan, should be pursued by beautiful women wherever he went and that columnists should make copy of this fact.

When I was about ten or eleven, I became conscious for the first time of raised quarrelling voices in my parents' rooms. Sometimes I would hear the violent slamming of doors and Father's footsteps stamping angrily off. Often they quarrelled about trivial things, such as the fact that, although Father preferred showers to baths, Mother refused to instal any in our homes. I think she thought them un-English. So whenever Father wanted a shower he was forced to go to one of his clubs.

More and more Father chafed at the restrictions of the role Mother wanted him to play—the distinguished host, the charming lunch and dinner companion, the frequenter of gentlemen's clubs.

When the pressure grew too strong, Father fled to his yacht or went off on manœuvres with the National Guard. As a soldier, he lived in a tent, doused his face daily with icy water at daybreak, ate army beans and hard tack, and frequently slept on the ground.

Mother, however, came to treasure more and more what were known as 'creature comforts'. I could not help resenting the fact that she seldom visited me at boarding school because she was then forced to sleep on a train or in some country hotel.

Mother's attitude is best expressed in a letter she wrote describing a 'harrowing' experience she once endured while travelling between French Lick, Indiana, where she had taken the cure, to Hot Springs, Virginia, for a 'nach' cure, or aftercure. She and Aunt May had interrupted their train trip to spend a few hours in Cincinnati with Speaker of the House Nicholas Longworth and his wife, Mother's great chum Alice Roosevelt.

'The Longworths met us in Cincinnati,' Mother wrote, 'and took us off to dine. At five the Longworths kindly took us to the train. I got in Car 2 and Aunt May in Car 3, both having staterooms in these cars. Before the train started they began to make the bed in my room so I said I would go talk to Aunt May a while.

'The porter said Car No. 3 had been placed three cars further back on the train, so I walked through three cars, but could not find Aunt May's stateroom. I turned and walked back, thinking I would return to my own room when, low and behold! I came to an engine!

'Frantically I said to a conductor, "Where is my Car No. 2?"

'He said, "I don't know. This is a special to Hot Springs."

'I said, "I must get back to Cars No. 2 and 3." But, alas, they had both been switched off and I was in a train full of men—electrical engineers who were coming as delegates to a convention at Hot Springs! Finally we discovered my train across the platform, *just leaving*. Imagine my horror! They tried to stop the train, but off it went with Aunt May and two maids and Sophie and all my luggage —I didn't even have a coat, but I did have my purse.

'The conductor, when he heard my story, said he could give me a stateroom for the night for which I paid eight dollars!! And there I sat, frightened to death all night. I had the bed made up and I took off my hat and covered up with the old car blankets!! Of course I never slept all night. In the morning I used the *car soap and towels* and made myself as presentable as possible. Isn't it funny to think of your poor little Mother off by herself, having to put up with all these discomforts? But I was thankful to find myself en route for Hot Springs and "beggars cannot be choosers" I was *very* glad to have the blankets, soap and towels!

'I wired Aunt May who, of course, was frightened to death until she got word from me about eleven that evening. Now it all seems a very funny episode, but at the time it was all *very terrifying*!'

Back in his office at 30 Pine Street, after leaving me at St. Paul's, Father wrote: 'Have the older boys "hazed" you much? I hope not but you *have* to expect some and don't think it will last, for in a very short time everyone settles down and you get quite a different and more homelike feeling about the place . . . I hope the Latin exam went well, and am anxiously awaiting news of it . . . Let me know all the news.'

Mother stayed on in Germany and then went to England for the christening of my little cousin-once-removed. After nine years of marriage, the Duchess of Roxburghe (Cousin May Goelet) had given birth to an heir. Aunt May, who was with her daughter at Floors Castle, wrote to Mother: 'May is improving and little Lord Bowmont (as the nurse likes to call him) is sleeping and eating and growing splendidly . . . The King has written a charming letter beginning "Dear Bumble" and saying he and the Queen wish to be godparents to the son and heir. It is very unusual for both King and Queen to be godparents. Isn't it wonderfully kind and nice of them? If May only knew how to take advantage and make friends . . .'

The baby was christened George Victor, Marquis of Bowmont, with Queen Mary and Aunt May as godmothers and King George and Lord Alastair as godfathers. In the family, little George Victor soon became Cousin 'Bo-bo'—his own childish way of saying 'Bowmont'. 'Bo-bo' is the present Duke of Roxburghe.

More invitations for gay parties in England kept Mother postponing her return to New York. She was too occupied even to find time for her usual hurried notes.

'I suppose Father wrote you about the wire we had from Mother,' Sister wrote me early in December, 1913, 'saying to arrange all about our party as of course she will be back 60 times too late. Well, I have been setting to work at it, also with the kind help of Mrs. Baylies. We decided, after all, it is best not to have fancy dress but to have a dancing party and cotillion like last year. I am having a most strenuous time arranging about the invitations etc., etc., etc. Please answer me at once, *immediately* returning the *two lists* I sent you, of boys and girls. Mrs. B. said to ask about 60 in all as a lot surely will give out. Please mark the boys and girls you don't want me to ask.

'Is it not better to omit all those boys we have never had before, as Mama generally only wants those we know the parents of, etc. Therefore be quick, marking those you think you do not want. Write instantly please. I think the school is awfully nice but you are the only boy, of course, in it. All the others pooh! Crowds of love, Sister.'

At St. Paul's I succumbed to terrible homesickness. I had been away to boarding school once before, but that had been to a small school of some twenty students called Pine Lodge, in the pine barrens of New Jersey. Each of the boarders there brought a horse, and the emphasis of the school was mainly on riding. 'Pine Lodge did not advance my studies,' I summed it up in my diary, 'but promoted love of nature and horsemanship.'

Because he had his heart set upon my entering Yale, his alma mater, Father had decided that it would be wiser for me to attend a school like St. Paul's with its strong emphasis on classical education. I felt lost and bewildered in a school of four hundred boys. Even at this age, I felt a strong sympathy for the underdog, inspired perhaps by my hero Teddy Roosevelt, and dreamed of exposing the plots against the poor by the unfeeling rich. Such an attitude did not endear me to the highly class-conscious student body, and when I attempted to build a hydroplane—a project which delighted my scientific Father—and it sank at the moment of launching, I was—as I noted in my diary—'much mocked by the whole school'.

Father's brisk, down-to-earth letters did little to cheer me up. He wrote me in his cramped, inhibited-looking hand, extremely difficult to read, on thin white office stationery. His letters came regularly once a week, but the contents revealed little of the affection and concern which his friends assured me he felt towards his only son and namesake.

'How do you spell "sure" and "rehearsal"? Look them up in the dictionary and remember in writing.' Or, 'Do you need any more allowance?'

'Come on, Neil,' my classmates urged me at St. Paul's. 'Let's go down to the drugstore and you can buy us all chocolate sundaes.'

'But I don't have any money,' I protested.

This was greeted with hoots of disbelief. 'His dad's Cornelius Vanderbilt! And he doesn't have any money!'

'I only get fifty cents a week,' I maintained stubbornly.

'Then charge it, charge it!'

'If I did,' I said feelingly, 'my father would come up here and give me the licking of my life.'

They called me stingy and selfish. I just couldn't make them understand that my father's millions had nothing to do with me.

One drizzly grey spring day, when I was recuperating from an attack of *grippe* in St. Paul's infirmary, the nurse brought in a pale-grey letter with 'Master Cornelius Vanderbilt' scrawled on front in Mother's large, firm, exuberant hand. It was postmarked from Germany, and she had written it on my birthday.

'My poor little son,' Mother wrote sympathetically: 'It is too dreadful to think of you being so sad and lonely. This idea of sending children away from their homes and parents seems a strange thing to me, but by most of the people in the world it is considered the best way to form the character of a boy—and also a better means of education than remaining at home. You know how *I* hate it! And how very, very difficult it was for me to make up my mind to allow you to go away, but you and I will have to *try our best* to put up with the separation and be very brave.

'I went to Paris Tuesday 22nd and stayed at the Ritz three days. That was *pandemonium*, dressmakers etc, etc. every minute—and the telephone ringing, and French friends calling to see me etc. Then, after giving my orders for clothes and Sister's, I left Paris

Saturday night at nine o'clock and got to Frankfort at eleven a.m. Sunday 27th. Princess Charlotte had asked me to join her there for the day. So I immediately drove to the Frankfurter Hof where she received me and we talked until luncheon time. Then I took a bath and put on a 'swell' frock and joined the Princess and her Sister, Princess Frederick Carl of Hesse, and went with them to a sort of Horse Show where good-looking officers were showing off horses. It was great fun.

'We sat in a large box (two bouquets of flowers for the two sisters of the Emperor!) in the centre of the stand, and after a while went down and stood by the show ring and afterwards had tea on the lawn . . . Monday I saw the doctor. He says my heart is weak but not so bad as two years ago. Today I have had my second bath and will finish here about May 28. Then two weeks of rest somewhere . . . I am going to send this by way of New York so Sister can read it first, as I really can't write it all over again. Much, much fond love and many, many affectionate kisses from your devoted Mother.'

It did not help matters that during my stormy years of young adolescence, Mother was so seldom home. During the year 1913 she was in New York City only three months. By this time, she was so caught up in the exhausting demands of her busy public life that she felt the need of longer and longer recuperative visits to the various spas of Europe. From her letters, I knew she missed us. I wrote to her almost every day, pouring out my youthful grievances, large and small. When her letters in reply finally came, they were always brimming over with sympathy and affection.

Before we acquired 640 Fifth Avenue, there was a lot of discussion about building a house big enough for Mother's splendid entertainments. Mother, who greatly admired Aunt Belle's house in London, wrote to her to look for an architect who would submit plans. At this time Aunt Belle was a widow; Sidney, her oldest son, was at Oxford, and Michael was preparing to go there.

Aunt Belle, not at all pleased by Mother's commission, replied rather acidly from London: 'It is a perfect waste of time for me to see architects alone. I would gladly do so if I could settle anything, but if you are to build a big and beautiful and costly house and have it planned, you must come over and see and study houses here where they know how to build them, or else have it built at home under your own instructions. I know getting a man to work hard on designs *without* consulting you would be nonsense . . .

'I am sending you 45 yards of silk. I think it is such a lovely colour so I have bought it for your new bouffant evening dress. It is a damask or brocatel and is just coming into high fashion here, even though it is of Italian origin, but with yards and yards of tulle under it, you will be the most beautiful whirling dervish in Newport.

'I am enclosing the bill. Please send a draft to the people direct immediately, as I have promised to have them paid within three weeks. If possible, I would have the draft made out without mentioning your name, as I am afraid if I say "Vanderbilt" I shall never get anything cheap there again . . .'

The closely knit Wilson family circle had been broken. Two years before Grandfather Wilson's death, in November, 1910, Grandmother had died. Aunt Belle and Aunt May, both widows, spent much of their time in London, the South of France, or Italy —rarely returning to the United States.

Aunt May Goelet explained why she shunned summers at Newport in a letter which she wrote to Mother from the Ritz in Paris: 'I hope to sail about June 25th but, aside from the joy and happiness of being near you, I am not looking forward to my return or summer at Newport. It will mean such a lot of trouble and endless domestic worries, running that big establishment—just a housekeeper for the 27 servants, the 8 coachmen and grooms and 12 gardeners. I feel Ogden intended Ochre Court as a home for his children as well as for me, so I hope to gain some sense of pleasure in fulfilling what I believe to have been his wish.

'I haven't enjoyed anything so much in years as Belle's and my little journey to Italy and it seems such a waste of time coming back here when there is so much that is interesting to be seen in travelling. Now I am missing Belle as she returned last week to London.

'I see the Duc de Luynes nearly every afternoon with that perrectly horrible Fouquier, Boris' friend, which means mischief. I met Boris [the Russian Grand Duke Boris] the other day, gay boy as ever and looking decidedly fat. He now weighs over 300. Belle perhaps has written you about meeting him at Cherbourg with his little lady! A fine thing to do, going there openly with her, but they don't care what they do here in France in high society. Just so long as they are high enough. Grand Duke Alexander was seen dining with Harry Lehr the other day. How the Russian Court has fallen!

'What are you doing about clothes? There is actually nothing very pretty and the prices are dreadfully high. Not an evening dress to be had at Callot's which are much the prettiest, for under $85. There is a new style now about to break. Some of the fashion papers call it "paniers". It is all done with an effect of drapery, using up scores of yards of damask and linen and lots of tulle. There is a little inclination to drapery in the day clothes, too, which has really looped up skirts. Not very pretty as it shows the ankles, which is what you might expect on boulevards but not on the Rue de la Paix.'

In the early spring of 1912, Aunt May, who must have been somewhat astonished, had sent this inquiry from London to Mother who was in Paris: 'Teenie Mills told me that you are much interested in politics. Perhaps you can tell me who is to be our next President?'

It was true that Mother was deeply interested in the outcome of the presidential election that year. Theodore Roosevelt, having served three years following President McKinley's death while in office, and one term to which he was elected, had refused the nomination in 1908 and gone to Africa to hunt wild game. Four years later, with the Republican party split into two factions, one for the re-election of President Taft and the other against it, Theodore Roosevelt was urged to run again. The Roosevelt followers were called 'insurgents' by the opposition (later christened by T.R. 'the Bull Moose Party'.)

The convention was held in Chicago in late June, and Mother rushed across the Atlantic to attend. Before she left Paris she wrote to Father: 'Today I lunched at the Gays' and had a treat, meeting the Conservateur of the Arts Decoratifs and also the Conservateur of the Louvre and the Luxembourg. You can imagine how interesting the talk was. Yesterday I sat next to Rodin at a luncheon at our Embassy and had Gaston Calmette of the Figaro on the other side . . . Charlie Carroll tells me that Elsie [Mrs. William Woodward] went to a prize fight the other night. Rather a vulgar taste, don't you think? He seemed quite surprised and shocked by it and said New York society would shun her parties from now on. I also heard *she has taken up smoking*. Isn't that too crude for words! . . .

'It now looks as if Roosevelt will surely win and you can then go to Germany (as U.S. Ambassador) and I will come and stay in

Berlin. You *must* arrange this. Just think how exciting and interesting it will be. Remember I am not joking—this is dead serious . . .'

Father and Mother both attended the Republican convention which opened June 20 in Chicago. Mother went every day to sit in a box in the Coliseum, usually between Nicholas Longworth and Father's close friend Richard Crane, the plumbing king, whose empire Mother referred to delicately as 'a pipe business'.

Mother had never before experienced anything like those convention scenes. Since the swarming crowds made it almost impossible to leave and return to their box seats from the time the convention opened at 11 a.m. until it adjourned at 6 p.m., Mrs. Longworth and Mother took to carrying box lunches with them.

It was a short convention, with never any question of the outcome. The Taft group was in complete control. Remarked Chauncey Depew, a member of the New York delegation, two days before the final balloting, 'It has all been so well arranged that it is merely a matter now of which of the corpses gets the most flowers.'

That was the end of Mother's hopes for an ambassadorship for my father. When Woodrow Wilson defeated both Taft and Roosevelt in the November election and became the next President, he appointed James W. Gerard as Ambassador to Germany. Gerard had been one of Mother's beaux before her marriage and was always a devoted friend.

'But it's a girl's hat! You don't mean I've got to wear a silly thing like that. Honestly, Mother, it's crazy—it looks just terrible!'

Bitterly I yanked at the silver brocade, twisted into a turban, on my head. The feather duster of blue ostrich, which rose at the back of the turban, billowed out over one of my ears.

Mother straightened the turban. 'It's a little loose,' she said. 'Miss Henderson, will you see about that?' Turning back to me, she went on: 'Of course you're going to wear it, darling—and look very handsome. It's just what a young prince at the Persian court would wear. See how beautiful this blue and silver coat is? Slip it on, Neil —oh, Sister, there's something wrong with the way those pearls are fastened. Nana, will you straighten them for her?'

We were in the playroom at Beaulieu, where Mother had come to see Grace and me try on the costume which had arrived that morning from New York. Mother, dressed in an amethyst-coloured linen suit and a black cartwheel hat laden with roses, would be leaving soon for Bailey's Beach. She had dropped her ruffled black lace parasol and gloves on my desk. Miss Henderson, the secretary, unobtrusive in the background, was scribbling in a notebook. On the floor was the box, from which foamed great sheets of glistening white tissue paper, in which the costumes had been packed.

Grace, now the centre of attention, turned slowly, displaying her rose-coloured skirt and creamy blouse, the loose cloth-of-gold coat with jewelled edges. Nana, like a hen mothering a single chick, fluffed out Sister's curls, and fastened the clasp holding ropes of artificial pearls beneath her chin.

'Very sweet.' Mother nodded with satisfaction. 'Yes, Baby, you look lovely. Very, very sweet. Neil, aren't you proud of your little sister?'

'It's all right for girls,' I said sulkily, 'but I don't see why I can't wear something like that boy we saw in the circus. The one who rode the elephant——'

'This is not a circus party,' Mother interrupted firmly. 'It is to be an Oriental ball. You and Sister are going to be a little Prince and Princess of Persia. When you see the magnificent costume your father is wearing you'll understand. Now I *must* rush!'

She took up the parasol, smoothed on a glove. 'Miss Henderson,' she said, 'you must personally check the costumes for the Persian quadrille. You have the list, haven't you? The purple gown is for Mrs. Tiffany, the blue one for Mrs. Herbert Harriman, the green for Mrs. Drexel, and the pink for my sister-in-law, Mrs. Richard Wilson. We must know tomorrow morning by telephone.'

The last words floated back to us as Mother and the secretary disappeared into the hall and down the broad, curving stairway.

Nana hurried us out of our Oriental splendour, shushing my muttered objections. I knew as well as she did that they were useless. Beaulieu in August of 1912 was a bubbling cauldron of activity, of strangers coming and going, of commotion outdoors, where a stage was being hammered together and a dance floor laid, and of tensions within the house, as an enlarged staff of servants worked with strained faces. Grace and I scarcely saw our parents.

It was exciting, if not entirely comfortable for us, since it was to be the first time we were to be allowed to attend a grown-up party.

Down at 30 Pine Street, in Father's New York office, no financial crisis could have involved more generalship, more diplomatic skirmishing, more attention to detail, or more boldly imaginative planning than Mother and her assistants gave to the Oriental ball—'the most extravagant affair of its kind ever seen in Newport', in the opinion of the New York *American*.

Again, as for the Fête of Roses, a tent theatre was built on the lawns. The Schubert theatrical company sent *The Merry Countess*, a musical comedy version of *Die Fledermaus*, which was playing in New York. 'I can give you the entire second act,' J. J. Schubert wrote, 'which includes a new ballet, a very remarkable dancing number done by the Dolly Sisters and some solo dances by Mlle. Dazie. I will send the entire scenic equipment, stage manager and orchestra conductor.'

The tent theatre was built high enough to 'clear the flower beds', lighted by four hundred lights and twenty Oriental lamps standing eight feet from the floor. There were three hundred chairs for the guests, as well as twenty divans, each eight feet long, covered with Oriental material and placed along the wall to form one huge divan 180 feet in length.

The theatre tent cost $900 for the evening, while constructing the pavilion and engaging a crew of electricians and master carpenters came to another $11,800. (All these bills and the correspondence are before me as I write.) Mother, who had recently inherited $3,000,000 from her father's estate, also paid for the costumes her friends wore in the four quadrilles.

My Aunt Gladys Széchényi led the Gypsy Quadrille; Mother danced in the Russian one; Aunt Marion Wilson headed the Persian ladies and gentlemen; and fifteen *débutantes* participated in a figure dance called the 'Four Seasons'. Sixty-three men and women took part in these quadrilles, and the cost of their costumes was slightly over $5,000.

Grace and I saw none of the dancing. After *The Merry Countess* and ice cream and cakes, we were turned over to Nana and sent to our beds.

Alice Roosevelt Longworth recalls the Oriental ball as 'such a heavenly party. I went as a Turkish princess and danced one of the midnight cotillions with Craig Wadsworth. The party went on and on until dawn and, after a marvellous breakfast, we all drove off to the Ocean Drive where I can remember gathering armfuls of golden rod.'

Emily Post, an old Newporter, wrote my mother next day: 'Dearest Grace, I want to add my congratulations to the many you have received. Your Ball was the most beautiful, brilliant and original one that has ever been given in this country or any other.'

Charles Dana Gibson, the artist and brother-in-law of Lady Nancy Astor, said: 'This *bal costumé* was really quite the most beautiful, and artistic entertainment I have seen either here or in Paris. There was so much imagination and thought in the whole conception, the Oriental colours of the whole pageant, the quadrilles, the dances and the music, it quite fired one's poetic senses.'

To Mrs. J. Borden Harriman, the Oriental ball was 'the most delightful evening I have ever spent,' and the Bey of Tunis, who danced in the Gypsy Quadrille, declared, 'I will never forget the delightful hours I have spent at Beaulieu and the splendours of the Arabian Nights Ball will remain impressed forever before my eyes.'

It was at this party that a guest offered the toast, 'To the intoxicating women and the intoxicated men of Newport.' Mother was so shocked that she never entirely forgave the man who said it.

When I returned to St. Paul's for the second term, Mother tried to help me get rid of the nickname 'Limey'. 'Do you think you would be more comfortable,' she wrote, 'if I got you a short jacket lined with sheepskin and corduroy knickers lined with leather like the workmen I saw in Concord? I asked where I could get them and they said in Boston. Surely none of the boys would jump on you for this, as they are American and workmen's things . . . I have been lunching and dining out every day and going to opera matinées— and dancing a good deal in the evenings. So you see how frivolous your Mother has been, but it is so nice to see all our friends again after all my cures last Spring and Autumn. I think I am feeling a great deal better these last days . . . Tomorrow Father begins his three days of drills and inspection.'

Father wrote: 'Sister is frightfully lonely without you and of course we all miss you *very* much indeed. I could not go away for Sunday, as I had to go with General O'Ryan to "review" the aeroplanes at Garden City. I went up in one of the Wright machines and stayed high up in the air for about 10 minutes. It was most interesting and I enjoyed it even more than my first flight of two years ago. Please write me soon and tell me all about yourself—how you are feeling and what you are doing.'

My father was as fascinated by airplanes and the possibility of travelling by air as he had been by Marconi's wireless. Father's first flight was something we all remembered because Mother was so upset about it. She was deathly afraid of flying. Even during the Second World War, when I urged her to make a trip by air because I thought it would be easier for her, she replied, 'I'll never fly except to escape from the enemy!'

Mother was at Newport on that Sunday when Father drove out to Garden City with General O'Ryan. There Father climbed into a flimsy-looking wooden crate piloted by George Beatty. Father was wearing large black goggles and, under his English tweed suit, a stylishly cut padded vest with a huge flaring collar. His hands, gloved in the softest of grey French suède, rested calmly in his lap. Looking every inch the impeccable gentleman that he was, Father waited with perfect composure for the take-off.

During the ten minutes that they circled the field, although they were only five hundred feet in the air, Beatty managed to do a heart-stopping dip and spiral.

'What will my wife say?' was Father's aghast remark as he stepped from the plane.

In an interview afterwards, he said that he had ordered a plane from the Wright brothers and intended to learn to pilot it himself.

Mother, when she heard about this incident, must have said a good deal. She changed his mind about buying a plane; he never did own one. She even persuaded him not to invest money in the crazy new flying machines. The only chance Father got to fly was when cruising with his cousin Willie K. Vanderbilt, Jr., who had a small private plane attached to the deck of his mammoth steam yacht.

'Your mother is a bully,' Father told me once, with a profound sigh. 'If she can't have her own way, there's simply no use arguing with her.'

At St. Paul's I kept a little diary which I have still. Here is one entry: 'My second term at St. Paul's was not as bad as my first, but during it my sister Grace was operated on for appendicitis. She had a very serious time and was in bed for a long time. Then my Great Uncle George Vanderbilt died. He and Father had never been on speaking terms but at his death we received the George Vanderbilt home on the corner of 51st and Fifth Avenue; also some 133 pictures of the best schools which are now at the Metropolitan Art Museum. Then I sprained my ankle . . .'

The new home which Father inherited after the death of his uncle in 1914 was 640 Fifth Avenue, cater-cornered from St. Patrick's Cathedral.

This mansion had been built thirty-five years earlier by William H. Vanderbilt, son of the Commodore, who was determined that it should be the finest private residence ever erected in this country. He gave his architect absolute *carte blanche*, and for two years six hundred labourers (including sixty sculptors specially imported from Europe for the job) toiled on the mansion. Although the outside of the warm-coloured brownstone was quite plain, as befitted the owner, who had begun his meteoric career as a Staten Island farmer, the interior was so lavishly conceived that when movie producers were looking for a house elaborate enough to copy for Rhett Butler's mansion in *Gone with the Wind*, they chose old photographs of 640.

William H. willed the house to his son George, with the stipulation that if George died without male issue, it would pass to the oldest son of my Grandfather Vanderbilt.

And so, unexpectedly in the spring of 1914, when Uncle George died, leaving no son, my father inherited 640.

'Why, it's the Black Hole of Calcutta!' Mother exclaimed as we walked past the great Ghiberti bronze doors into the central great hall. 'I couldn't possibly live here!' Yet a larger mansion than the one we occupied was needed for Mother's parties, which had grown steadily grander.

Father decided to remodel the house completely and, since he had considerable talent as an architect, worked on the plans himself. Later he turned these over to Horace Trumbauer, a Philadelphia architect.

The renovations and redecorating of 640 took over two years. When it was finished, transformed by light and air and a collection of Louis XVI *boiseries*, Gobelin tapestries, Savonnerie carpets, petit-point chairs, and suites of furniture, some from Versailles, it was generally considered the most impressive and elegant house in New York City.

The summer before the First World War broke out, our family, as usual, was abroad on the *North Star*. There had been a fire at St. Paul's in the late spring. Mother at once removed me from the school, where I had been so unhappy, and took me abroad. Sister and Father were to join us later.

Grace, who knew what it was like to be in Paris with Mother, wrote me on June 1. 'I wonder what you and Mama are doing. I am sure Mama is very busy, but what can you be doing? Do you ride or wait outside of Callot's? . . . One week more and we expect to leave on the Kronprinz Wilhelm. It seems a small and creaky ship to me, but Father seems to like it.'

After the voyage on the 'small and creaky ship', my sister and I, with the governess and tutor, were dispatched to St. Moritz in Switzerland, where Grace and I were to have lessons in tennis and golf, spending as much time as possible in the open in order to benefit from outdoor life.

Mother was in Paris, shopping and dining, and Father was on the yacht near Le Havre when, in late June, the news of the shot fired at Sarajevo was flashed around the world.

By the end of July we knew that Austria and Serbia were at war and that the Russian, German, and French armies were mobilizing; a few days later we learned that the German troops had marched into Belgium. On August 4 came the British declaration of war.

Immediately communication facilities between Switzerland and the Allies to the west were frozen. At St. Moritz we were completely cut off from our parents. They could neither communicate with us nor come and fetch us, as all trains had stopped running and the sale of petrol was suspended. Father sped to London, where he obtained an emergency passport from the United States Embassy. Then, in Paris, he received a special permit from the French war office and special supplies of gasoline and set off by automobile for Switzerland.

In the dead of night, in our St. Moritz hotel bedrooms, my sister and I were awakened, hastily bundled into clothes, and led to our father. He was almost tottering with fatigue, covered with mud and dust, and—quite inexplicably—bulging and clanking in various parts of his anatomy. Loaded on his person in moneybags and belts were enough pounds of gold to bail out all the stranded Americans in Switzerland. The gold came from the American Embassy in Paris.

Quickly Grace and I were shepherded into the car to drive beside him through the rest of that night and all the next day. Early morning brought us to the Crillon in Paris, where Mother swept us into her arms amid a bevy of excited French friends crowding her luxurious suite.

We set sail at once from Le Havre to England, where Father gave our magnificent yacht, the *North Star*, to the British Government. The Admiralty shipped her to Scotland, where she was stripped of her pale silk walls and French ormolu lights and outfitted as a hospital ship. The portraits of the arrogant Kaiser and Prussian princes and Russian grand dukes disappeared from her walls, as they and their glittering courts were to disappear, perhaps for ever, from the face of Europe. Painted an antiseptic white, the *North Star* served an honourable career as a mercy ship. When last I heard of her, she was plying a coastal trade in the China Sea, a derelict of peeling paint and scarred mahogany.

When we had left Switzerland on that midnight drive to Paris, our German governess had remained behind. Many of the servants at 677 were English or French, deeply worried over the war and what might be happening to relatives across the Atlantic. Grace and I often heard discussions about whether or not the United States should join in the war.

Aunt Belle wrote from England, where her sons, Sidney and Michael Herbert, were both in uniform. One of her letters Mother showed to Theodore Roosevelt one evening when he and Mrs. Roosevelt came to dinner. A few days later the former President, characteristically emphatic, sent Mother an eight-page typewritten letter:

'My dear Mrs. Vanderbilt,' he wrote, 'I am much interested in Lady Herbert's letter. I understand entirely why it is natural that there should have been a growing feeling of irritation in England about the American attitude. Moreover, I recognize that there is much justice in this attitude because a nation must be largely judged by the actions of its government; and I would be the first to say that Messrs. Wilson, Bryan, Daniels, McAdoo and their associates are wretched representatives of the United States in this crisis and have wholly failed, partly from timidity and folly and partly from even worse causes, to do their duty either to their own country or the world at large . . . This letter, of course, is not for publication. But Lady Herbert is quite welcome to show it with discretion to people of influence in England who ought to know the facts and help shape public opinion.

'I hold very strongly that as a signatory power of the Hague Conventions, we should have promptly interfered by protest and to any further extent that was found necessary when Germany invaded Belgium and subsequently committed at the expense of the people of Belgium (as well as of Northern France and of the bombarded English coast towns) acts of wrong doing which were in flagrant violation of the Hague Conventions . . .'

My Uncle Alfred, staunch in the Allied cause, sailed for Europe in the spring of 1915 to offer his services to the British Red Cross.

'The Germans would not dare to attack this ship,' he said as he boarded the *Lusitania*. 'They have disgraced themselves and never in our time will they be looked upon by any human being valuing his honour, save with feelings of contempt. How can Germany, after what she has done, ever think of being classed as a country of sportsmen and of honour on a par with America, England and France?'

So saying, he stepped on the 45,000-ton liner.

Neither of my parents went to see Uncle Alfred off on his voyage; the first hint of disaster reached them in the form of a cable from Ireland a week after he had left. Two German torpedoes had struck the *Lusitania* amidships. Twenty minutes later she disappeared from the surface of the ocean, ten miles off the head of Kinsale, Ireland.

'Find all the kiddies you can, boy,' Uncle Alfred directed his valet at the first explosion. Together my uncle and his manservant directed women and children to the lifeboats. Then Alfred, who had always been a poor swimmer, gave his lifebelt to a lady. Quietly he joined Charles Frohman and three other passengers.

'Why fear death?' asked the famous producer. 'It is the most beautiful adventure life gives us.'

The five men joined hands. 'They've done for us; we'd better get set,' remarked Frohman at the final lurch of the liner.

'Vanderbilt was absolutely unperturbed,' a survivor recollected.

'He stood there, the personification of sportsmanlike coolness. In my eyes he was the figure of a gentleman waiting for a train.'

In England the Bishop of London cried: 'When Alfred G. Vanderbilt was face to face with death, he said to his valet: "*Come on and let us save the kiddies.*" Those words will run round the world the way no millionaire's ever do.'

When the news of the *Lusitania* disaster first reached New York, it was reported that all passengers had been saved. (Actually, 1,198 drowned.) Mother's letter to me at boarding school, written on the night of the sinking, makes no mention of Alfred: 'Darling Neil: The terrible news today (at two o'clock) of the torpedoing of the "Lusitania" was a great shock for all of New York. Wild excitement everywhere and great indignation! And now deep thankfulness that the passengers' lives have been spared, as far as we can make out from the various reports. How terrible and terrifying it all is!

'Tonight we were to have dined with Willie K. Jr. [Father's cousin], but owing to all this uncertainty over passengers on the "Lusitania", we gave it up. Last night I sat next to the Maharajah of Kapurthala, an Indian prince, at dinner at Mrs. Billy Hoffman's. He was rather nice looking, a charming voice and seemed very clever and agreeable. His wife (his sixth!) is a Spanish woman—very odd of the Hoffmans to ask her to their dinner, I thought, as she does not go about in Paris or London. Tomorrow our fleet will be here and Father's duties begin!'

Sister wrote: 'My darling brother, Concerning the horrible disaster of the "Lusitania" and the losing of Father's brother, we know as yet nothing definite.

'We heard the news first at 2 p.m. Friday from Father on the telephone. It gave Mamma an awful shock. A few minutes later the ominous cry of extras rang out in the hot, crowded streets and all day long from hour to hour new extras were issued, always saying more or less the same. People bought and bought every time, just to see. We kept in touch with all the papers all day. Of course Father could not go to welcome the Admiral on account of the uncertainty. The fleet is all in the river. Love, Sister.'

By noon of the day following the disaster, the flags of Uncle Alfred Vanderbilt's hotel dipped to half-mast. Father, as the new head of the house, was receiving bulletins every ten minutes from Ireland, but our Aunt Margaret, Alfred's second wife, no longer understood them as she lay half-unconscious in the top suite of the family's magnificent skyscraper hotel, the Vanderbilt.

And at Grandmother's great cold chateau at 57th Street, Alice of the Breakers sat in dark seclusion in her Italian Renaissance bedroom. The multimillionaire's widow had buried a five-year-old daughter, a twenty-one-year-old son, a husband struck down in the prime of his vigorous life. She refused to admit that death had also taken her dashing Alfred.

Widowed Aunt Belle was quick to send her sympathies to Father from England. Both her sons were now in the fighting in France.

'My dear Neily,' she wrote, 'I have felt so full of horror at what has happened and so certain of your great distress that I have felt it difficult to write . . . I try to send you my real and affectionate sympathy. I realize that just because of these years when you have not been able to see much of each other, all the other years of your youth and childhood will seem very near to you, and you will be very unhappy; and if you will let me say how sorry I am for your Mother.

'The papers have all told of the courage and nobility of his last moments and his death—perhaps it does not help much to hear—yet I am sure it is helping us all during these awful days to see how goodness and courage are triumphing—and I am sure that it will help you to bear the tragedy to know that your own blood has died as a hero dies. We are living from day to day simply surrounded on all sides by tragedy and misery . . .'

Mother wrote me from 677 Fifth Avenue ten days after the *Lusitania* went down: 'Darling Neil, A very eventful day has just passed. At 10.45 the sailors began marching past—splendid looking men, well set up—many officers—friends of Father's. Some looked up at him! At 11.30 a telephone message came for Father—President Wilson wished to see him at the Hotel Biltmore! He made a lightning change of clothes into 'morning coat', top hat, etc. and dashed away to his interview. The President received him quite alone in a small room (crowds of Naval officers were waiting outside to be received) and was very gracious and nice and said he wished to thank Father for the way in which he arranged the reception for the Fleet and said everyone had told him it was so well managed etc. They had a very nice talk of about ten minutes.

'Father had not been to any of the public entertainments—nor could he dine with the President this evening alone (as he had been invited to do) but the Admiral received him informally on his Flag Ship, Wyoming. This Father enjoyed *very* much. I am glad he has been *forced* to attend to all these duties these past days as it has somewhat taken his mind off the sad and distressing death of his brother. I hope you will write and tell your Grandmother how sorry you feel for her. She told Father yesterday that if she heard nothing more by the end of this week, she would arrange for a memorial service. They are now trying to send down *divers* where the ship went down. Isn't it awful?

'The feeling here is not at all for war. *No one* believes Germany will continue to provoke. They think she will find *some* way of answering the President's message satisfactorily . . .'

The following day Father wrote me for the first time in weeks on letterhead with the inscription 'Mayor's Committee for the Entertainment of the U.S. Atlantic Fleet': 'My dear boy—I have been meaning to write to you for some time but have been frightfully busy. Mother has written you about the loss of my brother on the "Lusitania". It is such a terrible catastrophe that it seems impossible to realize. Of course I feel most awfully about it—more than I can say—and it does not seem possible that it can be true.

'Grandmother will not give up hope that he may still be alive, and in some remote port in Ireland but I fear there is practically no hope of this, after the length of time that has elapsed.

'The Fleet's visit has gone off better than I had hoped, and it is a great relief to have it over. Lots of love, Father.'

I can recall getting special permission at school to rush home to 'comfort' my father over the loss of his brother.

My busy parent brushed aside my stammered words of sympathy. And then, for the first time, I perceived how deeply, irrevocably, my father had been hurt by Alfred's long years of indifference. Long before he died, Uncle Alfred and my father were as far apart as the planets.

Chapter Eleven

WITH the death of Uncle Alfred, and the increasing irre-
sponsibility of Uncle Reggie, there no longer seemed to be
any question about Father's being head of the House of
Vanderbilt. His mother and sisters turned to him with renewed
protestations of affection, but their recognition came too late. By
now Father's tormented spirit showed clearly in his dark and
melancholy face.

I began to suspect that his frequent absences with the National
Guard and on railway-inspection trips served as a convenient excuse
to avoid Mother's incessant parties. And, while at home, he spent
much of his time closeted in his upstairs sound-proof laboratory.
More than once he skipped one of Mother's important dinners to
dine alone on a tray in his study.

The more Mother cajoled and entreated, the more distant and
polite and unco-operative Father seemed to become. He made no
bones about the acute boredom induced by dining with the same
fashionable people night after night and listening afterwards, over
liqueurs and cigarettes, to the richest man present telling all the
other millionaires how he made his money!

But what Father seemed to resent most of all was Mother's
invasion of his privacy. She frequently opened his mail and listened
in on his phone conversations until he finally installed a private
outside wire in his bedroom at Newport and also in New
York.

Sister and I were also furious over Mother's poking and prying
into our affairs, and we used to envy Father his many avenues of
escape.

Mother's failure to mould Father into an amiable host and man-
about-resorts only served to accelerate her efforts with me. Every
morning after her social secretary brought her the list of people we
were entertaining for luncheon and dinner that day, Mother would
sit up in bed with her card rack and diagram of the table or tables
and work out her complicated seating plans. The cards were different

colour for men and women and each had a name written upon it. My sister and I then had to spend several hours alternating the men and women about the table in their proper social stratification down to the plain 'Mr.' and 'Mrs.' down by the salt. Mother and Father always faced each other across the middle of the table, English-style, with the most honoured guests clustered about them.

Sister and I were also given lessons in proper table settings. Followed by the butler bearing various dishes and condiments on a huge silver tray, Mother led us around and around the gleaming sixty-foot mahogany table. Before I was nine, I knew precisely which dishes remained and which disappeared during a complete seven-course dinner.

Nothing in my training as a future perfect party host was left to chance. And when I was away from home, Mother kept up a barrage of hypothetical problems, enough to furrow the brow of the most adept party giver.

Father had been giving a good deal of his time to the work that was being done on the house at 640 Fifth Avenue. Months before it was completed, however, he was sent with his National Guard unit to the Mexican border to help quell the Pancho Villa raids. My mother was very unhappy about this. A few days before Father's departure I was at home for a weekend visit. When I arrived Saturday morning I found that Mother had left this note for me: 'Welcome Darling: I shall not be awake when you arrive, and Father will be gone—to return or call by for you at eight if you are not too tired and would like to go with him and see a regiment *en train* or start off. Then please come back *immediately* to see me, as I want to see you badly and talk over *plans*. There is a police Review or something down at Sheeps Head Bay and we might go, you and I, if you like. I do not want you to start off for the yacht before Sunday. I do pray Father will not be actually sent off to Mexico, he should recruit here! Love and kisses, Mother.'

Nevertheless Father, with his usual ardour for all things military, was one of the first National Guardsmen to be off for the Mexican border.

A few weeks later Theodore Roosevelt wrote my Mother to congratulate her on becoming chairman of the Active Service Auxiliary of the New York National Guard. Aunt May was a member of this group, too. The purpose of the organization was to help support needy families in which the husband or father had been sent to the border as a member of the National Guard.

'I am very much pleased,' the former President wrote, 'to learn of the formation of the Guard Auxiliary. Thanks to our national folly in not having provided a system of universal training and universal service, any action taken in support of the country is at present necessarily taken at the expense of the most patriotic and high-minded citizens. It is a matter of duty as well as common sense patriotism to help organizations such as yours . . .'

On Christmas Day of 1916 my father, with the officers and men of the Second Battalion of the Twenty-second Regiment of Engineers, was back in New York. They arrived by train at Hoboken, crossed the river on the ferry, and marched up Fifth Avenue to 59th Street and Columbus Circle to the applauding shouts and cheers of crowds that had gathered along sidewalks all the way.

Mother, who had a childish love of bands and parades, gave a big luncheon. Afterwards we sat in the big windows of 677 facing Fifth Avenue and waved flags and cheered my handsome father—now a full colonel—as he rode by.

Mother never referred to any of our various domiciles as 'home'. Our Newport place was always Beaulieu, and when she invited friends to dine in New York, it was 'Come to 677'. Later on, when we moved to our most famous Fifth Avenue address, its number, 640, became as well known among society circles abroad as in this country. Father humorously said that most well-connected foreigners told taxi-drivers to take them to 640 Fifth Avenue five minutes after they were through customs.

We moved into 640 the summer of 1917. The process took a long time, for Mother wanted nothing less than perfection. Bevies of upholsterers, curtain makers, importers of rugs and furnishings filed in and out, with their samples, their drawings, their estimates. There was also the demanding task of engaging new servants and the even more demanding one of seeing that the new staff worked in harmony. Mother needed all her executive ability and experience—of which she had acquired a good deal.

When I think back to the growing signs of discord between my parents during the time of the First World War, I feel I should mention Mother's strong German sympathies. Her many friends among Prussian royalty had something to do with this, and she was also quite close to the German Embassy group in Washington.

Naturally, she was very sympathetic with the English, too—the trouble was, I suppose, that she didn't take sides as Father did. She wanted to believe that the war would end without the United States becoming involved.

Father was particularly annoyed at her friendship with the German Ambassador, Count von Bernstorff, a handsome Prussian type very much sought after by New York hostesses. 'Dear Mrs. Vanderbilt,' the Count wrote my mother from Washington in 1912, 'I hear that you are back in New York, so you can imagine how I am longing to see you again. To begin with, I wish you most heartily a very happy New Year in which I hope to have the great pleasure of seeing you very often. Is there any chance of your coming here this winter? I missed seeing you so much at the Crillon this summer. Very sincerely yours, J. von Bernstorff.'

In the summer he wrote her at Newport: 'I just heard from Mrs. Longworth that you are not coming to Baltimore [where the national Democratic convention of 1912 was held] and that I will not have the pleasure of seeing you there . . . Should you still have the gracious intention of allowing me to pay you a visit in Newport, I shall be very much obliged for a telegram. I could manage to get away from here the end of the week, having taken leave of the President and Mr. Knox. If you are not going to Newport now I hope to meet you in Europe where I generally have such good luck to go. Looking forward to your gracious order by wire . . .'

So much has been written about Mother's dinner for Count von Bernstorff in Newport when he was our house guest that I feel I must give the true version here. In the first place, Father was extremely annoyed when he heard that the Count was coming. Father, who—in addition to serving as a lieutenant-colonel in the New York National Guard—was on the staffs of the Commanding General and the Governor of New York, did not want to seem to be exhibiting any friendliness towards Germany. He pointed out to Mother that she ought to be ashamed to be entertaining the German Ambassador when her many French and English friends were engaged in such a terrible war and her two English nephews, Aunt Belle's sons, were in front-line trenches.

Mother laughed her little silvery laugh, turned her head away as if that was the end of that, and said, 'Well, I still think Count von Bernstorff is a very nice person.'

When the dinner party was arranged, Father managed to be absent, I believe, but many of Newport's most important people came. The Count had the position of honour at Mother's right. As she sipped her *consommé double* Mother's practised eye swept over her guests, the five immense gold bowls of American Beauty roses and Japanese iris, the footmen deftly pouring wine; without an apparent break in her rapt interest in her handsome guest of honour, she noted that an argument of some heat had broken out between two guests down by the salt, that a male guest was wearing a particularly handsome set of black pearl vest buttons, and that Gerald, our immensely fat English butler, looked slightly distrait.

The footmen began removing the white Sèvres soup plates with their deep blue and gold borders. When they seemed unusually slow about bringing in the fish, Mother caught Gerald's eye; he bowed and hurried noiselessly out into the butler's pantry. He did not return. Mother missed the thread of what von Bernstorff was saying; she smiled radiantly, but one slender white hand began tugging at the side of her flame-coloured chiffon gown—always a danger-signal. As Mother's servants well knew, an eight-course dinner must be served in an hour flat, even if slow eaters dropped three courses behind. So forceful was the effect of Mother's personality that the servants trembled to fulfil her every whim; this was particularly remarkable because they knew that, however heinous the offence, she could seldom bear to fire anybody.

Five minutes passed. Ten minutes. No Gerald. No food. Little pauses in the conversation were now apparent as Mother's well-bred guests cast surreptitious glances about the room and down to Mother's end of the table. After what seemed an interminable amount of time, one of the Irish kitchenmaids appeared with a small white note on a heavy silver salver.

Complete silence fell over the dinner-table as Mother carefully unfolded and read the note.

After a moment she announced in her gracious, cultured voice, 'Most of my servants are English or Irish. My chef is French. I regret to say that they refuse to serve the German Ambassador. Please accept my apologies.' And she motioned gracefully for them to rise from the table.

At first, everyone sat stunned. Then one of the guests suggested jokingly that the men serve the dinner, which they did, bringing in the food from the stoves and butler's pantry amid much hilarity. It was quite the sensation of Newport. But, humiliating as the affair was to Mother, she did not fire a single servant. She said that it was unfortunate but that she could understand their point of view. Shortly afterwards, war was declared by the United States, the Count was recalled to Germany, and his friendship with our family ended.

Soon after the declaration by Congress that 'a state of war exists between the United States and Germany', my father left for Spartanburg, South Carolina, where he assumed command of the 102nd Engineers. General John O'Ryan, commanding officer of the New York National Guard, wrote us that 'Neily is so well-liked by both officers and men that if his present popularity continues he will be our next President.'

Filled with pride in my soldier father, I envied him and longed to follow in his footsteps. Meanwhile, many of my boarding-school friends had enlisted and gone overseas; whenever I encountered the gaze of Uncle Sam, pointing an accusing finger at me from recruiting posters and saying 'Your Country Needs YOU', a throb of guilt shot clear down to my toes.

But Mother would not even discuss the subject of my enlisting. In the first place, she pointed out, my health would not survive the rigours of boot training. Also, she had big and important plans for my future. The most important thing for me to do was to enter Yale and complete my education. Only in this way could I fill the exalted position waiting for me in life. And so I entered what was known as a fashionable 'cramming school' for college at Norwalk, Connecticut.

All that spring of 1917 I was torn by my burning patriotic desires —an almost suicidal urge for self-sacrifice. At the same time, disobeying my mother or causing her a moment's anxiety or pain seemed inconceivable.

But mainly I was troubled about my father, whom I admired so much. Ever since I had left St. Paul's he seemed to grow progressively cooler towards me, until finally he seemed as prickly as a porcupine. Almost everything I said and did seemed to irritate him, and more than once he ordered me out of the room because he said I made him nervous.

For a long while I accepted Father's attitude contritely and humbly. I knew I was a disappointment to him.

But presently I began to rebel. I had tried as hard as I could to please him. If slavishly following his wishes would not win his approval, then I would do something bold and dashing and heroic, something he would be bound to approve and admire.

I was a painfully skinny lad of nineteen—over six feet tall and under a hundred pounds—on that spring day of 1917 when I became a buck private.

Mother had been resting at the Homestead with Grace; when news came of my enlistment, she headed north on the first train. Back in New York, she pulled every string she knew to make me a civilian again. But I had enlisted in the United States Army and there was little she could do.

Our old friend, General O'Ryan of the National Guard, replied to her cry for help by writing: 'Dear Mrs. Vanderbilt: This from the New York Sun of today may interest you. The young soldier was beaming with pride when I last saw him. Sincerely, John F. O'Ryan.'

The newspaper clipping which was enclosed bore the heading, 'YOUNG VANDERBILT, LIKE DAD, ENLISTS', and beneath it: 'A tall, slender, blue-eyed lad of 19 stood before a recruiting sergeant of the newly organized Field Artillery section of the Ammunition Train, New York Division, yesterday morning. The sergeant looked him over with a sweep of his eye, grunted his approval and then reached for an enlistment blank.

'When the dotted lines had all been filled out and the score of questions answered the sergeant glanced over the paper and repeated aloud the name.

' "Vanderbilt—well, well," he mused. "Cornelius Jr. Any relation to the Colonel, young fellow?" he asked.

'The boy blushed and then answered, "He's my father, sir."

'So it was that young Vanderbilt—and it's a certainty that will be his title for many a day at least—joined the colours yesterday. In a jiffy he had passed the military examination and was ordered to report after lunch. An hour later he gave a very creditable salute. He was uniformed in natty khaki that looked very much as if it might have been hand tailored. Five minutes afterward he was busy with a mass of papers next to a smiling happy lad whose father is a motorman on a Third Avenue street car.'

Next Mother appealed to Theodore Roosevelt. In his reply to her, he enclosed this letter: 'Dear Neil, Your dear mother, of whom, as you know, I am very fond and whom I greatly respect, and I do not agree about you; and if she is willing, she is to send you this letter.

'I am *very* proud of you; I sympathize absolutely with the course you are taking; I feel that you are doing exactly what, if you were my son, I would wish you to do.

'I advise you to stay where you are, perfect yourself in your work, and get abroad with your division, into the fighting line, as soon as you can. I am exceedingly glad that you do not wish to go to Washington to join the slicker-and-slacker brigade. I do not care a rap whether a man is an enlisted man or a Major General; so long as he does his duty, and gets into this, why, I'll take off my hat as quickly to one as to the other. If I had my way, every man would have to serve a year in the ranks before being permitted to try for a commission.

'Of course study steadily, at every chance, so as to fit yourself to try for a commission when the time comes. But if I had the command of a division, I'd take you with me far quicker than I would any man, no matter how well educated, who had not done as you have done. I regard you as showing the true American spirit; the spirit of a man. I am proud to greet you as your comrade, an old ex-colonel, Theodore Roosevelt.'

But that letter didn't change Mother. When she found there was no way to get me out of service, she tried to keep me from being sent overseas. After I had gone through training in the mud and rain in South Carolina all winter, I wanted more than anything else in the world to be among the first to get to France. Mother tried to prevent this. The night before I was to leave for overseas she telephoned to Secretary of War Newton D. Baker and got a stay to keep me in this country two more weeks. Then General O'Ryan saw to it that I was put on a list of men to accompany the staff officers to Europe. General O'Ryan did this, I think, partly because he liked my Father and partly because he knew I spoke French fluently.

The night before we were to leave for France, Mother invited General O'Ryan and Mrs. O'Ryan and a great number of other people to dinner. My father was then busy building Fort Belvoir, Virginia. I had received a twenty-four-hour leave to say good-bye to my family. When the taxi left me at the corner of 51st Street and Fifth Avenue that spring evening of 1918, the first thing I noticed was the huge service flag with two stars hanging over the front entrance of 640.

My parents' new home was an oblong stone house with rooms built around a very large square hall which ran up through four stories to a huge skylight, not unlike the arrangement of the Breakers. There was a basement with the kitchens, servants' dining-rooms, laundries, wine cellar, etc., and a sub-basement where the menservants slept, the maids being on the fifth and sixth floors. Altogether there were some seventy rooms, most of them huge, and thirty-three bathrooms. Almost every room had its own telephone. I was told that at this time 640 had more miles of telephone wire than New York's Biltmore Hotel!

This mammoth pile of stone and marble was heated by coal furnaces, fired by hand. As I remember, we employed a man to do nothing but attend to these furnaces. We had, as well, thirty-five other persons as hired help, most of whom lived in, but some, like the French chef and English butler, had apartments of their own in the city and reported to work each day.

When I arrived that April evening, I saw that the red velvet carpet had been brought up from the sub-basement and laid over the Fifth Avenue front steps and over the sidewalk to the street. It was obvious that Mother considered my farewell dinner a very special event and this, plus the service flag, so patriotically displayed, gave me hope that she was reconciled to my going overseas and that the evening would pass without any trying emotional scenes.

I ran up the red-carpeted steps of my parents' palace into the small front foyer, where Mother's English social secretary, Miss Henderson, was checking the invitations. Several Army majors and a Navy admiral, resplendent in their full-dress uniforms, were talking to her. Miss Henderson nodded at the skinny, khaki-clad private who came suddenly to attention and saluted. Then I hurried on past into the inner foyers.

Miss Henderson was a tall, spinsterish type whom my sister and

I called 'Hen' and cordially disliked; however, Mother found her indispensable. In her card file could be found the likes and dislikes, birthday, marital status, number of children, etc., of each of Mother's hundreds of friends. Thus, when we had house guests at 640 or Beaulieu, they would find on the beside table the latest books of their favourite authors, their own brand of cigars or cigarettes, the flowers they liked best, a large ash-tray, pad, pencils, and a thermos of their pet going-to-bed refreshment, whether that was milk, orange juice, champagne, or a particular brand of Scotch whisky. No wonder Mother's house guests were so sublimely comfortable! 'If you ever need a job, I'll offer you $100,000 a year to be my head housekeeper,' J. Leslie Kincaid, the hotel-chain owner, used to tell Mother jokingly.

In the inner foyer stood Gerald, the butler, in tails and black tie. He looked so distinguished that there were times when guests who did not know Father mistook him for the host and went up and shook hands. This never disturbed Gerald's aplomb, although it was a mortifying experience for a guest.

Lined up on either side of Gerald were six footmen in maroon knee pants and tail coats, white stockings, and black pumps, and as many maids in black dresses with frilly white organdie aprons and caps. I handed my private's hat to a footman, who gravely carried it to the dressing-rooms. These rooms were as large as a theatre's and could hold five or six hundred coats. I then moved over to a silver tray on a small table and found a small white envelope with my name on it. Inside was the name of the lady whom I was to take in to the dining-room and whom I would sit next to at dinner. Many hostesses, I knew, did not bother with these cards, but Mother always said it was well to be forewarned, as this gave one an opportunity to think up topics of conversation. Also, if you didn't know your dinner partner well, there was time to find out a little about her beforehand from the other guests.

Crossing the marble foyer, I passed through a pair of towering bronze doors, blazing with gold leaf, and into the great hall which stretched up four full stories. Green palms and beautiful seventeenth-century Brussels tapestries lined the galleries; nothing else detracted attention from the chaste, clean lines of the Caen marble walls and columns crowned with alabaster.

In the centre of this great hall stood an immense vase, eight feet tall, on a bronze pedestal. It was fashioned entirely of the green semi-precious stone malachite; its twin stood in the St. Petersburg palace of the Czar Nicholas. (The malachite vase is today in the Metropolitan Museum of Art, a gift from my mother.) Grouped about its base and filling the air with their heady fragrance were hundreds of pots of gardenias and lilies, French lilac and jasmine— Easter gifts from Mother's hundreds of friends.

The day after a dinner party Mother often received fifty or sixty flower bouquets. At Easter time Miss Henderson sometimes acknowledged as many as a thousand plants. (Most of these, of course, were donated to hospitals.)

Mother was receiving in the library. Of this room Frank Crowninshield, a valued friend of Mother's, wrote: 'Of all the rooms in this great house, the library, dark and crowded with the mementos of a lifetime, is Mrs. Vanderbilt's favourite. Far more like a *salon* in Paris than a room one might expect to find in New York, the library tables are loaded with bibelots, with ornaments in mutton-fat jade, with vases filled with flowers, with books—some autographed, with photographs, all ceremoniously signed.

'A beautiful jumble of damasks, petit-point, tapestry and velvets, this room is thoroughly lived in. The small tables are covered with fringed velvet in the style that was so fashionable in the Paris of Proust's day, and that is just now becoming fashionable again in this country. The room has French Regency woodwork of oak and Regency furniture, some pieces covered in a ripe, raspberry-red silk, others in the French fashion, covered in the same yellow-green damask as the walls.

'But the chief glory of the room is the tapestry, which was made in Brussels sometime in the seventeenth century. It represents the famous visit of Alexander the Great to Diogenes in Athens. (At that time, Alexander, master of the known world, asked the impoverished philosopher if there was anything that he could do for him. "Yes," said Diogenes, "you can stand out of my light.") It is beneath this tapestry that Mrs. Vanderbilt receives her intimate friends, and serves tea every afternoon.'

As I entered this room that evening in 1918 the second man (second in the hierarchy of the footmen to the butler) announced 'Private Vanderbilt', and Mother looked up from the fireplace where a small fire was glowing. At forty-eight she was still a strikingly beautiful woman with lovely smooth shoulders and arms. She was wearing a silver lamé gown with perfect cascades of diamonds over her bosom and at her waist, four or five diamond bracelets on her arms, her long pear-shaped diamond earrings, and a band of the same gems in her white hair.

Now she extended two blazing arms and gave me a warm kiss and embrace.

'Happy birthday, darling,' she murmured. 'Nineteen years old!' And for an instant those extraordinary clear grey-green eyes blurred with tears.

She laid a soft hand on mine and led me over to a corner to introduce me to an Army colonel. From his insignia, I could see that he was from my division, the Twenty-seventh.

'The colonel would so love to see 640, darling,' Mother was saying. 'Would you mind awfully showing him around?'

We had time to stroll through only the ten entertainment rooms on the first floor before dinner. In the picture gallery with its dark-red tapesty walls and crystal chandeliers hung the Millets and Meissoniers and Corots collected by my great-grandfather, as well as other paintings purchased by my parents. My knowledge of art was limited, but Mother could give a complete history of every painting and its artist.

The small dining-room next to the picture gallery was designed for family meals and intimate luncheons of no more than a dozen people. It was an inviting little room with pale-beige and gold wall panellings of the Louis XVI epoch. Cleverly concealed behind one of the imported panels was Father's secret elevator. He made use of this elevator on many occasions when the atmosphere told him that a scene was coming on with my mother. He would murmur some explanation, hasten to the little side elevator which went down to 51st Street, and leave the house.

If Father made such an exit at luncheon, it was not very likely that we would see Mother at dinner that night either.

Sam Barlow, the famous conductor, once told me that he considered Mother's music-room the finest in New York. Here Rubinstein used to practise and Zimbalist and Iturbi often played; here Madame Melba and other famous divas of the Metropolitan came to entertain at Mother's musical evenings. The floor—a parquet de Versailles imported from France—was so beautiful that it never was covered. The walls were a soft, faded green, accented with gold leaf, and in the crystal chandeliers flickered dozens of white candles. Mother's gold harp, which she sometimes played for us, stood in one corner.

The ballroom, one of the largest in a private home, was an almost exact replica of the famous one in the palace of Versailles, with its red velvet hangings, huge mirrors, cream and gold wood-work, and gleaming bare parquet floors. Mother sometimes asked a thousand people to her balls, at which Alexander Haas' red-coated Hungarian gypsies played her favourite waltzes and schottisches until dawn.

Everywhere stood huge vases of Mother's favourite flower—long-stemmed American Beauty roses. Generally before every big party the florist sent over five or six different shades. Then Mother would hold a single sample rose against her red and scarlet damasks until she found precisely the right shade of rose for each room.

The dining-room was immense, with an expandable table that could seat sixty persons. Linen damask tablecloths eighteen yards long were ordered from London to cover it, and along its white expanse sat five huge gold flower vases. For the centrepiece the butler told me he generally spent from fifty to seventy-five dollars for flowers, and for the smaller bouquets, thirty-five dollars apiece. There were also five gold fruit bowls, and to fill these with out-of-season hothouse fruit the butler might spend between one hundred and fifty and two hundred dollars for a single dinner party. He used to pay ten dollars for the bunch of imported Muscat grapes which crowned the towering bowl of nectarines, peaches, persimmons, and pears. For a large dinner party, he also bought eight different kinds of candy. Mother generally knew the tastes of all her guests—she had a phenomenal memory for that kind of thing—and if she asked that the Turkish delights be placed next to Mrs. Carnegie and found the chocolate-covered caramels there, she and the butler would really have a row. Our family candy bill, he told me, ran around three hundred dollars a month. Of course Mother had a terrific sweet tooth herself. Since she never drank, and ate sparingly, I believe this is one way she kept up her amazing vitality.

The dinner that night tasted delicious to me, after months of leathery steak and congealed fried eggs and the usual army chow. Only sherry was served before we sat down. Not until the end of

Prohibition did Mother begin serving cocktails and then *never* with appetizers. The meal began with chilled balls of different kinds of melon prepared hours beforehand and kept chilled in our huge ice-boxes, which were large enough to hold crates of oranges on their lower shelves.

Next was a clear turtle soup. (I am checking this against the menu for that evening, written in French and filed away by the efficient Miss Henderson, along with a list of guests and how they were seated, and whether after dinner they listened to music or danced or played cards.)

The fish was brought in on a huge platter, still with its head and tail on, as it is served in Europe. It was a boiled whole salmon, surrounded with very thinly sliced cucumbers and tomatoes.

Next came turkey with chestnut stuffing and little pieces of bacon twisted around hot olives and tiny sausages. With the main course, the footmen stopped pouring sherry and sauterne and began with champagne, which kept up through dessert.

Instead of the salad course, Mother had that evening immense hothouse asparagus. These had to be lifted off the serving plate with a pair of tongs and, as they were dripping with melted butter, it was always quite an achievement to get them on the plate in front of you.

All during the dinner Mother kept at hand a small notebook with an ivory cover. Occasionally she would jot something down—a suggestion to give to the butler or cook, or some favour somebody wanted her to do. Mother was for ever arranging things for people. I am reminded of a cousin of ours who married a dentist from the deep South. Mother was absolutely horrified; doctors were 'possible' for tea, or perhaps luncheon, but a dentist was absolutely beyond the social pale, to her way of thinking. She got to work at once, introducing the cousin's husband to all the right people. He is now vice-president of a very large beverage concern.

This is not one isolated example; Mother 'fixed' things for everybody. She did all this through the goodness of her heart, for she liked to make people happy. The only trouble was that she wanted to arrange her children's and husband's lives, too, and that's where many of our family troubles started.

Mother loved ice cream for dessert, and she and her chef had frequent arguments about this, all in French, as they never spoke any other language to each other, although his English was excellent. The chef wanted Madame to try some other dessert for a change, but Mother usually won. I loved his *crème brûlée*, an immensely rich vanilla custard of eggs and cream baked until it had the thinnest and crispest of butterscotch crusts. This was served with a sweet sauce of red cherries. Lots of Newport hostesses copied this dessert of Mother's. But her favourite was raspberry ice and vanilla ice, covered with a rich chocolate sauce with a very faint peppermint flavouring. After this, fresh fruit was served on small gold plates, followed by coffee and liqueurs.

My sister was also at this dinner. She was eighteen then, and an extremely pretty girl. Frequently she looked at me across that huge table with its dazzling array of diamond bosoms and aigrette-studded coiffures; the appeal in her blue eyes was disturbing. Temperamentally very much like my father, Sister was feeling his absence keenly; to have me, her closest confidant, also headed for the battlefields of France hurt her cruelly.

By eleven o'clock most of the dinner guests had gone, and while I was talking to Grace in the small salon, trying to cheer her up, the butler announced from the doorway that my mother would like to see me in the library.

I jumped up, as we all did when Mother commanded. Even if my sister was in the middle of having her hair shampooed when Mother sent for her, Mademoiselle would wrap her head in a towel and rush Grace to Mother's boudoir. Now I followed Gerald back to the library with its dozens of fondly inscribed photographs. Mother was sitting on the sofa, talking to General O'Ryan and his wife, and she looked as though she might begin to cry at any minute.

When I came into the room she said dramatically to the General, 'Here is my only son. His father is about to go to France. Isn't that enough? This boy should be in school, finishing his education so that he will be able to carry on his father's position in life. How can you send him away from me?'

General O'Ryan was a tough soldier, but a nice old fellow, too. He said, 'Private Vanderbilt, do you want to go overseas or do you want to stay here and take care of your mother?'

I clicked my heels together and said, 'General O'Ryan, I want to go overseas with my outfit.'

The General said to Mother, 'You heard what he said.'

And so, the day after Mother's party, I boarded a troop transport for overseas. This touching farewell note from my sister followed me. It was written on my nineteenth birthday: 'Brother darling: You know I am heart-broken at having you go and that I shall never get over it . . . I haven't the heart to tell my own darling Brother to go out to the greatest peril and adventure the world has ever conceived— and I can't ask you to stay for my sake because it is a weak and sentimental and too feminine wish . . . I knew from the beginning that you *couldn't* do otherwise—with your spirit. I shall never look upon it as an act of impertinence, and if any of the family do I shall always endeavour to correct that false impression. It is most regrettable that Mother cannot see it this way. I will try and make her see it the way I do.

'Family dissensions have always been a tragedy in my eyes and I deplore that you should have put yourself in such a light but I again repeat that I will do all in my power to make it otherwise.

'I am utterly, profoundly suffering at seeing you go—it is the most speechlessly distressing moment of my life and I want you to know it. Brother darling, if I have ever seemed mean or false or catty to you, I know you will forgive it.

'You are to me like a beautiful young knight or crusader of old. May God guide and protect you and bring you home safely. Your most loving but lonely little Sister.'

My father, busy with his troops, did not find time to say good-bye.

Chapter Twelve

MY sister Grace was now approaching marriageable age, a fact which increasingly occupied my Mother's mind and caused her some anxiety. Her hopes for her only daughter became fastened upon a brilliant match, preferably with the scion of some distinguished British family, a *coup* accomplished so successfully by her niece, May Goelet, now the Duchess of Roxburghe.

Because of the war it had not been possible for us to travel abroad since 1914, and this vexed Mother considerably. It was with a kind of chill disbelief that I became aware that not even the stunning impact of a world war could dislodge her from her purely social preoccupations.

No sooner had Father and I embarked for France than she and Grace travelled to Hot Springs for a spartan regime of hot mineral baths, long walks, and massage. While they rested from the ordeal of winter parties and regained strength for the next season, the staff of servants 'moth-balled' our seventy-room New York house. The glitter of the great entertainment rooms was masked in white muslin; the blinds were drawn; and moving vans were hired to cart away to Newport the Steinway, the Gobelin tapestries, the gold service, and trunkloads of silver.

When Mother arrived at Beaulieu several weeks later, everything was in place—aired, waxed, and polished—and the broad piazza ablaze with potted gloxinias and scarlet geraniums.

Father, in command of a unit of combat engineers overseas, was under fire much of the time. I was attached to a headquarters command and chauffeured officers on their inspection tours to the front. I found the misery of trench warfare appalling. War was not at all the gentlemen's sport I had so naïvely assumed.

Infrequently, thick letters on pale-grey stationery, wax-sealed in Vanderbilt maroon, reached me from home. One day as I sat with a group of mud-stained, gaunt, and weary infantrymen, I was handed this letter from my sister: 'This is the most heavenly place,' she wrote from Newport. 'Everything is as it has been since my first memories of earth—the crimson geraniums, the blue, blue, Atlantic with Gull Rock clamorous with white winged birds— Beaulieu basking in the sun, waving lazy awnings and a turkey-red hammock. The moss garden is at its zenith and hummingbirds are feeding from tall blue flowers . . .'

I glanced up from the letter as a hospital truck roared up. I could hear a stifled moan as casualties were removed one by one, on stretchers.

'Nice quaint wholesouled Williamson is digging about,' my sister went on, 'and carrying bunches of fragrant jasmine in baskets. In the morning they mow and mow the lawns with a clickety sound and big bluebottles drone in the rooms and in the evening a light fog arises and all the boats blow their faraway fascinating calls— signalling and answering—oh, the delights of it all!'

She complained of the lack of men, due to the war, but added, 'the mob is still flourishing and more inanely "jazzy" than ever'. Mother, she said, was knee-deep in arrangements for her coming-out party.

Few mothers had the audacity to plan *débuts* for their daughters that tragic summer of 1918, but to Mother, with her deep-grained sense of tradition, it was unthinkable that Grace should reach her nineteenth year without being properly introduced to society.

Although we served in the same area in France, I saw my father only once. This was on a night when a staff car I was driving was hit by shrapnel. There were two officers in the back seat of the car, and both of them were injured, one seriously. An ambulance took the wounded officers back to a hospital unit. After that I was obliged to remain until a British repair truck came by to tow away the car.

This took the rest of the night and part of the next day. Late that night we were going through a town called Canaples near Ouderzelle. Suddenly, in the light of some lanterns, I saw the out-line of my father's figure and, beside him, several other officers.

Excitedly I began honking the horn of the car furiously and yelling, and the truck which was towing me stopped. I jumped out of the car and ran towards Father, completely forgetting that I was a private and he was a full colonel.

'Father, Father!' I yelled.

He turned, stood perfectly still, and looked me straight in the face. It was a look that stopped me in my tracks, and I came to attention and saluted.

Father waited a long moment before he returned the salute. Then he said, 'Son, you're in the Army of the United States. You will obey the regulations.'

'Yes, sir,' I replied.

My father said: 'Return to your unit. Secure permission to see me in the right way and return here tonight.'

But by nightfall he had moved on.

I have often felt that World War I represented my Father's supreme hour. For exceptional service, he was promoted to Brigadier General on the field. Later, his sergeant told me of handing him the news of his promotion, just before the Meuse-Argonne offensive of the fall of 1918. The same telegram ordered Father back to the United States to help with the mobilization programme.

'Dammit, dammit, *dammit!*' swore my seldom-profane parent.

Father was reassigned to Camp Lewis in Washington. To be near him my mother deserted the New York social scene and travelled across the United States for the first time in her life.

She and Grace moved into a rented house at Gravelly Lake, near Tacoma. I think that Mother probably had lavish ideas about entertainments befitting a general, but unfortunately the terrible 'flu epidemic of the winter of 1918-1919 soon broke out. All military installations were immediately quarantined. Day after day Mother and Grace sat in their rustic retreat looking at one another and at the rain streaking down the window-panes.

When Mother returned to 640 three months later, still in time to catch the last of the opera season, she declared that she never cared to visit the primitive West again. And she never did.

Father emerged from the war with many splendid decorations. Mother made haste to order him new calling cards but was undecided as to the proper protocol. Now that Father had resigned from the Regular Army, although not from the Reserve, should his cards read 'former' Brigadier General, 'ex', or what? Prettily she wrote to General Pershing, asking his advice. That famous commander ordered a thorough search of his office files 'for some precedent or other', finally decided that 'a simple Mr.' would be the best thing, 'because,' he explained to Mother, 'his rank and services are so well known'.

Mother, however, from World War I on, invariably referred to Father as the General.

Father kept his commission as Brigadier General in command of the Seventy-seventh Division of the United States Army Reserve until 1935. Then he was relieved of his command at his own request and transferred to the unassigned list, ending thirty-three years of continuous service.

By the time I was discharged, in the spring of 1919, I had become a lieutenant. And I had come to some decisions. After two years in the Army, living and working beside men from all parts of the country from every variety of background (very few, though, like my own), I knew that the manner of life which my parents led was not for me. While I did not entirely realize it then, I was through for ever with Mother's 'well-rounded life'.

I will not recount here the bitter feud Father and I waged through the 1920s, a battle which made newspaper headlines more than once. When Father finally realized that he and I were cut from completely different bolts of cloth, he gave up trying to tailor me to his image. But he could never reconcile himself to my rejection of the careful, accepted formulas of his narrow circle.

When I heard my father's many devoted friends describe him as a shy, sweet, gentle person and a wonderfully sympathetic listener, I was filled with a sense of amazement. Only later, much later, did I come to realize why he was such a hard-driving perfectionist where I was concerned.

It was a devastating blow to discover that my mother—usually so loving and indulgent—sided wholeheartedly with my father in his disapproval of my newspaper career. For the first time, she and I exchanged heated words and, when the fracas was over, I stomped out, convinced that in spite of her many protestations of affection she was as obstinate and uncaring as my father!

If only my parents had taken me into their confidence! I can see now that pride kept them from revealing why they were so prejudiced against the Press. I naturally assumed that their opposition was based on nothing more substantial than the usual knickerbocker snobbishness towards the fourth estate. It was not 'respectable', they said, and that (to them) was that.

I soon became a member of the staff of the New York *Herald*; later I joined the *New York Times* and was sent to their Albany bureau. Occasionally I saw my parents, but I rarely attended Mother's parties either in New York or at Newport.

Meanwhile Mother had many new activities to occupy her. Wrote Evangeline Booth, commander of the Salvation Army, to my mother in May, 1919: 'I feel I cannot leave for the South without troubling you with a brief note to say that my very heart of gratitude is with you for the splendid, unselfish and efficient service you and the General are rendering our organization. I, as well as all my brave workers, will never forget the way you have championed our cause.'

Mother played the role of civic leader with immense dignity, unlike Mrs. O. H. P. Belmont, mother of the Duchess of Marlborough, who scandalized society by marching with other fervent ladies the entire length of Fifth Avenue in support of the suffrage movement.

'Don't cry, my dear,' the militant Alva reportedly comforted a weeping supporter who had been jailed for pouring carbolic acid into mailboxes. 'Pray to God, and *She* will help you!'

When the Red Cross asked Mother to lead a Fifth Avenue parade, in recognition of her distinguished leadership in this organization, Mother pencilled on the invitation for her secretary's information: 'Regret. What does she think I am—a suffragette?'

Mother's principal charities—to which she gave generously for almost half a century—were the Seamen's Institute, the Red Cross, the Salvation Army, and the Crippled Children's Association, but she also donated large sums to many other groups, usually anonymously.

Mother's rector, the fashionable Episcopalian Bishop Potter, summed up her own feelings on woman's new aggressive role in society: 'Once Woman was my superior,' mourned the Bishop; 'now, alas, she is only my equal.'

On my twentieth birthday, Mother gave a ball in my honour at 640. There I met a pretty, quiet-spoken, dark-haired girl named Rachel Littleton, half-sister of Martin Littleton, the distinguished lawyer. Rachel was one of eight children and an orphan. She was sweet and easygoing, a wonderful listener, and—most important to me—seemed to entertain no notions about the grandeur of the title Mrs. Vanderbilt.

Mother and Aunt May held an earnest conference in Mother's pale-grey and pink boudoir and finally came to the conclusion that Rachel would 'do'. Mother had hoped for years that I would fall in love with an English girl. But there was really no fault she could find with my gentle fiancée and so she went ahead with long lists of guests for the wedding.

Three thousand persons attended my nuptials—breaking all attendance records for St. Thomas' Episcopal Church. At the reception afterwards at the East 57th Street home of Rachel's brother, Grandmother Vanderbilt—gowned in her habitual black velvet—stood in the receiving line next to my mother and father. Upstairs only a smattering of our hundreds of wedding presents could be shown. My parents gave Rachel a laurel-leaf bandeau of diamonds valued at $300,000. Grandmother Vanderbilt sent a diamond necklace with a pear-shaped diamond pendant. From the Wilson aunts abroad came caseloads of antique silver of the George I period. Family friends sent gold coffee spoons, jewel-studded boudoir clocks, rare first editions, crystal, a pearl-inlaid writing desk, and many diamond bracelets, brooches, and watches.

My paper had assigned me to Seattle. Rachel and I planned to motor out, attending both national conventions on the way. This was quite an adventure in 1920, when flat tyres seemed to occur with disheartening regularity and, except for the great main arteries, roads were little better than wagon tracks through mud and weeds.

Once on a visit to me at boarding school, Mother had been forced to climb out of the Vanderbilt Rolls Royce into the mud with Father and Sister and the chauffeur and push. Mindful of this dreadful experience, she insisted upon our taking a Vanderbilt footman on our honeymoon.

The day after the wedding, on my birthday, Mother sweetly wrote this letter which reached me in Hot Springs, Virginia: 'Many many *very* happy returns of this day, darling Neil—and may each day bring greater happiness into your life! Father, Grace and I drank your good health and many happy returns of the day at dinner this evening. We are all quite exhausted from yesterday's wonderful wedding and reception, and all the strain and excitement that went with it—for us—your loving parents and little Sister. It was more of an ordeal than I had contemplated, the giving away of my own and only son! But I am comforting myself with the thought of having *gained* a loving daughter, but only *time* and life can make me realize this, and although at present I truly love and admire Rachel, we shall have to grow to feel a mother and daughter love for one another!! Do you understand?

'How dear of you two happy little frauds to wire us from Trenton that you wished we were with you!! Ha Ha! How I laughed when I received it last evening, and I cried all night with your loving telegram under my pillow!! God bless you, my darling Son.'

Although I have been married more than once, none of my wives seemed to measure up to Mother's idea of what a daughter-in-law should be. In public she treated them with great graciousness, but when we were alone together she had the disconcerting habit of never answering their questions directly. And often her clear grey-green eyes looked through the junior Mrs. Vanderbilts simply as though they did not exist.

Back in the 1890s another Mrs. Vanderbilt, the famous Alva, had sailed with her daughter Consuelo to introduce her to society overseas.

Now, a month after my wedding in April, 1920, Mother, Father, and Grace were in England, and they returned, summer after summer, until Grace's marriage in 1927.

My sister, an extremely attractive girl, had my Mother's social tact coupled with a most appealing shyness. When beaux first came to call upon her at Newport, she was often found hiding behind the curtains. Her gentle breeding and exquisite manners soon won her a secure niche in the English *haute monde*.

My sister was presented to King George and Queen Mary at Buckingham Palace in June. Father, having given the *North Star* to the British government in 1914, had chartered a yacht, *Sheelah*, and Mother set to work to collect a group of entertaining, attractive guests for a yachting party.

Lady Alice Lowther, accepting the invitation, wrote: 'Grace dearest, I am so thrilled over your and Neily's really wanting me on the yacht. By the way, what is her name? The yacht, I mean? And I am enchanted at the prospect of being with you both. You were asking me about different men you might have room for, and I am sending you the addresses of those we spoke of, those who have nothing especial to do and must therefore, of course, be gentlemen. Dimitri (Grand Duke), His Imperial Highness, Ritz Hotel. I could write to him and sound him out, and you could meet him here on Monday or Tuesday week and talk it over and look him over. He is, I think, not doing anything particular in life except wondering whether he will ever be Czar.

'Then there is that veritable *darling*, Rudolph de Trafford. He would amuse us. He is just too delightful, 39 Portland Place. Lord Lascelles is a very nice fellow, too, Chesterfield House, but he is always 'busy' I fancy at Court. Argyll is 28 Clarges Street. Peel is 52 Grosvenor St. Cowans is in Paris, but will be back on the 15th of August, 72 Curzon St.

'Lord Stanmore, 186 Ebury St., is a very nice, dear, quiet fellow but would not make us laugh. Almaric Paget is a dear friend but not as gay as Coke or R. de Trafford, but somewhat younger. He is 39 Berkeley Square. Lord Islington is also a dear, but I fancy busy with government work and married. Evan Charteris, charming but sleepy—always sleepy when I see him. Don't know why he never seems to get enough sleep. Sydney Greville is full of fun but rather detached at heart, though very eager in appearance. What an absurd letter this is for a grandmother to write! I will do any 'sounding out' you want, dearest Grace. Just telephone.'

From the *Victoria and Albert*, the royal yacht, the unmarried Prince Albert (later to become George VI) wrote on August 6, 1920: 'Dear Mrs. Vanderbilt, my sister and I are delighted to be able to come to luncheon today with you on board Sheelah. We will be on board by 1.30 if that is all right. It is most kind of you to ask us. I remain yours sincerely, Albert.'

His older brother, the Prince of Wales, came to Mother's parties on the yacht and in London. One evening he presented a tall, strikingly handsome young man to Mother. 'Dickie', he said, 'this is Mrs. Vanderbilt. She knows more about my family than I do.'

'Dickie' was his cousin, Dickie Mountbatten. A few weeks later Father and Mother sailed across the Channel to dine with the King and Queen of Belgium, whom they had entertained at 640 in New York the year before. Mother invited Dickie Mountbatten for the sailing party as well as a lovely, slim, blonde girl to whom she had introduced him at a party at Claridge's, Miss Edwinna Ashley.

In that most romantic of settings, a perfectly appointed, luxurious yacht, Dickie fell head over heels in love with the delectable Edwinna. When they returned to England he wrote Mother on thick coronet-crested and wax-sealed stationery from St. James's Palace: 'My dear Mrs. Vanderbilt, I am sending round the photo you asked for, though I fear it isn't a terribly good one. I feel certain you know just how wonderfully I enjoyed myself during the fortnight you had me aboard the Sheelah. I don't make a noise unless I am happy, so you can judge from the continual roar that proceeded from me the state of my bliss.

'I also feel that you know me well enough not to expect a lot of 'hot air' about the trip. All the same I do want to thank you very, very much and of course the General and Grace, too, for the wonderful fortnight. Voila, voici, N'est-ce pas? Mais Hélas. Ici, ici, ici. Dickie Mountbatten.'

During the twenties Father was playing the market heavily, as were most of his family. At that time the aggregate wealth of all the Vanderbilts was estimated at $800,000,000. One of the first things Father bought with his stock-market profits was the beautiful $750,000 sailing yacht, the *Atlantic*.

I am told that this lovely plaything excited the liveliest interest at the Cowes Regatta in 1923. She was 188 feet long, with a very slender black hull and three sailing masts soaring over a hundred feet into the sky, each carrying a huge expanse of sail. One of the fastest and sleekest of her class ever built, the *Atlantic* had won the Kaiser's Cup in pre-war days by sailing from New York to England in twelve days. She was diesel-powered as well, and Father cruised on her over practically every ocean in the world.

One day Dickie Mountbatten persuaded our ship's carpenter to make him a crude aquaplane, a sport which was just coming into vogue. Then he got Bertie to try it out. From the deck of the royal yacht, *Victoria and Albert*, King George looked across at the upright figure being towed behind the *Atlantic's* motor launch.

'There's that damn fool Dickie showing off again,' he complained.

His equerry raised his binoculars to take a look. 'Not this time, I'm afraid, Your Majesty,' he contradicted. 'It's your own son, Prince Albert.'

After Cowes, Mayfair society migrated to Scotland, where my sister continued her friendship with Prince George, who was then a Navy midshipman at the Naval Academy. Before long English and American newspapers were publishing rumours of an engagement. 'Dollar Bride for Britain?' speculated the tabloids, showing pictures of my attractive sister and the laughing Prince with arms slung about each other's shoulders on the deck of the *Atlantic*.

'Nothing to it. They are merely friends,' Father denied the rumours. Grace told reporters that no engagement existed. Mother said nothing.

Often news of the parties which Mother gave, the trophies the *Atlantic* won, and my parents' visits with kings and queens came to me by way of wire-service news reports long before letters from the family reached me.

By this time Mother had given in to the idea of my being a journalist, for the sake of family harmony. Relations between me and my father remained as strained as ever. I finally decided that we were hopelessly incompatible, but I felt miserable when 'on the outs' with Mother. Eventually I grew to accept her shortcomings and to appreciate her virtues, which were many. I learned to listen to her constant advice and admonitions kindly and tactfully, while proceeding to do pretty much as I pleased.

'None of us can really change Mother's nature,' my sister wrote to me. 'One just has to protect oneself as best one can, from being *imposed* upon or completely *swallowed* up.'

My sister was now in her middle twenties, and still Mother would not allow her to leave the house without a chaperon. After every date and party, she was supposed to knock on Mother's bedroom door, no matter what the hour, and give her a full report of the evening. Often Grace complained that Mother had a perfect phobia about who people were, for Mother insisted upon being personally acquainted with the parents of every friend Grace made, and was constantly urging her to drop this or that person who did not measure up to Mother's ideas of family excellence.

Mother now embarked upon the most exciting and glamorous period of her fabulous life as the premier hostess of her era. Her entertainment bills began to run between $250,000 and $300,000 a year. During this time her guests included King Albert of the Belgians, the Queen of Spain, the King of Siam, the Crown Prince of Norway, Lord and Lady Mountbatten, the Duke of Kent, Calvin Coolidge, Herbert Hoover, and Winston Churchill, among others. Some of this expense she paid from her own funds.

One of Mother's pet economies was renting things, although this was often a false economy in the end. For instance, we rented Beaulieu at a cost of $25,000 a season for almost thirty years; then bought it for $140,000 and spent another $100,000 in redecorating. I was amazed to discover that the big Steinway piano which was crated and shipped between Newport and New York every year was rented at a cost of $650 a year. At Beaulieu Mother paid $237 a summer to rent fourteen pots of palms. She also rented boxes of begonias, hydrangeas, and gloxinias for the season.

Another expense connected with Beaulieu was 'covering all the bedroom carpets on second and third floors with paper and supplying gum camphor in the other twenty-two rooms, $290. Removing in spring, $268.'

When Mother rented Lord Brownlow's house in London in 1921, she had all the third-floor rooms and passages done over, adding a new bathroom, buying new carpets and new blinds throughout, and installing new electric wiring in all the rooms. All this for a house she occupied for only a few months! Father complained bitterly about such extravagances.

A bill from Howard, Ltd., London, reads: 'To Hire, pair of Chinese vases and pair of large gilt candlesticks, from June 5 to August 6, 18 pounds [$90].'

Mother dickered with half a dozen linen places in London for supplies for the summer, since she could not transport her linens from New York and back again without paying full duty on them. Finally she rented from Harrod's for family use thirty-six bath towels, seventy-two fine face towels, sixteen table cloths, each from four to six yards long, a dozen tea cloths, and a few other odds and ends for $585 for the season. She spent another $340 hiring linens 'sufficient for sixteen servants'.

In spite of her extravagances, Mother was often a penny pincher. She bought two brands of champagne and, although the difference in price was only a dollar a case, she gave the servants strict instructions to serve the cheaper brand 'at all dinners of more than twenty'.

However, she bought on 1865 Rémy Martin brandy. 'Gentlemen taste their brandy,' she admonished her secretary in a scrawled note. 'It must be good. They gulp Scotch whisky and champagne.'

'What beautiful crystal!' I have heard guests exclaim at one of Mother's really large dinner parties. As often as not, the stemware they praised so extravagantly was made of glass and rented for the occasion.

Bertie, the Duke of York, was honeymooning with his Scottish bride, Lady Elizabeth Bowes-Lyon, at Polesdon Lacy, near Dorking, in the spring of 1923, when Mother, Father, and Grace arrived in England. Mother, in an enveloping cape and hat of fawn colour, with luxurious fawn-coloured suède gauntlets to her elbows, carried her little dog Dwika down the gangplank. With the family was the usual retinue of secretaries, maids, valet, chauffeur, and other servants. They settled down in Brook House, Park Lane, W.1, which they had taken until November. It was the London residence of Dickie and Edwinna, Lord and Lady Mountbatten, one of Mother's most successful matches.

The first party Mother gave was a ball at which the petite blue-eyed Duchess of York, in white satin and diamonds, twinkled at her Duke as they danced to 'Who' and 'Rio Rita'.

Mother, wearing a gown of coral lace and her longest pearls, had the Prince of Wales at her right during dinner.

'That's a good man,' the Prince said, aware that Mother was watching one of the footmen, a well-set-up chap over six feet tall. 'Used to be steward for my uncle, Prince Arthur of Connaught, in South Africa.'

The footman, Stanley Hudson, later became our butler at 640 Fifth Avenue. He came in 1927 and remained in charge of the household staff until 1951, except for three years during the Second World War when, as a British subject, he returned to England and was steward for the Lord Mayor of London.

While Mother was launching her daughter into English and Continental society, Father went on longer and longer cruises on his yacht. Sometimes, my sister told me, he stayed in England only for Ascot Week and the Cowes Regatta, then sailed with a group of congenial friends for ports unknown. While Mother was maintaining three splendid residences in New York, London, and Newport, Father became a kind of homeless nomad and wanderer.

I was aware, as all his friends were, that Father was beginning to drink heavily. My Mother, a teetotaller herself, held strong beliefs on this subject. Her butler had orders to evict, forcibly if necessary, any guest who became objectionably drunk, and anyone who arrived intoxicated for one of Mother's parties was seldom asked again.

For Mother's great opening ball at Brook House, Father arrived on his yacht from Spain just one day in advance of the party. This caused much speculation among their friends, but as Father stood by Mother's side that evening he appeared as polite and devoted as ever. Mother's smile, as it rested on him lovingly, belied rumours of a rift and a separation.

Steeped in the Victorian proprieties of her day, my mother never, never confided to friends any personal difficulties.

She even found it increasingly difficult to confide in her sisters as the following letter to her sister May indicates. It was written from a hotel suite at Claridge's in the summer of 1924, when May was in Paris: 'Darling Sister: A thousand thanks for all your dear letters—another one this morning to cheer and help me! I am feeling so terribly disheartened this evening—and am writing to ask advice, as I am really at the *end* of my resourceful mind!

'The situation is this (and very, very, sad for all of us). Neily, poor darling, was *so* very *drunk* this evening (our first appearance since landing!) in the restaurant at dinner that, before we had our dessert, Reggie Pembroke very kindly put his arm into Neily's and led him through the dining-room and up to our rooms where he left Neily asleep on the sofa.

'Poor darling Neily is *continually* drunk—every evening. I really do not know what to do or where to go—it is horrible. I do not know whether I should try to take a house, or what on earth to do. I know quite well what I should have done if I could have managed to get him there; I should have gone to Hot Springs or French Lick before coming abroad. Just to give him a chance to get his balance —for you know how terribly he drank over here last summer. When he met us on our return home last winter he was in a frightful state. I was simply heart-broken to see it.

'I am frightfully grieved and feel treacherous in telling all this

253

so frankly—so bluntly—but now that he has made this unfortunate public exhibition it will be the talk of London—and of the world. I could consult no one this winter but poor Neil, as I did often, and he tried so hard to help. I have all these years managed to get Neily straightened out by taking him along for cures and doing something —but now the devil seems to have got hold of him and I cannot combat whatever it is. I've always been able to get him away to go on a cure and get him straightened out for a while—and perhaps if I had insisted, I could have done so this time.

'Now the question is, what shall I do? If we suddenly decide to dash over to Paris (I wired today we wouldn't come) but after this evening I realize the impossibility of checking him here. I wonder whether it would be more impossible in Paris—or less terrible to cope with, and whether you could help or if there are any doctors who could and would do anything for him and for me.

'I believe that I shall just leave the house question unsettled and go over to Paris. We have seen only the Horlich house that I would care to have—as you say, it is so clean and comfortable and delightful—bedrooms, baths, etc.—but, alas, today late, Sir James Horlich said that he would not let his house. I've seen Alford House and several other houses. I agree with you again about Cargill House—too old and dingy. Have seen Lord Dudley's—rather small. The Salisbury's—no w.c. near any bedroom. They are all *on the stairs*! Every blessed one of them. How curious to place them directly on the stairs!

'I really could not take a house with those inconveniences. So I've seen nothing I really like and is it possible for us to come here at all with this terrible anxiety? However, by the time you get this I shall have decided our fates, and I send this so that you will understand a little and be au courant. Please, darling sister, help your devoted Grace.'

My poor, unhappy, forlorn Mother! By this time—in the middle 1920s—the sister she admired and relied upon so much—the romantic, moody Belle—was gone.

Her brother Orme (who married Carrie Astor) was dead, and so was brother Dick. Of the immediate Wilson family—so devoted to one another, so willing to share each other's burdens and triumphs—only Aunt May remained, and she seldom left her villa in France.

To make matters worse, the women of the Vanderbilt clan,

whom Mother treated with no more than a kind of chilling polite-ness—had taken Father back into their sacrosanct little circle. With Reggie and Alfred no longer living, Father was at last receiving respect and consideration due the head of the House of Vanderbilt.

When Consuelo Vanderbilt, her marriage to the Duke of Marlborough successfully annulled, decided to marry that charming, untitled Frenchman, Jacques Balzan, it was my father who gave the bride away. Grandmother Vanderbilt and her two daughters, Gertrude and Gladys, were spending many months of the year abroad; frequently they stayed with my father on his yacht (seldom, however, when my mother was there) and sought his advice in business and personal matters. When Aunt Gladys' husband, Count Lâszló Széchényi, unfortunately lost his eye in a duel, Grandmother in Switzerland notified Father before anyone else in the family.

As my parents began to drift quietly but inevitably apart, my sister Grace sided more and more openly with my father and the Vanderbilts. Then, quite suddenly, Aunt May died. Mother was left with no one but me to turn to for help, and I was thousands of miles away, in plenty of difficulties of my own.

After several years of reporting, I had decided to launch my own newspaper chain. My dream was a clean tabloid, to sell for a penny, which would uphold the highest standards of journalistic excellence.

The Los Angeles *Illustrated Daily News* hit the news-stand September 3, 1923 (Mother's birthday), my San Francisco paper came next, and then the Miami *Illustrated Daily Tab*. From the very beginning they attracted readers. For two and a half years we fought for labour, for social legislation, and against entrenched interests, and our circulation grew phenomenally. We were all amateurs, all hard workers. I still believe my newspapers need not have failed. At the critical moment, the financial support which I had counted on from my father did not materialize. It was a battle to the last ditch—and we lost.

When the Vanderbilt Newspapers, Inc., suspended publication I was as penniless as my great-great-grandfather, the Commodore, had been in the days when he was peddling vegetables.

Fortunately I had learned the trade of newspapering, and Arthur Brisbane offered me a job on the New York *Daily Mirror* as Associate Managing Editor. With a few sheets of folded copy paper in my pocket and my favourite old grey felt hat on the back of my head, I went to work again as a reporter. Before long I had begun the roving assignments which were to keep me crossing the United States and travelling about the globe until World War II.

Soon after I lost my newspapers, I was also divorced.

One summer day in 1927 my sister telephoned from 640 and asked me to meet her at the Little Church around the Corner. She was eloping with a young Princeton graduate and mining engineer, Henry Gassaway Davis, of West Virginia.

I was the only Vanderbilt present at the brief ceremony. Grace, carrying a little handbag of clothes, headed for Seattle with Henry, and then to a mining camp in British Columbia.

For three months no word came to them from my family. Grace told newspaper reporters that she had eloped with Henry to avoid marrying 'an English suitor' selected by Mother. She had chosen to settle down in a tiny backwoods shack, with no servants or comforts, to be with the man she loved.

In 1929, however, when Father learned that Grace was expecting a child, he telephoned her in British Columbia and said that he would like to have his first grandchild born under the Vanderbilt roof. And so Grace came home to 640. Soon afterwards her husband gave up engineering and, to my mother's great satisfaction, joined a stock-brokerage firm.

Chapter Thirteen

AS Father's drinking became more pronounced and his absences from home more and more prolonged, Mother was forced to find substitutes for a party host among her many male admirers.

The secret of a good party, she used to say, was not brilliant conversation but extra men. Mother's social secretary kept lists of 'men who will dance', 'men who can play the piano', 'men who can lunch', 'men who will go to the theatre but not the opera', and so forth. As late as 1951, when Mother was eighty-one, her list of eligible male dinner guests still contained 138 names.

Of course the real reason Mother was able to give such superb parties was that her staff was so beautifully trained. She knew exactly what she wanted and how to give directions. She never paid the highest wages and she expected her servants to do their work to perfection, with very little time off; yet few ever left her employ.

At 640, the number of servants varied from twenty-six to over thirty. Stanley Hudson, our butler for more than twenty years, was in charge of all of them except those in the kitchen, where the chef ruled supreme. Hudson never wore livery like the footmen, though he changed his clothes three times daily, progressing towards more and more formal attire until at dinner the only thing which distinguished his costume from that of the host was his black vest.

Our butler never opened the front door or answered the telephone, relegating such tasks to the footmen. However, he did greet guests in the foyer, always speaking in the third person, such as 'If Madame will please be seated, I shall see if Madame is in.'

He supervised the six footmen, clad in maroon breeches and jackets, white stockings, and buckled shoes, who set the table for luncheon and dinner, served meals, poured wine, and later washed the dishes. The butler was solely in charge of supplies for the pantry, which consisted of wines and liqueurs, soft drinks, all the food necessary for teatime, and the fruit and flowers. After a dinner party, the chef left for his home as soon as the guests rose from the table, leaving in the butler's pantry trays of sandwiches to be served at the close of the evening.

Whether my mother was at 640, at Beaulieu, at Claridge's in London, at Hot Springs, or anywhere else, her day began at about ten o'clock each morning, when her maid drew the curtains back and brought in the breakfast tray.

Propped up by pillows, with a little pink woollen jacket over her white linen monogrammed nightgown, and with a lacey cap over her hair, Mother always ate exactly the same breakfast—an egg, two slices of toast, a little marmalade, and tea. Then she read her mail, which was brought in with the tray, together with messages which had been prepared by the social secretary. The letters from friends Mother devoured happily. All the others had been opened first by the secretary, who attached to each a memo telling what it was about: 'thank you' notes, invitations, bills, even letters from people who did not know my mother, criticizing (or praising) her for something she had done.

A large part of Mother's mail came from acquaintances in Europe, introducing friends who were coming to America. Some of these notes were kindly evidences of friendship. Others were like this one, sent to Lady Mary Herbert, Uncle Mungo's sister, by an English acquaintance.

'Dear Lady Mary: I wonder if you would ask your sister-in-law, Sir Michael's widow, if she would give C—— and me a few introductions to the rich Americans such as the Vanderbilts who entertain in New York and give large parties. I am told I ought to have some letters to those sort of people. We are off for six months in the U.S.A. in hopes of collecting some dollars . . .'

If the newcomers were really friends of people whom Mother liked, she was usually delighted to invite them to tea or luncheon and to arrange for them to meet the people they most wanted to see while they were in the United States.

'Telephone the Secretary of State in Washington and the Greek Ambassador and ask them to dinner some day next week,' she would instruct the secretary. Mother never knew what day but expected her secretary to arrange the scheduling.

Sometimes the secretary would report back, 'I'm sorry, Mrs. Vanderbilt, but it's impossible to reach Mr. So-and-So.'

'Nonsense,' Mother would retort, 'Call the mayor's office,' or,

'Call the governor's secretary at Albany.' Or, 'Call the protocol office of the State Department in Washington. Tell them that Mrs. Cornelius Vanderbilt would like to know at once where Mr. So-and-so can be reached because she would like to ask him to a dinner party.' And sometimes she would say, 'Call the White House.'

The secretary also read the social columns of the newspapers every morning to brief Mother on the latest arrivals from Europe, who was getting married, divorced, and so forth. The secretary kept a dossier on all Mother's friends, aided by 114 social registers. Burke's *Peerage*, and the *Almanak de Gotha*.

While Mother was still in bed she would talk to her friends by telephone. When a call came for her, a secretary would answer and then ring Mother on the private house telephone. If the house telephone rang three times, it meant the call was from someone Mother knew very well. If it rang twice it was an acquaintance, and Mother would pick up the house phone to ask the secretary what the call was about. If she didn't want to talk to this person, the secretary would say on the outside wire, 'I'm very sorry, Mrs. ——. Mrs. Vanderbilt is unavailable,' or, 'Mrs. Vanderbilt and the General are talking.'

The menus for the day were also sent to Mother every morning. At about eleven o'clock the French chef would come up from the kitchen and stand in the boudoir outside Mother's bedroom to discuss them. She would say to him in French, 'Masse, why are you having truffles with lamb?' or, 'Don't you think it's too warm today for hot lobster?' When they had decided together what the menu should be, the chef himself went out to market for the food.

He was responsible for everything that happened in the kitchens; the butler was in charge of the pantry, the dining-rooms, and the entertaining-rooms. And no matter how many different French chefs and English butlers we had, they were always terribly jealous of their prerogatives. Woe betide the chef if he ever set foot in the pantry and vice versa!

Under the chef was a second cook, who substituted for him at times and cooked for the household servants. There was a kitchen-maid, a second kitchenmaid, who scrubbed pots and cleaned vegetables, and a scullery man to handle the garbage, scrub the floor, and do the heavy work.

Down in the basement where the kitchen and the servants' dining-room were located both at 640 and at Beaulieu, there were three laundresses who washed and ironed all the household linens and personal laundry of the family. The very long tablecloths they handled in sections in tubs, scrubbing them on tin boards, and also ironed them by hand in sections. In addition, there was all the bed-linen, which, for the family, our guests, and servants, ran to somewhere between 180 and 200 sheets a week.

Hudson felt that in fashionable households all the bed-linen should be changed daily, but Mother said twice a week was enough. She didn't own an electric washing machine or mangle until after she had moved to 1048 Fifth Avenue in 1945.

The household linens all came from England or Switzerland. Everything was white, and the tablecloths and napkins were heavily monogrammed. Part of the footmen's work was to gather up the tablecloth and napkins after each meal and shoot them down the chute to the laundry.

It was also part of the footmen's work to polish silver. The 'silver well' which was in the pantry at 640 was three stories high, completely lined with cupboards filled with silver. At almost any time you might go there one of the footmen would be sure to be polishing silver.

Upstairs three chambermaids cared for the bedrooms, the boudoir, and library, in addition to doing the pressing and personal laundry for guests. A parlourmaid kept the entertainment rooms on the first floor dusted and in order, and a 'useful maid' cleaned the servants' rooms and washed the dishes after their meals. The men-servants' bedrooms were in the basement, the women's on the fifth and sixth floors.

Mother's personal maid was a privileged character who kept aloof from the rest of the household staff and was allowed to eat her meals on a tray in her room. She kept Mother's clothes in order, did the packing, and accompanied her whenever she travelled. The maid always waited up at night until my mother returned from a party or the opera, though this might be at two, three, four, or even five in the morning. The maid would put the jewels Mother had worn into the wall safe, hang the evening wrap and gown in their wardrobes, brush Mother's hair, and put it up in curlers while Mother chatted about the evening, whom she had seen, and so on.

Once a week the maid shampooed Mother's hair, which she then brushed dry, winter or summer, in front of a small bedroom fire. Then she curled it, rolling it up over brown-paper curlers fastened with silk-covered hairpins purchased in England. All the tooth-brushes and hairbrushes in the house also came from London.

Once when Father's valet, for some reason, was unable to go to Europe with him, Hudson was taken in his place. My parents were at the Crillon in Paris, about to leave for Madrid. Father decided to send Hudson to London to order some suits and coats so they would be ready for fitting when Father arrived later. Hudson was quite set up about being given this responsibility.

But Mother's maid told him witheringly, 'You think you're going to London to order those suits! What you're really going for is to bring back two pounds of "Her Majesty Queen Victoria's tea". We need it to rinse Mrs. Vanderbilt's hair.'

As it turned out, Hudson did bring back the tea. After Mother's hair turned white, she never dyed it, but the tea rinse gave it a faintly golden gleam.

The other servants at 640 were Father's valet, two chauffeurs, a houseman, and a night watchman. Mother's financial secretary kept an office away from the house and came in for a few hours daily.

When bills were received they were itemized under such nota-tions as 'window cleaner, twice a month', 'elevator maintenance service', 'piano rental', and so on. The cost of running the Fifth Avenue house and Beaulieu, including entertaining close to 10,000 guests a year, came to $20,000 a month or $250,000 a year.

'Do I have this much money?' I heard Mother ask her financial secretary naïvely one morning as she signed cheques totalling $80,000.

One of the staff at 640 said to me recently: 'What I remember best about Mrs. Vanderbilt is the way she felt about different religions and races. Once when a titled Englishman came to dinner and was ranting about Irish Catholics, Mrs. Vanderbilt reprimanded him right in front of the other guests.

'She said, "Most of my servants are Irish Catholic and I do not want to hear their religion or anyone else's disparaged in this house."

'The English peer shut up at once, looking very much sur-prised.'

Although Father lost heavily in the crash—he used to say he lost

$8,000,000 in paper profits in twenty minutes—this did not prevent him from selling the *Atlantic* in the fall of 1929 and buying an even more expensive and faster yacht, the *Winchester*, formerly owned by 'Broadway' Rause.

Father's new yacht looked like a navy destroyer—long, low, grey, and very, very fast. Extremely narrow in her beam and 225 feet long, she was also a 'holy roller' and a wet ship in a seaway.

Mother supervised the decoration, as she had on all the other yachts. The deck house, with delicately panelled walls, two-inch-thick carpets covering the floor, overstuffed divans, Chinese lacquered chests, and taffeta curtains and cushions could have been a *salon* in a Newport Villa.

The *Winchester* was especially conspicuous on the New York Yacht Club cruises and races when, because of her great speed (over 30 knots), she acted as a kind of dispatch boat.

William Taylor, writing about the Vanderbilt yachts, said, 'When the big windjammers get away in a fresh breeze in a reaching run along the coast, and the race committee in its tug can't be sure of getting to the finish line ahead of them, it is the "Winchester", black smoke pouring from her funnels and her sharp ploughshare of a bow turning up a great white furrow through the sea, that slides down the coast and times the early finishers.'

Father had three great passions—engineering, soldiering, and yachting—but I believe that he was happiest at sea, cut adrift from Mother's tight scintillating social world.

Treasured among his possessions, I found this letter written to him by his mother, my Grandmother Vanderbilt, just before she died: 'Dear Neily, I would like to give you a present for the summer and it would be such a pleasure to me if you will put the "Winchester" in commission for three months. I know how you enjoy her and want you so much to have her this summer. Love, Affly yrs. Mother.'

Although Father conscientiously paid for half of the expenses of running our different houses, Mother never contributed to the up-keep of any of his yachts. Since it cost Father about $7,000 a month just to keep the *Winchester* tied up at the dock, and at least twice that on long cruises, Grandmother's gesture was a generous one. And Aunt Gertrude and Aunt Gladys, both of whom were now immensely rich (the Countess, a true offspring of the Commodore, by this time controlled all the street railways in Budapest) also found ways to take care of some of Father's yachting expenses quietly.

After Grandmother Vanderbilt's death in 1934, in her eighty-ninth year, Mother's calling cards were straightway changed to bear the sublime inscription 'Mrs. Vanderbilt', but she had no ambitions to occupy the Breakers. During the summer of 1926, following Reggie's death, Grandmother had invited my parents to move into the Breakers while she was abroad. This they did, but Mother found the enormous villa so unlivable and made so many changes and alterations that Grandmother, understandably put out, did not repeat the invitation.

In Grandmother's will she left the Breakers, her great Newport palazzo, to Aunt Gladys, as well as her New York house. The Countess also received nearly two-thirds of the $7,000,000 trust fund left to Grandmother by her husband. To Father, Grandmother left the Gwynne Building in Cincinnati, which had come to her through her family. To my mother she left nothing, and to me, a photograph of herself.

It was not long after Grandmother died and was laid to rest in the immense Vanderbilt mausoleum on Staten Island that Father's richest uncle died. This was Uncle Fred, who owned the great Hyde Park estate within a short drive from Franklin D. Roosevelt's home.

At the time of Father's marriage, Uncle Fred had said a great many unkind things about my mother, for which she never forgave him, but we were quite fond of his wife, whom we called Aunt Lulu.

According to Cleveland Amory, Eleanor Roosevelt considered our Aunt Lulu to be a perfect example of the Old Order. Every day, regardless of the weather, promptly at three o'clock Aunt Lulu went for a solitary drive with her coachman, and later with her chauffeur. One day the President's wife asked her politely what she thought about on these drives.

'Why,' replied Aunt Lulu, 'I do my mental exercises. First I do the kings and queens of England, forward and backward, with their dates. Then I do the presidents of this country, forward and backward, with their dates, and sometimes, if I take a long drive, I get to the kings and queens of France.'

Uncle Fred had been a widower for many years before he died, and since he and Aunt Lulu had no children, there was much speculation about his fortune and to whom he would leave it. Although Mother and Father were fêting the Crown Prince and Princess of Sweden at Beaulieu, they cancelled the affair to attend the funeral.

After the reading of the will they came back to 640, Mother walking very stiffly, her shoulders erect and head high, Father wearing a look of compressed outrage.

Uncle Fred had owned nine mid-Manhattan properties, including a large Fifth Avenue mansion. All of these, plus the Hyde Park estate, and all his furniture and paintings and tapestries and silver, all his yachts and automobiles and jewellery, and most of his $72,000,000 he bestowed on the pretty head of his wife's niece, Mrs. James Van Alen.

He did not leave a single penny to any of the Vanderbilts. It was quite the scandal of the year.

Some time later Daisy Van Alen came to Mother's for a luncheon party. She left her mink cape draped about her shoulders, for the day was chilly. Unnoticed by her, the cape soon slipped from her chair to the floor.

Now Mother, in her later years, became so devoted to her little brown rae pinscher dogs that she allowed them to sit on her lap at lunch and nibble at her plate. During this particular luncheon little Teepee, as her dog was called, jumped down, and soon sounds of furious battle came from beneath the long gleaming mahogany table.

The guests, greatly surprised, peered under the tablecloth. There was Teepee, savagely tearing to bits Mrs. Van Alen's new mink cape.

Like most of their friends, my parents thought that the New Deal administrations of Franklin Roosevelt were a calamity. Mrs. James Roosevelt had for years been a close friend of Mother's; in fact, when Mother wanted me to know how thoroughly she disapproved of my book *Farewell to Fifth Avenue*, she arranged a luncheon at which I was seated beside the President's mother. Mrs. Roosevelt said that she had read my book and that I was 'a traitor to my class'.

Father said the same thing about F.D.R., only in much stronger language. Father knew that F.D.R. was my hero.

Both my parents were aboard the *Winchester*, watching the

Yale-Harvard boat races one spring, when a change in the tide suddenly brought the stern end of their yacht against the stern of Vincent Astor's *Nourmahal*.

President Roosevelt, whose love for sailing was like my father's, was sitting on the deck of the *Nourmahal*. He looked across and, seeing my parents, waved to them.

'Hello there,' he called. 'Why don't you come aboard?'

Father replied stiffly, 'Mr. President, we would be delighted to come if we were invited.'

'Well,' said F.D.R., 'I invite you now.'

But Father answered, 'It is the custom in yachting circles for the owner of the ship to ask the owner of another ship aboard, and not for one of the guests to do it.'

This made the President laugh. 'Well,' he said, 'I waive all those customs.'

My father began to look angry. He could not be rude to the President of the United States, but he was embarrassed, and he would not give an inch in the observance of the ceremonious yachting code.

Then my mother got up from her deck chair and moved over to the rail. 'I don't like you, Mr. President,' she said. 'I don't like you at all.'

F.D.R. smiled. 'Well, Mrs. Vanderbilt,' he called back, 'lots of people don't like me. You are in good company.'

Mother said, when she told about this later, that she thought it was a fine, sporting kind of reply. Besides, she knew how the President felt about me.

By this time Vincent Astor had come over to the rail of the *Nourmahal*, and he called over the side, 'I would like to invite you, General and Mrs. Vanderbilt, to come aboard and pay a social call.'

Mother said there was quite an argument then between herself and Father and some of their guests about whether or not they should go. Finally the fast launch was ordered alongside, and my parents went over to the *Nourmahal*.

Vincent Astor came down the gangway to the edge of the sea and said to Father: 'The courtesy of the sea is to let you, as former Commodore of the New York Yacht Club, go up first. But I think the real commodore in your family is your wife, so I'm going to waive the courtesy of the sea and ask her to go up the gangway first.'

Father replied: 'You may waive the courtesy of the sea, but I will not. I will go first because I outrank everybody here.'

Vincent Astor was laughing, but Father was not. Then my mother stepped forward and went up the gangway. When she arrived on deck, F.D.R. greeted her with, 'Well, well, I want to greet the first female admiral in the United States Navy.'

My father laughed then and went over and sat down with F.D.R., and they had a long discussion about the Panama Canal defences. Father had been through the canal not long before on the *Winchester*. By the time the tea party was over, everyone was chatting away and having a wonderful time.

When my parents were ready to leave, F.D.R. said, 'Grace, come here, I want to speak to you.' My mother leaned down, and the President reached up and kissed her cheek. 'You were born a good Southern Democrat. What changed you?'

'I married a good Republican from the North,' Mother told him. 'But the General and I both appreciate a good fighter. From now on, Mr. President, I won't vote for you, because I don't believe in what you're doing, but I won't vote against you.'

So far as I know, she never did.

When F.D.R. ran for election the third term and won, it was impossible for two Newporters to talk together for five minutes without roundly damning *that man*. Each week it seemed, another yacht was sold, another fleet of cars reached the auction block, another great Bellevue Avenue mansion was boarded up—all because, they said, of the President's socialistic notions.

Finally, at one of Mother's parties, her guests' malicious comments about F.D.R. became more than she could tolerate. Rising to her feet, she announced a toast to her tableful of disgruntled multi-millionaires.

Not until every glass was raised with hers did she announce sweetly, 'Let us drink to my President and to yours!

'And,' she added quietly after the toast was drunk, 'let us have no more treasonable statements about our Commander-in-Chief.'

While Father was living on his yacht, Mother would frequently join him for a week or ten days. Sometimes the whim to see him would seize her late at night, as her dinner guests were leaving.

'Pack my bags, Ingrid, and meet me at the station in an hour,' she would carol up the stairs to her Swedish maid. 'We're going to Miami.'

The *Winchester* had some fourteen guest cabins, and whenever Mother came aboard they were soon filled. At home, every day of the year, she entertained at lunch and tea and dinner seldom under fifty or sixty people. Occasionally she would consent to dine at the home of one of her friends, if she approved of the guest list, but she always arrived late, with an apologetic murmur, and sat uneasily in her chair, as if she felt she should be signalling the butler to refill the wine glasses and reshaping conversational groups after dinner. It was almost impossible for her to relax at somebody else's party.

Our guest rooms at Newport and 640 Fifth Avenue were occupied so much of the time that the butler had difficulty distinguishing between the incoming and outgoing luggage. Mother asked her secretary for a roster count each morning to discover just who was there, and for how long. On Sundays, as many as a hundred people would 'drop in' for tea, while on Christmas Day a thousand or more people milled through the great Fifth Avenue house with its twenty-foot Christmas tree blazing in the Corot- and Millet-lined red damask picture gallery.

'It's just like Grand Central,' Father complained on his rare visits home, crossing the great foyer through dozens of strangers, guests in his own house.

And of course Mother did far more than merely entertain her friends. She arranged introductions, found better jobs for promising young men, helped to organize benefits, induced her friends to contribute to finance drives and—last but not least—made many brilliant matches.

The demands upon her tact, time, and energy grew so great that when she finally arrived at Hot Springs for her semi-annual rest, she was close to exhaustion.

'This having to keep *en evidence* all year! We society women simply drop down in harness,' Mrs. John Drexel once exclaimed.

At the Homestead—one of the last great feudal estates left in America, sprawling over 14,000 acres—Mother seemed to crave only the shelter of anonymity. Here she retreated into a large suite insulated at each end and overhead with empty rooms so as to exclude all possible sound of human voices. She came to dread the stir her arrival caused at the imposing Greek-columned front entrance, and slipped in and out of an inconspicuous door at the rear used for unloading guests' baggage. Here her carriage waited to pull her sedately through the quiet forests on her afternoon drives.

At the Homestead, Mother gave no parties and attended none, and seldom dined downstairs, preferring instead to eat alone by the fire in her large private living-room. Her personal waiter, John, had orders to bring her entire meal at once, to remove the silver covers, and depart.

I remember one day watching her sitting by her hotel window, a pink French blanket across her knees, her brown dog on her lap. The room was filled with high, dark, old-fashioned mahogany furniture which the management kept just for her visits. That day I thought I detected a deep weariness in her cameolike features, her gentle voice.

I wanted to tell her that I thought her public role had become too much for even her immense energies. I remained silent, because of course she would never admit this. And after total rest and quiet for five or six weeks, she would be ready to begin again. Father remarked that her hospitality had become a kind of blind, overpowering instinct. 'Your mother has become a waltzing mouse,' he said.

Gradually I began to understand that being a leader of society was not a hobby with my mother, or even an avocation, but a full-time profession which taxed all her resources every waking moment.

Although I had made Reno, Nevada, my permanent home, Mother and I talked by telephone almost every day during the 1930s. Then I spent a year and a half in the Orient, crossing Russia by way of the Siberian railroad and visiting half a dozen European capitals as correspondent for *Liberty* magazine. Mother's loving wires and cables followed me everywhere, and when I returned we spent long hours together discussing the world scene and my interviews with people like Hitler and Mussolini and Stalin. Mother seldom read anything—not even the newspapers—but got all her information firsthand through people in strategic places. Although she scorned gossip, she loved to discuss world and domestic politics. Talking together, sharing experiences outside her narrow social sphere, my mother and I grew very close.

My father had suffered a series of minor heart attacks, and finally he moved more or less permanently to the *Winchester*, attended by a doctor and several nurses. I rarely saw him, but my sister, with her daughter, Cornelia, spent a good deal of time with him. My sister was then in the process of divorcing Henry Gassaway Davis.

'It's a sad thing for us in that we've never had a *real* home with Mother,' she wrote me from Florida, 'and we just have to play a *game* most of the time in order to keep her from absorbing all our lives.

'Luckily neither of us has grandiose ideas or aspirations to big handsome houses or places—or "social entertainments". In fact, we are pretty well fed up with all that kind of thing—having *seen* how hollow it all really is . . .'

However, in 1935, when her divorce from Davis was final, Grace crossed the Atlantic with Mother to attend Cousin Bobo's London wedding. 'Dearest Neily,' Mother wrote to Father a week after their arrival in London. 'It is the middle of the night but I must write, hoping these lines will go by the Europa tomorrow. I am delighted you are feeling a little better, and that the pulse and blood pressure are lower—and pray God you may be much better when we return. Grace tells me she wrote to you at length. Since our arrival I have never dreamt of anything like the wonderful times we are having. It is impossible to describe the kindness and hospitality we are having showered upon us—never have I dreamt of anything like it!!!

'I will relate today's engagements. Lunch at Lady Cunard's. A lot of very gay, amusing, clever people. Emaraud and others asking for you. Then a drive with Sidney Herbert who is deep in the elections. Then I went to tea at five at Buckingham Palace with the beloved King and Queen. It was all very interesting and wonderful. They received me quite alone and we sat at a small tea table, the Queen pouring tea for the King and me! They kept me with them one hour and we talked of everything and everybody—of course a great deal about you, and he said you did not like 'going out' any more than he did!!!

'They were awfully sorry to hear you were not well, and sent the most charming messages. As I was leaving, the Queen said, "I am very sorry never to see your husband any more, as we get on so well together and understand each other." Lots of other messages, too. He told me many things. I was so overcome by their frankness and kindliness that I came away feeling in honour bound not to relate anything to anyone but *you*—on my return. It seems he never stays more than 20 minutes at tea and then leaves, but today he stayed *all the time*—one hour! He is looking much better than I expected to see him and they were both so dear and kind and touching, I felt I was with very dear and true friends—more like one's family than just friends.

'Then I rushed home, jumped into my prettiest gown and, with Grace, drove off to Crewe House for a large and beautiful and most delightful dinner where they kindly put me on Lord Crewe's left, the Turkish Ambassador on his right. There were lots of our mutual friends and we stayed until 12.'

Mother then described the exhausting round of luncheons and dinners and theatre parties that had occupied her during the week, commenting that Father's sister Gladys had been especially kind and hospitable.

'And next week it all continues—I am almost dead!' her letter goes on. 'Completely overwhelmed by kindness and don't know how I should be able to survive another week of it. Grace seems to enjoy it all and Margaret Drummond Wolffe is trying to persuade me to leave Grace here, but I do not quite like the idea and think she had better return with me and come over again in the spring. I wonder if I am right? But I do not like staying away from you any longer, and I rather fear leaving her alone . . .

'We have been very comfy here and are spending a terrific sum of money on rooms, motor, etc. I've bought nothing so far and have sent no flowers or presents to anyone. I should have done so, but have been too busy. I have had flowers from about thirty people. *Beautiful*, bushels, etc. etc.—it's all like a wonderful dream—only I wish I were not so dead tired all the time. You never could have stood the strain—it is killing, but well worth while. Well goodnight —or good morning, darling Neily. And lots of love from your devoted Grace.'

There is a joke among society people that a dinner invitation, once accepted, is such a sacred obligation that if you die before the dinner takes place, your executor must attend.

Mother felt so strongly about guests who 'gave out' at the last moment, thus ruining all her carefully worked out seating plans, that such a person was not asked again to one of her parties for a long, long time and sometimes never.

I remember that Mother was giving a dinner party for some thirty people the day the great hurricane of 1938 struck Newport. Beaulieu's clipped lawns were strewn with magnificent specimen elms and maples, stripped white of their bark by the fury of the wind. Several of our chimneys blew down, and part of the roof. We had no electricity or telephone, and the terrified staff feared a tidal wave would dash over the cliff and drown us all.

At six o'clock Mother began to dress by candlelight in her usual calm and deliberate way. At seven she was standing in the candlelit drawing-room, exquisitely gowned and groomed as usual, ready to receive her guests.

Of the thirty she had invited, twenty-seven braved the teeth of the colony's worst gale to come.

Mother never expected them to do otherwise.

My sister soon married another American, Robert Stevens of the well-known Hoboken family, founders of the Stevens Institute.

Grace's daughter by her first marriage, Cornelia, was by then a very pretty and vivacious teen-ager.

'Of course she is bored to death with Mademoiselle or any chaperone, rules, conventions, etc.,' my sister wrote me about her daughter. '*No* governess is *ever* exactly right—and the nurses are even worse—but they are certainly a *necessity*—Cornelia is sweet and really awfully pretty—but a *handful* when she gets going and just a little "madcap"—very vague and flighty and completely *naïve*—and is apt to do the *silliest* things when she gets carried away having fun—and just never knows when to stop. She hasn't the foggiest idea of finding out *who* people are—is astonishingly childish in those ways and therefore it is terribly dangerous not to have somebody to check up on her and clamp down on a lot of wild plans and schemes. . . . Naturally a terrible bore to share a room with Mlle,—but all *those little* things won't hurt her a bit.'

After the Second World War broke out, Father gave his million-dollar *Winchester* to the Canadian government to use as a submarine chaser. Then he moved to a hundred-foot chartered yacht tied up in the Miami Yacht Basin.

'Every Vanderbilt son has fought with his father, and every one has increased his fortune except me,' Father often remarked bitterly. This was not true, as Uncle George of the 'Biltmore', North Carolina, and several other Vanderbilts ran completely through their money, but Father seemed determined to think of himself as a failure.

From time to time he had received offers for 640 Fifth Avenue for as high as $9,000,000 (when it was being considered as a site for Rockefeller Plaza). But, although he badly needed the money, Father refused to be tempted, knowing the pride and pleasure Mother took in living there.

Finally, in 1940, when the daily property taxes on the seventy-room mansion had reached $168 a day, my father sold it to the William Waldorf Astor estate for $1,500,000, with the proviso that Mother could continue to live there, paying rent, until one year after his death.

On a bitter morning in February, 1942, news came to me in Washington, D.C., where I was serving with G–2, General Staff, that my father had suffered a cerebral haemorrhage in Miami. I at once telephoned Mother in New York to learn that airplane reservations had been made, changed, and remade half a dozen times as she wavered between the need for speed and her lifelong abhorrence of flying. Finally, after hours of tortured indecision, Mother, her personal maid, and my sister got on a train.

It was a very slow train. By the time they reached Jacksonville it was late in the evening. Mother rushed to a telephone to call the Yacht Basin at Miami.

'This is Mrs. Vanderbilt,' she said. 'I am calling about the General. How is he?'

There was a pause at the other end of the line, and she repeated, 'How is he?'

A strange voice answered: 'The General is dead, Madame. He died ten minutes ago. Master Neil is here. And so are the General's sisters.'

The personal maid took mother's arm and, together with my grief-stricken sister, led her back to the train. In Mother's compartment were photographs of Grace and me as children in royal attire—

white leggings and fur hats and sable-collared coats. There was a photograph of Father, dark and handsome in his general's uniform, wearing all his decorations.

On the drawing-room bed were Mother's monogrammed Irish linen sheets and fine French woollen blankets and a silk coverlet. On the wall brackets hung her thick monogrammed towels.

Her maid told me later that Mother moved towards the bed as though she were going to fling herself down and sob her heart out. But, almost at once, her lifetime habit of rigid self-control overcame the impulse. She stood quietly and submissively as the maid undressed her with swift and gentle fingers and helped her into her fine white handkerchief-linen nightgown. Then Ingrid brought her night-cap and thermos and snapped off the light.

All night long, as the train rocked and rolled and stopped and jolted down the Florida coast, Mother tossed from side to side, occasionally uttering a small moan, but when morning came there was no sign of tears.

She did not cry when she stood, finally, by Father's side. Nor did the tears come when we accompanied the coffin home on a private train with a military guard of honour, nor when, by ferry-boat, we crossed the grey and gusty harbour to Staten Island.

That night when she returned to 640 Fifth Avenue, Mother went into Father's study and remained there a long, long time.

To me, the final twist of irony to the collapse of my parents' marriage was that Grandfather Vanderbilt, whose animosity to my mother caused so much grief and suffering, had finally been proved right. Two people of such opposite temperaments, with such different goals in life, should probably never have married. Although he grew profoundly disillusioned and unhappy, Father never changed from the shy, retiring, serious-minded inventor, and Mother—even in her eighties—never outgrew her need to be a reigning social belle.

'Why don't you get a divorce?' I used to urge my parents separately in the waning years of their marriage.

'People in our position do not get divorces,' Father would say with a shrug.

Mother protested, 'But I love your father!'

On the night of Father's funeral, after she came out of his study,

Mother turned the key in the lock and never entered his room again.

Father's privacy was inviolable at last.

Mother's lovely face was flushed and red, and her green eyes swollen. But her back was as straight and proud as ever.

Chapter Fourteen

ALTHOUGH Mother continued to be society's most respected and elegant arbiter, her declining years were desperately lonely and unhappy ones, and it became obvious that her brilliant fêtes and soirées could no longer masquerade the emptiness of her days. She became cantankerous and difficult, with only flashes of her former captivating charm. When her maid tried to bend that implacable will, Mother threw hairbrushes at her.

Almost every day she telephoned me, if I was somewhere in this country, or cabled me overseas. 'When are you coming home?' she invariably demanded plaintively. 'I miss you so, Neil darling. Why must you always be so far away? Why don't you come home and stay with your poor lonely Mother who loves you so much?'

My mother's affection and need for me, however, were never allowed to interfere with her outward composure. She was a great admirer of British aplomb—of imperturbability during the most severe domestic crises. Once, shortly after my father's fatal stroke, when Mother and I were lunching alone together at 640 Fifth Avenue, I suffered a fainting spell. I rose from the vast gleaming mahogany table and started for the door, only to fall unconscious upon the carpet a few feet from Mother. When I came to a few moments later, the butler was leaning over me with a concerned expression. Mother, her eyes on her plate, was calmly finishing her dessert!

During my youth I both resented and adored my beautiful and glamorous mother. Now, looking at her through the eyes of mature adulthood, I came to understand and, in a sense, to pity her.

In her last years, her eyesight began to fail. She had only 'spots' of clear vision, as if she were looking through the wrong end of a telescope. Her oculist felt that her condition could be much improved by glasses, but although Mother was constantly ordering new pairs, she was much too vain to wear them. Now as she sat upon a red velvet settee in a gold lamé gown, a golden bandeau about her snow-white head, greeting the hundreds of friends who always came to her big glittering receptions, she could only recognize those who came within her very narrow range of vision.

'Who is it, darling? Who is coming now?' she would inquire brightly, clinging to my hand.

I never liked the Duke of Windsor so well as the night he sat next to Mother at dinner and carefully, with an air of tender solicitude, cut into small morsels the slice of roast beef she could only dimly perceive in front of her.

I cannot help feeling proud of Mother's great courage and indomitable spirit. Whereas World War I had found her preoccupied with the social launching of her only daughter, she viewed the storm signals of another great conflict with genuine distress. Perhaps because there had been so little peace in her own personal life, she abhorred the idea of war on a world scale.

So in spite of the repeated warnings of friends in high places that World War II was expected to begin any moment, Mother sailed to England in July of 1939 on a personal peace mission to Buckingham Palace. She took with her another doughty dowager, Mrs. James Roosevelt, and together with Queen Mary they thrashed out the problem of averting war, at tea.

Many people laughed at my mother about this, but had she been able to get the leaders of the East and West to one of her incomparable dinners (as she tried many times to get Gromyko), who knows what course history might have taken?

'Darling Mrs. Neily,' wrote Lady Mountbatten to Mother during the terrible bombardment of London in September, 1940, 'the children have been writing so happily of all the wonderful times they have been having and of your sweetness to them.' The two Mountbatten daughters, Patricia, sixteen, and Pamela, eleven, had been invited to make 640 Fifth Avenue their home for the duration.

'I cannot tell you how touched and grateful Dickie and I are,' Lady Mountbatten continued. 'Life here is pretty exciting and we are full of determination and optimism. I wish I could give you some news but I cannot!

'The Duke of Kent has just been staying and sent you many messages of love and I send you lots and also to little Grace. Affectionately, Edwinna.'

During the years that the girls with their French governess remained at 640, Mother grew very fond of her young charges. She loved to tell about the time a society friend of hers, feeling sorry for the English refugees, offered to give them a ball.

'While Father is at sea and Mother is working in air-raid shelters, surely you don't expect me to go to a *party*,' loftily rejoined Patricia Mountbatten.

During World War II I was a major in the Army. Since I was stationed for some time in New York, I spent many of my off-duty hours at 640, for even with a staff of thirty and a night watchman, Mother disliked spending a night in the great echoing house 'alone', as she called it.

One of the most painful moments of her often difficult life came when she was forced, finally, to vacate 640 Fifth Avenue. Three years after my father's death she bought another mansion, much smaller, but still very *chic*, farther uptown on Fifth Avenue.

As I drove up to see her one afternoon I saw the wrecking crews demolishing 640. Stone by stone they were tearing down my great-grandfather's baronial brown palace. Already my fifth-floor bedroom and Father's handsome walnut-panelled study and sound-proofed engineering laboratory had vanished. Mother's famous pink boudoir still remained on the second floor, its undraped windows staring blindly down at the Avenue Mother had dominated for fifty triumphant years.

Stanley Hudson, our English butler, moved uptown with Mother. 'There is hardly a household left in America for a first-class butler, except your Mother's,' he mourned to me. 'Why, these days we're even supposed to *dust the furniture*!'

Mother first opened her blue eyes in 1870 to a world of creaking black *moiré* and lace lappets, of gentlemen with imperial beards and stovepipe hats, and plain brownstone houses filled with black horse-hair and mahogany, with kitchens exuding the comfortable smells of anthracite and coffee.

By the time she had grown into a young lady, America's new multimillionaires were attempting to outdo one another in acquiring Old Masters, Greek statuary, Gobelin tapestries, and other symbols of Old World culture. I suppose that by surrounding themselves with objects of great antiquity, they hoped successfully to camouflage the brevity of their family trees.

277

It was not surprising that Mother, who had visited the courts of Europe every summer since she was a child, under the best of auspices, should later become the leader of this new millionaire society and of the conservative knickerbocker element as well.

But many an ambitious American woman has attempted to found a *salon* in this country to find that she has merely succeeded in opening a restaurant.

Mother's following was unique in that she entertained not only the greatest names of this country but of England and the Continent as well. No American woman had ever before been on such an intimate and friendly basis with the great crowned heads and titles of Europe, its artists and statesmen, poets and musicians.

Mother's tremendous charm was inherited, I feel, from her father, that beguiling and astute Southerner Richard T. Wilson. His youngest daughter he both pampered and adored, while entertaining, I am sure, large ambitions for her future. His faith in her was abetted by the ready assistance and great affection of her two older sisters who, Mother often said, taught her everything she knew.

As a beautiful young belle, greatly admired both here and abroad, Grace Wilson must have felt as though the world were hers for the taking. Whether creating a sensation on Newport's Bellevue Avenue, or at Cannes, or Paris, or Bad Nauheim, she was, at the age of twenty-five, in no great hurry to select one of her numerous suitors.

There were few obstacles or disappointments in Mother's life, as far as I can tell, until she encountered the extraordinary animosity of the senior Vanderbilts. Knowing how strong-willed and proud my Mother was, I can see how their unyielding opposition, coupled with the slander they heaped upon her in letters to their son, was enough to induce her to look even more favourably upon the love-lorn Neily. She could not have failed to be impressed by all the sacrifices he was willing to make for her.

Once she was married, the continued highhanded disapproval of the Vanderbilts furnished the steel in Mother's resolve to become the top-flight hostess in the tight little group the senior Vanderbilts dominated. But in the eleven years it took to bring her mother-in-law to her knees, Mother's outstanding beauty, tact, and vivacity had won her a far more enviable niche in royal circles abroad.

With the Vanderbilt name and a small share of the family millions to back her, Mother stepped lightheartedly upon the social merry-go-round. As the years passed, it whirled faster and faster until she sensed disaster, whether she held on or let go. Hundreds and thousands of people crowded about her, until their faces merged and blended into white anonymity like the squares of cardboard she shifted and arranged endlessly in her seating rack for one of her splendid parties. Eventually her need to dominate and direct people according to her desires grew to be the most compelling thing in her life.

Despite her many vexatious faults, however, Mother possessed a sincerity, a loyalty, and steadfastness which were truly admirable. And when the First World War put an end to footmen in livery, chaperons, and cotillions, it was Mother more than anyone else who maintained the protocol of polite, elegant society with its emphasis upon gentle breeding and good manners.

This she did despite great personal heartache and at tremendous expense. Even when she was finally confined to a wheel chair and seldom left her boudoir, Mother went on giving parties and spending close to $250,000 a year running her magnificent establishments. Father had left about four million dollars to be divided among us, and Mother had several millions of her own. Still, taxes cut so heavily into her income that at the end of her life she was spending principal at the rate of $125,000 a year.

Wrote that discriminating *bon vivant* and editor Frank Crowninshield about my mother: 'While she may have erred, as Mrs. Astor did, in allowing her ritual to become a shade too rigid; in placing an over-emphasis on magnificoes and distinguished personages, her qualities of heart have more than made up for her preoccupation with ceremony. All in all, her influence has been restorative, her loyalties unswerving, and her hospitality at all times unbounded.'

Remarked a Wilson relative, herself a recognized society leader: 'Your mother succeeded, against the heaviest odds, in becoming the person she most wanted to be. Her life was dedicated to being the top-flight hostess of her era. If she trampled a few people in attaining her goal, it was no more than any other entirely successful person does, and from my point of view, the result was worth it.'

For the last two years of her life Mother was bedfast. With sight and hearing failing, she often asked to have me near. Hour after hour

I sat by her bedside on a spindly gilt chair and held her hand, exquisite as an old piece of ivory, as I talked to her about the people I had seen, far-off places I had been.

Often she seemed to slip away into a coma until some word or phrase of mine invoked tender and bittersweet memories.

One day I happened to mention visiting my Cousin Bobo's great Kelso, Scotland, castle, one of the most splendid in the British Isles.

'Ah, Floors,' Mother murmured with a beatific remembering smile. 'Floors!'

Often she lapsed into French and seemed to be back in the halcyon days of girlhood.

Mother passed away quietly in her sleep in her eighty-third year on January 8, 1953.

All the proud and haughty Vanderbilt clan came to her funeral service.

Afterwards, a fleet of limousines followed the hearse down to the ferry. I remembered, as we drove towards the Battery, how much Mother had loved the sounds of the New York harbour, the cry of gulls, the clanging of buoys, the shrill, impatient whistling of ships eager for the sailing.

As the ferry pulled out from its slip, we could see in the white foggy distance the great bulk of a splendid trans-Atlantic liner heading out to sea.

The rain began to fall in cold grey sheets that January day as we accompanied Mother on her final crossing, this time to Staten Island, where the saga of the Vanderbilts began. This was the birthplace of the Commodore, Cornelius I.

And there in the great stone mausoleum designed by Richard Morris Hunt for my great-grandfather, my mother finally joined the other Vanderbilts.

INDEX